RELIGION, MODERNITY, AND THE GLOBAL AFTERLIVES
OF COLONIALISM

CONTENDING MODERNITIES

Series editors: Ebrahim Moosa, Atalia Omer, and Scott Appleby

As a collaboration between the Contending Modernities initiative and the University of Notre Dame Press, the Contending Modernities series seeks, through publications engaging multiple disciplines, to generate new knowledge and greater understanding of the ways in which religious traditions and secular actors encounter and engage each other in the modern world. Books in this series may include monographs, co-authored volumes, and tightly themed edited collections.

The series will include works that frame such encounters through the lens of "modernity." The range of themes treated in the series might include war, peace, human rights, nationalism, refugees and migrants, development practice, pluralism, religious literacy, political theology, ethics, multi- and intercultural dynamics, sexual politics, gender justice, and postcolonial and decolonial studies.

RELIGION, MODERNITY, AND THE GLOBAL AFTERLIVES OF COLONIALISM

Edited by
ATALIA OMER
AND
JOSHUA LUPO

University of Notre Dame Press
Notre Dame, Indiana

University of Notre Dame Press
Notre Dame, Indiana 46556
undpress.nd.edu
Copyright © 2024 by the University of Notre Dame

All Rights Reserved

Published in the United States of America

Library of Congress Control Number: 2024941045

ISBN: 978-0-268-20847-9 (Hardback)
ISBN: 978-0-268-20848-6 (Paperback)
ISBN: 978-0-268-20850-9 (WebPDF)
ISBN: 978-0-268-20849-3 (Epub3)

CONTENTS

Introduction: Religion and the Legacies of Colonial Violence 1
ATALIA OMER AND JOSHUA LUPO

PART I. Religion, Politics, and Colonial Afterlives, or the Old Is Not Dying 23

CHAPTER 1. Seeing the Old in the New: The Coloniality of the Liberal–Populist Marriage 25
SANTIAGO SLABODSKY

CHAPTER 2. Deradicalization as a Fetish: The Threat of *Da'wa* and the Regulation of the Real 49
NADIA FADIL

CHAPTER 3. Afrofuturism, Islamofuturism, and Post-Western Modernity 77
S. SAYYID

CHAPTER 4. The Neoliberal Rationality of Secularism
LUCA MAVELLI AND EDMUND FRETTINGHAM 105

PART II. Challenging Colonial Paradigms: Nationalisms and Humanitarianism at the Edges of Modernity 139

CHAPTER 5. Modernist Epistemological Webs: The Complex Legacies of Missionizing and Humanitarianism for Decolonizing Religion in Africa 141
CECELIA LYNCH

CHAPTER 6.	Linking Identity and Solidarity: A Reflection from the Periphery SLAVICA JAKELIĆ	169
CHAPTER 7.	The Fires This Time GIL ANIDJAR	203
	List of Contributors	217
	Index	221

INTRODUCTION

Religion and the Legacies of Colonial Violence

ATALIA OMER AND JOSHUA LUPO

ORIGIN STORY

Religion, Modernity, and the Global Afterlives of Colonialism emerged from a series of conversations hosted by Contending Modernities (CM), a global research initiative based at the University of Notre Dame's Keough School of Global Affairs. Since 2010, CM has orchestrated empirical research and convened scholars from around the globe to focus on questions of science and the human person; reconfigured patterns of authority, community, and identity in sub-Saharan Africa and Indonesia; and practices of intercommunal organizing and new forms of cosmopolitanism and pluralistic exchange in the Global North. In June 2017, CM convened a Theory Working Group that has sought, together with CM's blog, to curate work on various theoretical issues in religious studies. This group aimed to build upon and push beyond the empirical research of previous years so that CM might intervene in and expand upon central questions and conversations that have shaped the academic study of religion and modernity. The current volume joins two earlier publications emerging from our conversation.

Religion and Broken Solidarities illuminated how national boundaries limit the horizons of solidarity, and *Religion, Populism, and Modernity* examined the intersections of race, Christianity, and nationalism during the populist moment of the 2010s and 2020s. The current volume examines the afterlife of coloniality in various locations around the world by focusing on global practices of nationalism, humanitarianism, neoliberalism, and deradicalization. As a whole, the volume also seeks to bring to light practices and imaginaries that exceed the colonial gaze and decenter a totalizing western and Christocentric storyline. Our approach is simultaneously genealogical and emancipatory. Through this approach, we move beyond the more cynical visions of critique, which often deconstruct hegemonic structures without pointing to possibilities that might follow them, and which have dominated religious studies, and the wider humanities, in recent years.

"The New Cannot Be Born" ... Yet

Famously, the Italian theorist Antonio Gramsci wrote that "the old is dying but the new cannot be born."[1] He was referring to the decay of the hegemony structuring his historical context and to the fact that this dying was not yet accompanied by the birth of a new horizon. This profound observation has animated emancipatory politics on the Left that have focused on racial capitalism, colonialism, and the matrices of domination and global structural violence. The contributors to this volume capture a similar set of foci in our reexamination of the relations between religion, colonialism, and modernity. We do so by analyzing the historical roots and the ongoing legacies of these phenomena. Through this examination, it is revealed that the dying of the old does not necessarily mark the beginning of an alternative future, as S. Sayyid reminds us in his contribution (chapter 3).

Sayyid and Gil Anidjar (chapter 7) write responses to the contributions herein that reflect on the ongoing challenge of imagining alternatives to the dominant neocolonial hegemony. Sayyid illuminates why a futuristic imagination of the world otherwise, emancipated from European modernity/coloniality, is too often either beholden to a romantic ahistorical "authentic" precolonial imaginary, or is a replication of western modernity, as we see in Dubai's skyscrapers—as if modernity was merely an architecture rather than an episteme and set of political projects. Either way, Christian

European modernity still anchors the discussion, and thus a true decolonial horizon—which requires epistemological and political alternatives—remains unrealized.

Anidjar, in his synthetic response to the contributors, likewise reflects on the (im)possibility of escaping from the all-consuming fire of Christian European modernity. He extrapolates this from an engagement with Luca Mavelli and Edmund Frettingham's contribution (chapter 4), which examines an internally colonizing neoliberal rationality/secularism. Anidjar navigates between the false/fictional and true/foundational (annihilating) fires with which the other contributors grapple. Occasionally, he finds them less than all-consuming and thus potentially generative of something new, as in Gramsci's assertion. This something "new" ostensibly needs to deploy a grammar different from the modern/colonial, but, as Sayyid and Anidjar suggest, a place of exteriority from the ongoing logic of modernity remains elusive.

Religion, Modernity, and the Global Afterlives of Colonialism centers a decolonial sensibility with regard to how "religion" intersects with neoliberalism, humanitarianism, nationalism, and the ethics of political solidarity. We collectively ask (albeit through different scholarly conversations) the following questions: Where are there openings for alternative, less totalizing, and more just futures? Are such new births even possible to imagine without decolonizing the imagination itself? And how might that look? Indeed, this volume asks what it means to decolonize the study of religion.

Part I, "Religion, Politics, and Colonial Afterlives, or the Old Is Not Dying," deploys decolonial and genealogical epistemological interventions to expose the onto-theopolitical underpinnings (despite their self-representation as "secular security") of "deradicalization" policies in Europe (as a part of a global reach of the "War on Terror") and to challenge the retreat to White liberal innocence in the face of reignited fascism in Euro-America in the early decades of the twenty-first century. A decolonial prism and genealogical approach are indispensable for such demystification, and the contributions by Santiago Slabodsky (chapter 1), Nadia Fadil (chapter 2), S. Sayyid (chapter 3), and Luca Mavelli and Edmund Frettingham (chapter 4) employ them.

This critical turn in the scholarship on religion connects the poststructuralist genealogical demystifying of "religion" and "the secular" as all-inclusive and universal categories with the critique of modernity/coloniality. Accordingly, the very presence of national boundaries—a feature solidified in the post–World War I and World War II secular liberal order—is a manifestation of ongoing coloniality and thus engaging with them as the site for emancipation risks erasing a still lurking colonial presence. The "secular" nation-state might appear enlightened and neutral on the surface, but a critical lens of the kind foregrounded by the authors in part I exposes its underside. We refer to this critical approach as "genealogical" or "archaeological." This method seeks to unearth the obscured features of various historical epochs.

Notably, religion is exposed via this archaeological approach as integral to the colonial grammar, as are secularist discourses that appear "good" on the surface. Such discourses—which might include democracy and economic development—are certainly not inherently bad. However, in their historical and ideological manifestations, they have often been genocidal, dehumanizing, and exploitative. Occasionally, critics seek to identify/rescue the "tradition" that anteceded the colonial/modern violence as the ground for an alternative horizon.[2] The problem, beyond the fact that such a precolonial space does not exist, is that such approaches rely on a closed account of religious traditions that reflects the colonial ossification of the cultural/religious. Such sedimented definitions of religion have been used by colonial powers to map, comprehend, and control colonized peoples, and are the hallmarks of modernity. If one wants to advocate for an emancipatory vision of religious traditions, as Slabodsky reminds us, they cannot do so through this naïve and fictional "return to religion"; indeed, this is not a return at all because "religion" is a classificatory category integral to colonial/modern structures.

According to the archaeological line of critique taken by the authors in part I, to the degree to which the analysis of religion and politics is subsumed within and naturalizes the boundaries of modern nations (which in turn conceals the violence their drawing and redrawing has entailed), the study of religion and politics remains colonized, both methodologically and epistemologically, and can only generate limited and nationalist accounts of religion and politics. However, in part II, "Challenging Colonial Paradigms: Nationalisms and Humanitarianism at the Edges of Modernity," Cecelia Lynch (chapter 5) and Slavica Jakelić (chapter 6) point to cracks in a totalizing critique. These two contributions consider interventions from the scholarship on coloniality in their reflections on the ethics of political solidarity and humanitarianism in Africa and the Balkans.

THE OLD DID NOT GO ANYWHERE, NOR IS IT DYING

A decolonial approach requires a long historical reach that begins earlier than conventional historical accounts of the category of religion. It requires reaching back to the Christian European colonial expansions that occurred alongside, and entangled with, modernist ideology, racial capitalism, and a scrutiny of what Slabodsky analyzes herein as the genocidal underpinning of liberalism.[3] The concept of coloniality captures modernity and colonialism as mutually constitutive and as enduring in their effects on the social, political, and economic realities under which people live around the world.[4] The contributors define "liberalism" in a variety of ways, but we consider it most generally to constitute a set of values that prioritize individual rights and the privatization of religion, which are enshrined in a worldview and set of political, social, and economic institutions meant to reinforce those values.[5]

"Coloniality" came to the fore as a concept meant to capture the afterlife of colonial rule in the postcolonial present. The effects of colonialism are felt beyond military and political domination. Therefore, it is a mistake to think that the problems introduced by colonialism came to an end with the conclusion of the formal colonial era (which is certainly ongoing in various places around the world). The colonial, in other words, goes beyond forms of "power over" human populations. It is also discursive and epistemic; it operates through bio- and necropolitics, controlling all aspects of life and death.[6] This means that an analysis of colonized people's interpretation of the world and of their conditions of marginality and dehumanization requires a conception of power as engrained beyond physical domination. To "decolonize," therefore, has come to mean the reclaiming of land *along with* cultural practices, epistemologies, and ways of knowing that decenter western European and Christian-centric universalizing epistemes.[7] As critics have pointed out, in spite of their desire to create universal values, these epistemes remain parochial in their outlook.

Coloniality dates to 1492. This is much earlier than where the comparative study of religion begins its own conventional examination of the colonial legacy of the category of religion (the European wars of religion are one starting point in this chronology of modern religion, and the study of philology in the nineteenth century is another). Such works trace the

Euro-Christian provinciality of "religion" as a definition deployed to map a world ripe for domination.

Scholarship that grapples with the study of religion's colonial legacy typically focuses on the deployment of the anthropological category of religion in the taxonomy of empire. The power to define, on these accounts, constitutes the power to control and contain.[8] The containment of "religion" has been carried out by colonial actors packaging it as a form of belief that adheres to a certain set of principles or dogmas. This has allowed them to identify and privilege key "religious actors" in their effort to further domesticate and fragment communities. European philosophy, theology, and political thought define, as cultural anthropologist Talal Asad has elucidated, the constitutive categories of the "secular" and "religious" and universalize them. This is a process of epistemic violence against which other theorists and practitioners try to resuscitate "tradition" from the claws of modernity as a supposed antidote to our current ills.[9] This binary framing, as Omer has argued elsewhere, reflects antimodernists' modernism.[10]

Still, these are important interventions. They introduce critical levels of disciplinary self-reflexivity. What they miss, however, is that an intersectional and decolonial analysis of "religion" needs to go back to 1492 and the onset of the Eurocentric Christian colonial project.[11] Recent interventions in the study of religion have drawn on insights from scholarship focused on the coloniality of power.[12] The CM blog, for example, hosted a sustained series of conversations by multiple scholars working in various subfields within the academic study of religion, including comparative religious ethics, Continental philosophy of religion, and theory and method in the study of religion. Collectively, they began to meaningfully connect modernity/coloniality scholarship to the academic study of religion and deepen the discussion around what precisely is meant by decolonizing the study of religion.[13]

Religion qua Christianity, as Slabodsky charts in his contribution, had been a mechanism entangled with the exploitative "doctrine of discovery," the consolidation of which coincided with the Inquisition and an emerging discourse about blood purity and identity.[14] Certainly, "race," even before race became a social/biological category, was already an instrument of nation-making during the Spanish Inquisition. The latter, it is important to note, coincided with Spain's colonial expansion. During this time, it deployed a racialization logic to justify dispossession and elimination through conversion and other forms of death, including cultural and epistemic forms. Religion as a racialized category, then, was deployed to identify those with the "correct" religion (Christians), "incorrect" or "false" religion (Muslims and Jews, or the two "others" of Europe), and those deemed to have no religion and thus to be less than human and targets for colonial control, conversion, and liquidation.[15]

Slabodsky, therefore, takes a long historical view in order to approach the contemporary configuration of religion and empire as expressed through the institution of the modern nation-state. The state confines the analysis of religion and politics to a comparative (hermetically closed) methodology rather than a relational one. The latter most clearly illuminates the links between *evolutionism*, or the discourse of false inclusion, and *dualism*, or forced exclusion. Evolutionism, which Slabodsky also interprets through a discourse of modern altruism, refers to Europe's inclusion of others via a discourse of progress. Such progress can appear in the form of accepting Christianity or in conforming to Europeans' understandings of democracy and "development." By *dualism* as forced exclusion, Slabodsky refers to the impossibility of erasing otherness. Accordingly, he states, "non-European populations, no matter how much they try to achieve the goal forced upon them, always remain suspect of not being Christian/civilized/developed/democratic enough and end their lives as 'terrorists,' exhausted laborers, or as 'collateral victims' in the advancement of the only truth. The altruism of modern liberation, then, is premised from a very early stage on a genocidal program."

Slabodsky's account of coloniality exposes the convergences and cross-fertilization between inclusive liberal values and genocidal legacies that live on in the contemporary manifestations of right-wing racist populist nationalisms of the kinds we examined in *Religion, Populism, and Modernity*. In light of this claim, the likes of Bolsonaro, Modi, Meloni, and Trump in the world must be analyzed through the lens of coloniality. This requires—and here, Slabodsky's intervention is decidedly different from Jakelić's contribution—one to resist a hermetic comparative lens in favor of a global decolonial outlook that can discern the matrices of coloniality and their afterlives. "Since its inception," Slabodsky writes, "coloniality has woven an intimate relation between (what we today refer to as) 'right-wing' genocidal practices and seemingly altruistic liberal discourses of inclusion," and so an analysis of the contemporary cruelty of political regimes must unsettle the persistent navel-gazing approach to history within which Europe is the only actor. Framing coloniality as an ongoing epistemic but also a political, sociocultural, and economic phenomenon helps Slabodsky clarify the need to unsettle methodological nationalism and show how the comparative approach is itself implicated in colonial afterlives.

Triangulating the critical study of religion with scholarship on coloniality and its genealogy, therefore, clarifies religion's complicity with empire and colonialism. It also shows how contemporary political theory and its intellectual inheritance dictate the present role assigned to religion in the "public sphere" (a contested space defined by the power of exclusion/inclusion). "Religion," therefore, as a "generic" normative category often denotes Christianity and its history of complicity with empire and the "nation" as a secular and political space likewise defined by western Christian modernity. This backdrop delineates the correct boundaries of "religion," what counts as one, and how it might relate to the thresholds of inclusion/exclusion into the discourse of citizenship.

Religion's complicity with the hegemonic epistemic modern/colonial constellation has manifested differently in various historical epochs. This includes an earlier emphasis on either the death or conversion of natives, and attempts to create a colonial taxonomy where subjects could be categorized and controlled across empires and colonies. This was done with the aim of dehumanizing people's sense of worth so as to exploit their labor, enslave them, occupy and displace them, and finally eliminate them. A genocidal logic, the decolonial outlook that Slabodsky conveys in his contribution, is not incidental nor is it a perversion, but rather it is central to modernity as a project that relies on racializing religion in nation-state making. Likewise, and in the contemporary moment, Fadil's analysis examines the dualistic logic of exclusion in technologies deployed to maintain the "secular, liberal" dimensions of the metropolitan centers of (former) empires. She specifically focuses on the regulation of political subjects' Muslimness in Belgium. What Sayyid points out as a foundational paradox between the pretenses of liberalism and the politics and violence of empire and (neo)colonial configurations, Fadil shows through a scrutiny of "deradicalization" policies in Europe, a vector in the global "War on Terror." She reveals the fragility of the modern political liberal order and its dependency upon singling out Muslimness as marked "religion" and "ideology." The "old" therefore did not die, it just changed its technologies and shapes.

Fadil's contribution also operates in an expository and demystifying mode, seeking to reveal the ontological and politico-theological dimensions of so-called deradicalization policies designed to prevent the manifestations of "religious extremism," where the "religious" is a marked category denoting the "other" of Europe, in this case the Muslim. Fadil illustrates how Muslims in Europe are represented as a "subterranean threat" to the political and social body and how pathological/medical metaphors such as "cancer" are deployed to rationalize invasive "containment" and eradication policies. Slabodsky's analysis amplifies Fadil's archaeology of deradicalization policies in Europe and the broader motif concerning the undying character of colonial formations and their reconfiguration. As in Slabodsky's piece, in Fadil's we find that inclusion within the liberal order's body politic requires a form of assimilation akin to annihilation. Sayyid thinks together with Slabodsky and Fadil about what their respective critiques of overt and covert Christian modernity/coloniality—as inscribed into necropolitical (and politically liberal)—violence means in relation to the broader conversation about decolonial horizons and what they might look like relative to concepts such as multiple and contending modernities.

If Slabodsky, Fadil, and Sayyid bring to the fore the political and social ramifications of colonial afterlives, Mavelli and Frettingham turn our attention to the economic sphere, bringing to light the religious anatomy of the hegemonic discourse of neoliberal capitalism. Their analysis is archaeological, seeking to excavate the metaphysical foundations of neoliberal theory and secularism. To this effect, they analyze the work of the "founding fathers" and architects of neoliberalism: Ludwig von Mises and Friedrich Hayek. They pay special attention to how these thinkers interpreted the place and role of "generic" religion (qua Christianity) in society. Mavelli and Frettingham subsequently argue that neoliberal secularism takes the market as a natural secular reality that constitutes the space from which religion is to be assessed for its function and use. This examination demystifies secularism and shows it to be an ideology that polices religion and promotes capitalism. Similarly, neoliberal practices assume spiritual and religious connotations and meanings. For example, philanthropy becomes a form of religious piety and, echoing Calvinist traditions, wealth signifies divine chosenness, a variation of which is the "prosperity gospel." The latter has taken hold and buttressed exploitative neoliberal policies. It has entrenched marginality in already marginalized and exploited regions in the Global South and marginalized and underserved communities in the Global North.

In their analysis of the metaphysical and theological anatomy of neoliberalism, Mavelli and Frettingham underscore the importance of studies in secularism for understanding and theorizing religion and modernity, and especially religion and colonial afterlives. Indeed, according to scholars versed in decolonial thought, neoliberalism is a contemporary manifestation of a colonial framework that morphed over the centuries from an initial Christian cosmological licensing of "discovery," plunder, exploitation, dispossession, slavery, and elimination to a discourse of "progress," "civilizational mission," "democracy," and neoliberal "development."[16] Understanding the neoliberal not only as a locus for colonial afterlives but also as the contemporary register of the same old colonial framework (or the colonial undying) requires the kind of careful analysis Mavelli and Frettingham extend to the metaphysical and Christian theological underpinnings of the "secular" as it features in the thought of neoliberal ideologues. They bring into the conversation mountains of research in the anthropology and colonial history of religion: "Secularisms are colonial epistemic regimes that construct 'the religious' as a universal, transcultural, and transhistorical dimension, thus concealing their contingent western-centric historical situatedness." Accordingly, their focus is on secularisms as "colonial epistemic regimes . . . that have been themselves colonized by neoliberal rationalities." They challenge the conceptual limits that the nation-state framework imposes on the analysis of secularism. Hence, instead of asking questions about French or Indian secularisms, they interrogate and distinguish what they call "political, economic, scientific, and even religious secularisms." They demonstrate the artificiality of national boundaries in their scrutiny of the secular challenges and disrupt the methodological nationalism still haunting the analysis of religion and modernity, an analysis that also involves a scrutiny of secular traditions. Slabodsky also supports this point when he critiques the hermetic approach to religion and nationalism for its conceptual blind spots. Indeed, such hermeticism supports the continued haunting of the nation-state by colonial afterlives.

Mavelli and Frettingham posit religion as a generic category that denotes "religion in general." This generic religion is of course the topic of countless critical works in the academic study of religion and adjacent fields.[17] In reality, the generic and comparative anthropological category of "religion" is not actually generic but specifically located in the theological, philosophical, intellectual, and political Christian-European projects of modernity. This insight is pivotal for any effort to extend, deepen, and illuminate creative openings for the study of religion and modernity. To this extent, Mavelli and Frettingham's reading of the intellectual genealogy of neoliberalism as an expression of secular modernity reveals that religious metaphysics has been lurking and colonizing all along. Even though the "secular" appears to colonize religion (through the ever-expansion of the market's logic), the "stand-alone" economic sphere of the market that seeks to apply a market logic to marketize all aspects of life is itself an expression of a colonized consciousness underpinned by a Christian political theology. Thus, Mavelli and Frettingham connect to the prevailing motifs put forward by scholars of coloniality who interpret religion as the midwife of empire, sometimes hidden but always lurking. If the colonial is undying, so is the religion that is hardwired into its political and economic projects, whether they are articulated explicitly through genocidal registers or more "nicely" through liberal political discourses. For Anidjar, who has written influentially about the Christian infrastructure of western modernity, this self-colonizing and ever-expanding neoliberalism, with its undergirding Christian cosmology, is the urgent all-consuming fire that is too often ignored, denied, and sublimated. At the same time, fictional fires, such as programs focused on the "deradicalization" of Muslims in Europe that Fadil examines, seek to redirect people's attention away from the real fires that consume them.

In this volume, Slabodsky connects the appearances of inclusivity with the eliminative colonial logic most explicitly. Indeed, for him, both are merely different shades of the same modernist logic that the concept of coloniality captures. Within critical scholarship on coloniality and comparative religions, "religion" appears as a nefarious actor, either lurking behind the scenes (in the "syntax" and "grammar" of coloniality), authorizing violence and domination, or disguising itself via the "secular" as a "public space" supposedly emancipated from the shackles of traditions. On this account, discourses of multiculturalism and democratic pluralism have replaced the older tendency to universalize and violently force conversion to Christianity. But such "nice" appearances do not confuse those aware of the underlying colonial logic that is still operative in liberal secular discourse.

Liberal concepts such as "multiculturalism" are merely a new guise for the same old Christian-centric and Eurocentric epistemology and geopolitics.

However, too often this demystification is/can be myopic. This is because its proponents seek to transcend the same situatedness they ascribe to the structures, actors, traditions, and ideologies they analyze. They claim to omnisciently see the matrices of control and all their intersections and totalizing upshots. At the same time, the empirical findings from CM's research in Indonesia, for example, shows how ethical concepts such as pluralism cannot simply be theorized away as merely a contemporary variation on an old theme.[18] Instead this context-specific work shows the importance of teasing out colonial afterlives without reducing the situation to one in which coloniality is the only defining feature of people's social and political life. For this reason, an acknowledgment of the situatedness of the scholar and of those they study is a necessary ground for critical engagement with religion, modernity, and coloniality.

Reaching for the Post-Abyssal

Thinking constructively about religion and its colonial afterlives requires exposing the ongoing role of religion in neocolonial grammars. However, the challenge is also to disrupt purist approaches to religious traditions that always read them through the same prism. Any critique that overcomes purism requires a simultaneous (intersectional and gendered) critique of the nation-state, colonial expansion, and racial capitalism. To advocate for a closed account of "tradition" that stands in contrast with "modernity" is itself a modernist move and is as problematic as the hermetic approach to nationalism that Slabodsky challenges.[19] Further, it leaves uninterrogated the multiple ways in which alternative syntaxes develop as a result of multi-directional exchange and porousness, a point that Lynch illuminates in her contribution. Such pluralism is captured in the decolonial intervention as an ongoing encounter that undoes what Boaventura de Sousa Santos calls "an abyssal thinking."

With the phrase "abyssal thinking," Santos refers to a colonial division between Europe and its colonized lands. A geopolitical line also constituted a normative one whereby those beyond the abyss were dehumanized as "subjects," "slaves," and "savages." Abyssal normativity differentiated the colonial metropolitan forms of sociability and ethics from what became acceptable on the other side of the line. The postcolonial moment, however, brought colonized communities to the metropoles, complicating clear-cut boundaries between the two forms of sociability, and exposing the inherent contradictions in the liberal discourse, as Slabodsky sketches in his chapter. The South is no longer merely a geography "over there," outside of Europe. Instead there are many "Souths" in the postcolonies that have come into being through the continued racialization of postcolonial "subjects." This is a point that Fadil demonstrates in her focus on deradicalization policies in Europe. The abyssal line divides social realities radically to "this side of the line" and "the other side of the line" in ways that resonate with other decolonial thinkers, such as Frantz Fanon and Sylvia Wynter, who focus on ontological divides of being versus nonbeing.[20] What defines this abyss, for Santos, is "the impossibility of the copresence of the two sides of the line." The line signifies the boundary between legality and illegality, reason and unreason, and truth versus untruth; it is where religion "proper" has been contrasted with "incomprehensible beliefs, idolatry, magic."[21]

Post-abyssal thinking, therefore, calls for decentering western epistemology through a focus on an epistemology of the South. It does so, however, without succumbing to the temptation to become a reactive eliminative project (in the way some neotraditionalist approaches do).[22] Indeed, this process constitutes a necessary mechanism for an emancipatory deployment of human rights. Santos reads human rights in part as a tool of colonial power that progressively (especially after the end of the Cold War) diminished the gains resulting from an expansive socialist interpretation of rights, which also included economic and social rights. Still, looking at the havoc wreaked by neoliberal violence, Santos seeks to recover the socialist genealogy of rights as one with an empowering potentiality for "turning despair into hope."[23]

The problem is that most of the scholarship that flirts with decoloniality stops with exposing the abyssal line, rather than also taking Santos's invitation to reimagine social justice in a way that moves past a logic of radical ontological and epistemological negation. Critics of religion who draw on the insights of decolonial theory, such as Nelson Maldonado-Torres, describe and redescribe the abyssal lines and religion's intersection with this violent ethical topography. This turn is necessary, but beholden to meta categories and narratives that sometimes, by design, detract from a historically and hermeneutically layered analyses that might reveal more liminal realities than those demarcated by this binaristic framework. Moving beyond this mode of critique is especially urgent when one finds herself in the midst of suffering, pain, and violence, which are not mere academic exercises but empirical realities to be transformed concretely and through modern mechanisms, such as human rights, international law, and democratic politics.[24]

The decolonial lens, of course, also operates within religious communities, and its proponents there engage in theological and rational debates that resist hermetically closed and "literal" accounts of their traditions. They also enhance the methodology of "double critique."[25] Here, reclaiming religious and cultural traditions disrupts purist antimodernist accounts of religious traditions that often also come with sociopolitical, patriarchal, and heteronormative frames. Double critique entails taking an anticolonial stance while resisting ahistorical reified accounts of religious traditions that reinscribe heteropatriarchal and other violent norms. Indeed, when religion is isolated from sociopolitical and economic contexts, as it so often is in ahistorical neotraditional approaches, we have failed to escape the colonial afterlife. This is because such a sequestering and ossifying (in ahistorical texts and dogmas/prescriptions) reflects a modernist discourse of authenticity that serves to depoliticize religiosity, a familiar colonial domesticating move.

However, this volume as a whole interrogates the colonial afterlives (the old that refuses to die) not only through an archaeology of religion that shows it to be a tool of empire and racialization in the postcolonial moment—and within the frames of nation-states that still define modernity's political organization—but also, in some cases, in its examination of how religion exceeds the bounds of coloniality/modernity. The contributions by Jakelić and Lynch offer instances to think about the meaning of decolonizing the study of religion in reference to the concrete themes of humanitarianism and political solidarity/nationalism.

All our contributors, through different intellectual genealogies (with occasional overlaps and cross-pollination), tackle the ways in which the old is not dead but lives on through different guises and registers. Schematically, the archaeological approach is pronounced in part I in the contributions by Slabodsky, Fadil, Sayyid, and Mavelli and Frettingham, who, when viewed together, identify, demystify, and expose the metaphysical and/or colonial and biopolitical underpinnings of "colonial afterlives." In part II, the chapters by Lynch and Jakelić, on the other hand, move beyond the diagnostic by imagining alternatives to the abyssal framework. Lynch focuses on the praxis of humanitarianism, and Jakelić scrutinizes the apparent tension between the ethics of identity and solidarity and argues that seeing them as opposed to one another is a product of a modernist framework that is inconsistent with the empirical realities of collectivistic identity. Grounded in a decolonial critical analysis of religion and humanitarianism, Lynch's contribution unsettles a binary construction that positions Indigenous traditions in contrast to colonial hegemonic religion and colonial political frameworks. Indeed, the morphology of religion and humanitarianism constitutes a complex colonial afterlife reflective of universalizing legacies where secular values themselves are underpinned by the colonial politics of defining the "secular" and "religious" for the sake of expansion and control.[26]

Still, even though religion (namely, Christianity) is implicated in the modern colonial infrastructure and expansion of "the west," it cannot be reduced to it. By examining the elastic and persistent manifestations of precolonial religious traditions on the African continent, Lynch exposes postcolonial humanitarianism as a site where, despite rhetorical claims otherwise, the old colonial practices seeking to reify religious traditions and practices of indigeneity persist. To this degree, the old is not dying but is simply reconfigured yet again through a different vocabulary.

Lynch's contribution, however, questions the possibility of truly decolonizing religion and in doing so raises the question of what decolonizing religion even means. A focus on the practices of humanitarianism and their articulations by Islamic and Christian aid organizations reroutes the analysis from a presumed destination of "decolonial religion" to more fluid, multiperspectival, and contextually/historically located contestations of religious and cultural traditions as they relate to human and environmental flourishing. Lynch's analysis, therefore, scrutinizes the colonial afterlives underlying the international and global practices of humanitarianism. This includes an interrogation of Christian missionary and cosmological imperialism and their complicity with modern colonialism. This interrogation, however, avoids reinscribing binaries and engaging in an anticolonial romanticism when scrutinizing postcolonial humanitarianism.

TENSIONS

To recap, Lynch scrutinizes the colonial afterlives of the humanitarian sphere of religion and the industry of global aid. At the same time, Mavelli and Frettingham expose the religious anatomy of a hegemonic discourse of neoliberal capitalism. In different ways, each contributor unearths the underlying logics of Euro-Christian colonial modernity. If Mavelli and Frettingham excavate the underside of the secular domains of an ever-expanding and colonizing neoliberal logic, Fadil uncovers the ontological and politico-theological rationality underlying deradicalization policies, and Slabodsky exposes how European Christianity is indeed at the core of a long history of coloniality, and he seeks to disrupt a comparative (and hermetic) approach to the study of nationalism. Jakelić is similarly concerned with the modernist construction of the nation-state. She ponders the dynamics of, and tensions between, an ethics of solidarity and an ethics of identity. Contemporary populist trends expose these twin ethics as central to understanding religion and modernity. They require an interrogation of the "we" that constitutes identities (often marked in flags and equipped with military forces).

Jakelić focuses on the Balkans as Europe's European "other" and thus she highlights the Balkans as constituting a site of instructive liminality that can puncture some of the critical assumptions hardwired into archaeological accounts of modernity/coloniality. One of these is that such an approach has struggled to seriously interrogate regional and national variations. This struggle is the result of such an approach's supposed interest in grammar rather than the details that an in-depth study of nation-state making and remaking from the margins produces. The archaeological/grammatical interest is in identifying subjects, objects, and syntax. This zero-sum approach allows no flexibility in terms of thinking through what Omer has referred to elsewhere as the "hermeneutics of citizenship,"[27] which denotes constructive interpretive horizons of imagining belonging that are born from counterhegemonic experiences and marginal epistemologies.

Jakelić reclaims Christian humanism in a way that seeks to avoid falling into patterns of dehumanization that have characterized it in the past. She, accordingly, examines the case of a religious actor grounded in Christian humanism and an ethical discourse of solidarity with (im)migrant/refugees in contemporary Europe. She asks whether collectivistic affect and a sense of belonging to particular communities also and necessarily delimit the boundaries and thresholds of solidarity. Pivotal to this analysis is the question as to what degree the relationship between identity and solidarity become teleologically bound together in ways that replicate secular progress narratives, even if the intent is decolonial. Indeed, one of the critical unknowns of decolonial futures is their lack of clear narratives about what vocabularies underpin the "common good within the pluriverse."[28]

Jakelić asks to what degree the confinement of the ethics of solidarity to the ethics of identity is a modernist phenomenon that once again expresses a colonial/modernist afterlife. Like Lynch, Jakelić unsettles a binary and modernist explanatory frame that, in this instance, assigned the ethics of identity and affective belonging to "tradition" and thus premodernity, and solidarity to a supposedly ethically transcending communal bond, and thus to "secular modernity." This binary script, which Jakelić also reads through Santos's notion of "abyssal thinking," itself overlooks a more nuanced analysis that exposes the very construction of tradition as a counter to "progressive" modernist ethics. Both "tradition" and "identity," as noted in our above discussion of antimodern modernism, are products of colonial modernity even if/when they posit themselves as anticolonial sites of resistance. Hence, Jakelić's focus on the Balkans and practices of solidarity through Christian humanism "uncovers," in her words, "another, liminal experience of modernity that gives rise to a productive relationship between the ethics of identity and the ethics of solidarity. This liminal experience of modernity is instructive for how we envision forceful—particular *and* pluriversal—challenges to antipluralism, exclusivism, and violence established by various forms of populist identitarianism and by 'identitarian essentialisms.'"

Jakelić's effort to illuminate liminal experiences and formations within the abyssal colonial framework and also grapple with the tensions between the ethics of solidarity and identity foreground the constructive potential of a post-abyssal engagement. What is at stake is not only the identification of the colonial undying through an archaeological demystification, but also an interrogation of the positive hermeneutical meanings that affective belongings can produce in imagining and reimagining belonging. Thinking beyond the binary of identity versus solidarity constitutes a critical intervention in our effort to open up pathways for theorizing religion and modernity that employ an archaeological demystifying investigative method, but also asks how religious meanings that exceed the colonial frame can populate a post-abyssal humanism and inclusionary political ethics. After all, it is not the case that the concepts of inclusion and belonging are in their essence bad, but rather that they function as a window dressing for undying coloniality.

Jakelić's contribution, therefore, gestures toward alternative horizons for articulating a politics of belonging that, in her view, is robustly collectivistic without being eliminative or genocidal as conveyed in Slabodsky's critique. The Balkans' liminality (and this is where Jakelić's intervention connects with Homi Bhabha's postmodern concept of hybridity) indeed disrupts an abyssal account and complicates decolonial theory when one grapples with the region historically, comparing colonialities.[29] The risk of Jakelić's effort to "save" Christianity from its entanglement with empire by positing a form of a universalizable Christian humanism and drawing epistemologically on European intellectual traditions is that it might re-import Christian cosmology through a different currency yet again. Jakelić's intervention draws on Santos's concept of the abyss, but it perhaps connects more robustly with a postmodern rather than the decolonial interpretive framework employed by Fadil, Sayeed, and Slabodsky in part I. From their point of view, a decolonial move that only focuses on hybridity or the semiperiphery of the Balkans without accounting for the deep history of the coloniality of power and the global frameworks of racialization and dehumanization does not constitute a decolonial proposal but rather a reform within liberal (inclusivist rather than eliminative) sensibilities.

Jakelić's contribution and the tension it has with the decolonial outlook surfaces the problems of actually practicing decoloniality within the study of religion and politics when the political imagination is delimited to the terms of coloniality/modernity and when market rationality, which is itself undergirded by Christian modernity, is all-consuming. On a related point, Sayyid quotes Wittgenstein, "A picture held us captive. And we could not get outside it, for it lay in our language and language seemed to repeat it to us inexorably." We will let the tension simmer and lurk in the background with the hope it can be generative for theory and practice.

We return to Gramsci's oft-quoted illumination, which declared that the old is dying while the new cannot yet be born. Applying it to this volume's analysis of colonial afterlives, we seek to move from analytic frames that expose, in effect, the old colonial as an undying phoenix to examining hermeneutical innovation and reimaginations of belonging and post-abyssal human rights. In doing so, we aim to highlight where the new is being born, here in potentially alternative scripts/grammars that affirm human life, equality, equity, and pluralism. Let us cite Sayyid's powerful words once again: "Can we use the logic of modern subjectivities to present the past without dehistoricizing it? Or can we make the assumption that one cartographic expression is exterior to another, when both formulations are the expression of the same cartography? This is a cartography underwritten by the gradual enframing of the planet through imperial racial-colonial logic. Modern/colonial epistemologies and liberal democracies are where critiques of modernity become possible and simultaneously contentious."

NOTES

1. Antonio Gramsci, *Selections from Prison Notebooks* (New York: International Publishers, 1971), 276.

2. E.g., Saba Mahmood, *The Politics of Piety: The Islamic Revival and the Feminist Subject* (Princeton, NJ: Princeton University Press, 2005).

3. On the development of racial capitalism, see Cedric Robinson, *Black Marxism: The Making of the Black Radical Tradition* (Chapel Hill: University of North Carolina Press, 1983).

4. The concept of "coloniality" was first articulated by Aníbal Quijano in his "Coloniality of Power, Eurocentrism, and Latin America," *Nepantla: Views from South* 1, no. 3 (2000): 533–80.

5. This definition follows closely the one laid out by Nadia Fadil in her contribution; see note 23 in chapter 2.

6. Achille Mbembe, *Necropolitics* (Durham, NC: Duke University Press, 2019[2016]).

7. Eve Tuck and K. Wayne Yang, "Decolonization Is Not a Metaphor," *Decolonization: Indigeneity, Education & Society* 1, no. 1 (2012): 1–40. See also Catherine E. Walsh and Walter D. Mignolo, *On Decoloniality: Concepts, Analytics, Praxis* (Durham, NC: Duke University Press, 2018).

8. For example, David Chidester, *Empire of Religion: Imperialism and Comparative Religion* (Chicago: Chicago University Press, 2014). See also Tomoko Masuzawa, *The Invention of World Religions; or, How European Universalism Was Preserved in the Language of Pluralism* (Chicago: University of Chicago Press, 2005); and Tisa Joy Wenger, *Religious Freedom: The Contested History of an American Ideal* (Chapel Hill: University of North Carolina Press, 2017).

9. For example, Talal Asad, *Secular Translations: Nation-State, Modern Self, and Calculative Reason* (New York: Columbia University Press, 2018).

10. Atalia Omer, "Modernists Despite Themselves: The Phenomenology of the Secular and the Limits of Critique as an Instrument of Change," *Journal of the American Academy of Religion* 83, no. 1 (2015): 27–71.

11. For example, S. Sayyid, "Empire, Islam and the Postcolonial," in University of South Australia's International Centre for Muslim and Non-Muslim Understanding Working Paper No. 9 (2012), https://apo.org.au/sites/default/files/resource-files/2012-07/apo-nid57054.pdf.

12. See Nelson Maldonado-Torres, "AAR Centennial Roundtable: Religion, Conquest, and Race in the Foundations of the Modern/Colonial World," *Journal of the American Academy of Religion* 82, no. 3 (2014): 636–65; Gil Anidjar, *Blood: A Critique of Christianity* (New York: Columbia University Press, 2014); and Anthony Marx, *Faith in Nation* (Oxford: Oxford University Press, 2003).

13. See the essays collected at https://contendingmodernities.nd.edu/category/decoloniality/.

14. See also Anidjar, *Blood*.

15. Nelson Maldonado-Torres, *Against War: Views from the Underside of Modernity* (Durham, NC: Duke University Press, 2008).

16. See Ramón Grosfoguel, "Decolonizing Post-Colonial Studies and Paradigms of Political Economy: Transmodernity, Decolonial Thinking, and Global Coloniality," *Transmodernity: Journal of Peripheral Cultural Production of the Luso-Hispanic World* 1, no. 1 (2011), https://dialogoglobal.com/texts/grosfoguel/Grosfoguel-Decolonizing-Pol-Econ-and-Postcolonial.pdf.

17. Talal Asad, *Genealogies of Religion: Discipline and Reasons of Power in Islam and Christianity* (Baltimore: Johns Hopkins University Press, 1993); Tomoko Masuzawa, *The Invention of World Religions*; Chidester, *Empire of Religion*.

18. Robert W. Hefner and Zainal Abidin Bagir, eds., *Indonesian Pluralities: Islam, Citizenship, and Democracy* (Notre Dame, IN: University of Notre Dame Press, 2021).

19. Examples of such "closed accounts" include Alasdair MacIntyre, *After Virtue: A Study in Moral Theory* (Notre Dame, IN: University of Notre Dame Press, 1981); and John Milbank, *Theology and Social Theory: Beyond Secular Reason* (Malden, MA: Blackwell, 1990). For a critique of this "new traditionalism" from the perspective of democratic political theory, see Jeffrey Stout, *Democracy and Tradition* (Princeton, NJ: Princeton University Press, 2004), esp. chaps. 5 and 6; for a feminist critique of communitarianism more broadly, see Susan Moller Okin, *Justice, Gender, and the Family* (New York: Basic Books, 1989).

20. Sylvia Wynter, "Unsettling the Coloniality of Being/Power/Truth/Freedom: Towards the Human, after Man, Its Overrepresentation—An Argument," *New Centennial Review* 3, no. 3 (2003): 257–337; Frantz Fanon, *Black Skin, White Masks*, trans. Richard Philcox (New York: Grove Press, 2008[1952]), xii. See also Lewis R. Gordon, "Through the Zone of Nonbeing: A Reading of *Black Skin,*

White Masks in Celebration of Fanon's Eightieth Birthday," *C. L. R. James Journal* 11, no. 1 (2005): 1–43.

21. Boaventura de Sousa Santos, "Beyond Abyssal Thinking: From Global Lines to Ecologies of Knowledges," *Review* (Fernand Braudel Center) 30, no. 1 (2007): 45.

22. For an example of this reactive approach, see William Cavanaugh, *Torture and the Eucharist: Theology, Politics, and the Body of Christ* (Malden, MA: Blackwell, 1998).

23. See https://criticallegalthinking.com/2020/01/25/toward-a-new-universal-declaration-of-human-rights-i/. See also Boaventura de Sousa Santos, *Toward a New Legal Common Sense: Law, Globalization, and Emancipation* (London: Butterworths, 2002).

24. Atalia Omer, *Decolonizing Religion and Peacebuilding* (Oxford: Oxford University Press, 2023).

25. Santiago Slabodsky, "Christian Hegemonies: Evolutionism, Analectics, and the Question of Interreligiosity in a Decolonial Philosophy of Religion," Colloquium on Coloniality, Race, and Philosophy of Religion, Harvard Divinity School, November 30, 2018.

26. See Cecelia Lynch and Tanya B. Schwarz, "Humanitarianism's Proselytism Problem," *International Studies Quarterly* 60, no. 4 (2016): 636–46.

27. Atalia Omer, *When Peace Is Not Enough: How the Israeli Peace Camp Thinks about Religion, Nationalism, and Justice* (Chicago: University of Chicago Press, 2013).

28. Claire Gallien, "A Decolonial Turn in the Humanities," *Alif: Journal of Comparative Poetics* 40 (2020): 29.

29. Manuela Boatcă, *Global Inequalities beyond Occidentalism* (New York: Routledge, 2016); Walter D. Mignolo and Madina V. Tlostanova, "Theorizing from the Borders: Shifting to Geo- and Body-Politics of Knowledge," *European Journal of Social Theory* 9, no. 2 (2006): 205–21.

PART I

Religion, Politics, and Colonial Afterlives, or the Old Is Not Dying

CHAPTER 1

Seeing the Old in the New

The Coloniality of the Liberal–Populist Marriage

SANTIAGO SLABODSKY

ABSTRACT

This chapter explores the epistemological implications of the hermetic Euro-American comparative political sociology that treats the centers of geopolitical power as the origin, theater, and motor of world history. It argues that maintaining hierarchical "area studies" silos makes it difficult to understand that certain political developments in centers of power are not new, but rather a continuation and adaptation of projects implemented years, decades, or even centuries before in the bodies and knowledges of non-Europeans in Global South/East locations. Following Afro-Caribbean, Arab, and Latin American scholarship, the chapter argues that this hermeticism led to misunderstanding the Holocaust as an "aberration" instead of a historical "norm," misnaming the post–World War II confrontation as a "Cold War" as it was boiling in heat outside the centers of power, and now may be occluding the antecedents that enable the "new" marriage between "right-wing populist" and "altruistic" inclusive liberal discourses. The chapter explains the implications of this exploration for the study of racism, in general, and antisemitism and Islamophobia, in particular, and shows how current scholarly trends are moving toward a broader relational project connecting decolonial and interimperial studies that can offer a more accurate account of current political developments.

Ending European Hierarchical Hermeticism

Between the early summer of 2018 and early spring of 2019, a group of global critical intellectuals met under the auspices of the University of Notre Dame's Contending Modernities Project co-led by Atalia Omer, R. Scott Appleby, and Ebrahim Moosa. During the first event, one of our common readings was the recent article "Between Nationalism and Civilizationism" by the acclaimed UCLA sociologist Rogers Brubaker, which is a sharp and incisive analysis of the European "populist" movements from a comparative perspective. Brubaker explains, probably better than the vast majority of scholarship, the transformations that have enabled a threatening phenomenon: the emergence of extreme "populist" movements throughout "the" Continent in the first decades of the twenty-first century. This movement takes a religious, generic Christian, civilizationist identity and brandishes it as a banner to unify its xenophobic nationalist aspirations throughout Europe and, with distinctive particularities, in the United States. In the European case, what seems particularly remarkable is the adoption of liberal inclusive social values for extreme "right-wing" programs. Today, perhaps for the first time since their defeat in World War II, these alternatives are actual regional options for state power.[1]

There is, however, one striking feature of this reading that should make us interrogate the scope of Brubaker's method. The political landscape seems to be changing globally. From the rise to power of Narendra Modi in India in 2014 to the electoral success of Jair Bolsonaro in Brazil in 2019, we have seen parallel phenomena taking over key spaces across the Global South. Some of the best analyses, by Brubaker, among others, interpret the sociology of European politics only in light of internal European (or Euro-American) dynamics. Bold readings may explain the repercussions that these developments have on the rest of the world, but the possibility that the rest of the world could influence the development of European politics is scarcely contemplated. This hermetic reading of the sociology of Euro-American politics invariably ends up identifying the Global North as the uncontaminated origin, theater, and motor of world history.[2]

In order to interrogate this phenomenon, I would like to reflect on Aimé Césaire's advice for geopolitical caution postulated in his *Discourse of Colonialism* at the outset of the 1950s. This text was written during the emergence of area studies, the very same field that enabled definitions of the Cold War as "cold" when it was boiling hot in southern and eastern locations. The Martinican social theorist identified an epistemological problem in the exclusive use of a geographically bounded European history to explain developments on "the Continent." He argues that what will be known as the Holocaust, unarguably a landmark for Euro-American self-understanding from at least the 1960s to our days, is interpreted erroneously when it is situated only within the bounds of Europe. Whereas Eurocentric intellectuals interpret the annihilation of millions of human beings as an aberration to Europe, adopting a longer-term and wider view from the rest of the world (populations in colonies, settler states, and migrants in the metropolis) illustrates how this genocidal bloodshed is actually the norm. For more than four hundred years, Europeans developed and perfected philosophies and programs of mass murder and annihilation of entire populations. These patterns of domination date from well before National Socialism/fascism, but Eurocentric epistemologies limit the comprehension of this phenomenon.[3]

Some intellectual movements never abandoned the importance of advising such geopolitical caution. To mention just one current example, today as part of the "Bandung of the North" grassroots project, Algerian-French activist and public intellectual Houria Bouteldja, an intellectual heir of Césaire, explains that not only Afro-Caribbeans in the colonies but also the descendants of Muslim colonized people in the metropolis recognize "Hitler" well beyond the history books or the programs of the new right-wing emergence. They find the Nationalist Socialist logic in the very same policies of the liberal imperialist republics that preceded the Holocaust, informed the genocide, and endured after it.[4]

The novel features of the current populist transformations are undeniable. But the relation between liberal inclusive values and genocidal programs, at least from a broader perspective that includes experiences of Afro-Caribbeans and Maghrebi-Muslims, is not necessarily new. It has in fact been the norm, not the exception. I am not proposing that we discard intra-European analysis because of its reductionist geopolitical perspective. We may recall that Edward Said frequently criticized Michel Foucault for the very same issue, but still identified as a Foucauldian.[5] But it is necessary to interrogate these perspectives within a broader framework. I would like to ask what we are missing when we read the political sociology of the new "right-wing populisms" exclusively according to Euro-America's internal developments. Just as some Eurocentric interpreters may have missed the boiling heat of the Cold War in other parts of the world or the historical genocidal programs that enabled the Holocaust, today we may also be missing systemic continuities. The fact that a particular connection (in this case, the marriage between inclusive values and genocide programs) is not seen with clarity from within Europe and North America does not mean that it does not exist or does not affect the majority of the world outside the North Atlantic. Furthermore, what we consider to be "new" may be part of a long-standing tradition that unfolded elsewhere and ultimately influenced the "center."

In order to put into practice this broader perspective, a relational methodology may be more helpful than a comparative strategy. Ella Shohat and Robert Stam propose that we may need to explore how discourses on race have been translated beyond the strict geopolitical units that were defined by area studies and frequently reproduce hierarchical patterns of influence.[6] This would allow us to trace how different political programs have traveled across continents and nation-states, and even used—as first happened during colonialism and imperialism, then the Holocaust, and finally the Cold War—spaces in the Southern/Eastern hemispheres to test and "perfect" extreme political programs with pernicious impunity. As such, what happens in the Global South/East may not be exclusively a consequence of developments in the Global North; rather, it may be well at the root of what will happen in Euro-America years, decades, or even centuries later. A relational method, then, enables a dynamic understanding of the navigation of ideas and political programs beyond the confines of area studies or unidirectional pathways. It also enables us to identify other locations as sites from which to interrogate the position of the Global North as the uncontaminated origin, theater, and motor of world history.

ᴄOLONIALITY, RELIGION, AND THE LIBERAL-GENOCIDAL MARRIAGE

I would like to explore in greater historical and conceptual depth two questions posed in the previous section. First, if we insist on the existing continuity of the relation between "right-wing" genocidal programs and liberal agendas for inclusion, how do we account for the beginnings and transformation of this discourse that fuses two seemingly opposed positions? And second, what theoretical tools do we have at our disposal to unveil and confront these discourses, especially as they pertain to two kinds of racisms that are central to our current volume, Islamophobia and philosemitism/antisemitism? Here, I will argue that some key features of current European discourse took shape outside of the Continent. They were part of a program of global domination that was established in the sixteenth and seventeenth centuries and helped shape the current political stage. This is to say that the current situation was deeply influenced by coloniality. By "coloniality," I mean neither "colonialism," which generally denotes the power of one political system over another, nor "neo-colonialism," which largely describes the multiple levels of dependency that follow actual political decolonization. "Coloniality" refers to the matrix created by the patterns of hierarchical domination that were developed during colonialism in colonial locations and are reproduced to structure and order global relations of power (knowledge, race, sexuality, labor) well after nominal political colonialism has ended.[7]

Since its inception, coloniality has woven an intimate relation between (what today we refer to as) "right-wing" genocidal practices and seemingly altruistic liberal discourses of inclusion. Here, I intend to discuss one influential trajectory that contributed to shaping the current context, but this is by no means the only one. In the seventeenth century, colonizing powers divided the world according to a tripartite system emerging from theological discourses. The first group was composed of people with the "right religion," namely, European Christianity. Their mandate was to spread this truth across the world through the use of redemptive violence, which they posited as necessary to accumulate the epistemological and material resources required to bring this plan to fruition. The second group was initially made up of Jews and Muslims and was described as having a "false religion." These communities were portrayed as rival projects to the first group's aims. They were seen as representatives of regressive traditions that were permanently plotting to destroy the advance of truth through open war or secret conspiracies that corrupted the body politic from within. It was precisely the alleged conspiracy, part of their supposed inability to fully overcome their impurified ancestry or blood, that made even those who submitted and were formally accepted (and/or forced) into the first group to remain permanent subjects of mistrust, persecution, and genocide.[8] The third group included people who were described as having "no religion," and whose humanity was thus questioned because religion became, in Catholic and then Protestant contexts, constitutive of selfhood. This group, initially identified with "Blacks" and "Indians," was forced to achieve an ever-elusive humanity by recognizing European superiority and becoming pawns in its project. Yet, neither courageous opposition nor aspirational submission would result in spiritual redemption or political liberation. Those who opposed "the truth" would most often be exterminated in "just wars." And those who submitted or were forced to submit would die under the duress of labor/sexual pawnship, or as a "collateral damage" of these just wars.[9]

It is precisely in the discourse about this last group that we see with clarity the connection between genocidal practices and liberal values. The altruistic dictum, "Convert—for your own good—or I will kill you," highlights the monopoly of the path toward salvation (then, that path was Christianity, and in the next centuries, civilization, development, and, finally, democracy). Not only were Europeans the exclusive owners of the "right path," they were responsible for bringing others to salvation. Religious, cultural, economic, or political liberation—modern symbols of liberal values—would ultimately end in permanent control under the threat of genocide or in genocide itself. The particularity of modern racism is that it was constituted through the interaction between two forces: (1) evolutionism (or forced inclusion) that operates when Europeans arrogate to themselves the ownership of the only "right path," define this path as a condition for achieving humanity, and "altruistically" force everyone to follow it; and (2) dualism (or forced exclusion), which is at work when non-European populations, no matter how much they try to achieve the goal forced upon them, always remain suspect of not being Christian/civilized/developed/democratic enough and end their lives as "terrorists," exhausted laborers, or as "collateral victims" in the advancement of the only truth. The altruism of modern liberation, then, is premised from a very early stage on a genocidal program.[10]

The religious dictum from the sixteenth and seventeenth centuries, "Convert—for your own good—or I will kill you," lived on in subsequent translations: during the eighteenth and nineteenth centuries, in a cultural key, "Civilize—for your own good—or I will kill you," and, in the (late) nineteenth and twentieth, in an economic-social format, "Develop—for your own good—or I will kill you." Finally, the overtly political dimension was added in the (late) twentieth and twenty-first centuries: "Democratize—for your own good—or I will kill you."[11] These were programs of forced inclusion (which "altruistically" saves, civilizes, develops, and finally democratizes non-Europeans), but were predicated on complete control of bodies and knowledges under the threat of—or under actual—genocide. Many resisted and were killed in scores. Others submitted (or were forced to submit) and died generating profit, from early modern accumulation to neoliberal capital expansion, for the centers of power and knowledge. But the promise of "liberation" did not, as Max Horkheimer and Theodor Adorno would posit within the North Atlantic, dialectically "turn into barbarism."[12] It was a genocidal project from the outset, premised on the partnership between liberal inclusiveness and right-wing exclusiveness on a genocidal spectrum of coloniality.

Antisemitism/Philosemitism and Islamophobia

The marriage between liberal inclusive values and genocidal programs eventually, or some may say in parallel and relationally, included Jews and Muslims. It is important, therefore, to interrogate the silos that are constructed between the multiple paths to describe the non-Europeanness mentioned above. From academic circuits currently dominated by Protestant, English-speaking perspectives, it is possible to argue that there was a transformation in the sixteenth century that divorced the modes of "the people with no religion" and "the people with the wrong religion." After all, in the latter mode others would be objected to for holding the wrong "beliefs," while in the former mode they would be objected to for who they are in their very "being" (or lack of), thus transforming a discriminatory theological difference into an ontological anthropology that will constitute one of the most influential, enduring, and cruel paths of modern racism. There is little doubt that this analytical distinction is important and has played an important role in the generation and reproduction of coloniality in some geographical spaces.[13] This is why Latin American decolonial theorists of the first generation—Walter Mignolo, building on Anibal Quijano's idea of coloniality, for example—make an excellent case when they point out how the distinction among racialized populations in the Occidentalist and Orientalist projects generate what Mignolo calls "colonial" and "imperial differences" respectably.[14] When decolonial theory was emerging as an epistemological scholarly option in the North Atlantic, this distinction was necessary to show the influential role Spanish and Portuguese discourses and practices in and about the Americas played in the global construction of race.

Now, more than two decades later, when this contribution is undeniable and is deeply influential beyond Latin American scholars, we can explore whether the sharp distinction may not limit our view. The path to see beyond analytical silos is already existent in the authors mentioned above. Quijano, already in his above-cited landmark text on coloniality, points out that Jews and Muslims suffered the "first experience of ethnic cleansing exercising the coloniality of power in the modern period."[15] Mignolo, years later, argued that the simultaneous conquests of the so-called south of Spain and the Americas led to genocides that, though in some regards were "analytically distinctive" in practice, were "logically linked to the colonial matrix of power."[16] Current scholarship has followed these early insights that open the scope of analysis. Javier García Fernández complements Quijano when he explains the economic transformations that led to the coloniality of power and labor imposed over former Muslim regions and inhabitants of what is today Spanish Andalusia.[17] And Manuela Boatcă and Anca Parvulescu challenge the uniform description of Europe and complement Mignolo by describing the usefulness of "inter-imperiality" as a framework for recognizing the role that economic structures and different racializations in peripheral and semiperipheral locations across the world play in an entangled global matrix.[18]

This is a productive path for a comprehensive understanding of the racism generated in what Enrique Dussel calls "the first modernity," a historical period in which the leading powers were culturally permeated by Catholic theology even when retrieving Greek political philosophy and setting up the genocidal ground for altruistic humanist thought. This helps explain the fluidity of racial tropes that traveled with Europeans to distinct populations, who then enacted persecution with relation to practices and not just beliefs.[19] For this reason, I ask us to start interrogating whether considering religion only as a matter of faith—as main branches of Protestant theology might—instead of a cultural phenomenon that includes, but is not limited to, faith, may not open up broader dynamic spaces of inquiry that blur geographical and identity boundaries. In other words, I am asking whether the more comprehensive Catholic understanding of religion that persecuted people because of their practices can explain why racialized conceptions—which transformed theological discrimination into anthropological ontological difference—traveled with such ease across spaces, identities, and categories. This does not downplay the importance of the ontological change in the modern construction of race. On the contrary, it demonstrates its full reach across the globe, which led to different but entangled statuses of non-Europeans on both sides of the Atlantic. This may give us the potential to talk about beginnings in the plural, exploring the multidirectional traveling of ideas, and putting into question the existence of one and only one origin and development of modern racism.[20]

Fortunately, some scholarship, especially in the last fifteen years, has started exploring key aspects of this dynamic relational possibility. Irene Silverblatt, an even earlier pioneer in her book *Modern Inquisitions*, reads Inquisition documents against the grain to show how in one of the central locations of the Spanish Americas, the Viceroyalty of Peru, the persecution of allegedly unassimilated Jews and Natives was discursively interrelated because of the assumption that their presumptuous actions (that may include but are not reducible to the narrow and compartmentalized conception of religion as faith) were perverting the purity of the body politics in the colony. She explores, for example, not only the parallel persecution of alleged anti-Catholic actions of Jews and Natives but also how the blueprint of modern conspiracies (connecting secret Jewish hidden organization and Native/Black rebellious labor) already existed in the colonial world of the seventeenth century. Silverblatt, therefore, offers a groundbreaking framework that intersects with Stam and Shohat's proposal of relationality.[21]

Current scholarship in Sephardic studies has also taken these lessons. For example, Jonathan Schorsch eruditely explores the "horizontal relations" that emerge from reading with deep care the archives portraying the "hidden lives of Jews and Africans" in the Spanish Americas. He makes a helpful distinction between the Spanish/Portuguese Catholic and the Dutch/English Protestant experiences. The lives of members of the explored communities sometimes run parallel, sometimes historically or discursively intersect, and usually occupy conflicting spaces within "underground societies in the Iberian World." Schorsch explores "alliances" and crossovers, both "real" and "imaginary," between and within these groups without dismissing verticality and difference but by explaining that the latter is not the full account of a fluid context.[22] Dalia Kandiyoti, in one of the most innovative works of the field, explains that, with all their differences, one of the key overlaps between Natives and Jews is that they were meant to "disappear" in a unifying and allegedly pure Catholic body politics of both colonialism and coloniality. Since the disappearance of bodies and of knowledges are intimately connected, these lessons did not make it to legitimized western archives. Instead of just lamenting the "missing archives," she ingeniously draws from the field of literature, memory, and cultural studies (including Silverblatt, Shohat, and Michael Rothberg's work, which is described below) and interrogates the extreme positivism and limited deconstructivism of Eurocentric historical analysis, proposing to make current narrative "archives" for the future instead of limiting ourselves to creating narratives from documents already legitimized by the system.[23]

Other frameworks and innovative research allow further exploration of the transatlantic multidirectional traveling of ideas among populations that can be divided in positivistic ideal types but are entangled in practices of systemic building. José María Perceval, for example, shows how the anthropological attempt to define some people as being "without a soul" (*desalmados*)—which was arguably first employed to interrogate the humanity and justify the colonization and enslavement of Africans and Natives—was quickly transported back to Europe to describe (sometimes in a phantasmagoric manner conspiring against the purity of the body politics) Jews and Muslims in the metropolis.[24] In another example, María Elena Martínez explores the transformation of the conception of the "purity of blood" (*limpieza de sangre*), from, first, its aim to limit the assimilation of Jews and Muslims in the European metropolis; second, in its attempt to manage Natives and Africans in the colonies; and then, third, its redeployment in both the metropolis and colonies to describe "New Christians."[25] Martínez convincingly argues that the genealogical construction reproduced a binary conception of gender that María Lugones and Ann Stoler argue is one of the axes of the modern/colonial system emerging in the first modernity and in the imperialism and colonialism of the second modernity.[26]

We can now return to Shohat and Stam to understand why the Portuguese saw "mosques" when arriving to the coast of Brazil. Given the "Orientalist unconscious" in the Occidentalist project we call the Americas we can still witness yearly rituals that reproduce Christian crusader triumphalism over Islam.[27] Gil Anidjar has already shown with his usual powerful insight that the western construction of Jews and Muslims has been necessarily entangled in the construction of a Christian European political theology (or better said, Christianity as a political theology).[28] It is thus important to learn the lessons and question the strict practical distinction between what is classified as interior to Europe and what is classified as exterior. In other words, even though the projects of Occidentalism and Orientalism have differences (between but also within them), they are mutually constituted.

This is not to say that critics have always recognized one another, and that the system has maintained the same role for the same populations in every space and time. In the context of coloniality, there are evolutionist systemic incentives that populations ontologically racialized in the matrix received in order to, consciously or unconsciously, reproduce the system. This makes the equalization between victimhood and purity a complicated endeavor.[29] This is why anti-Black and anti-Native racism surely exists in Jewish and Muslim populations. And it is historically undeniable that some of those populations have contributed to diverse forms of imperial projects, including settler and extractivist colonialisms, becoming at the same time victims and agents. Concurrently, other racisms, including Orientalism, exist among many other racialized communities. This is especially true when the system traditionally blamed Jews and Muslims collectively for global theological, political, and economic open wars or conspiracies in an attempt to occlude the west's own racist perpetration (from slave-trade to racial capitalism to religious fundamentalism). Or when racialized individuals in western or westernized contexts are systemically forced to join nationalistic enterprises spreading "salvation" through participation in state policies, ecclesiastical missions, or armed forces of western "democratic liberation." This creates a dynamic and diffuse structure of permanently changing relations not only between groups but also in between them. This is not to say that these communities cannot develop a westernized project. But it is important to differentiate between individual participation in aspirational incentives the system develops to divide and conquer, and structural ownership of state power.

These systemic mechanisms that make it difficult for critics to recognize one another have multiple consequences. For example, they not only occlude the existence of threads of coloniality that connect different populations, but also solidify intracommunal hierarchies that invisibilize those who do not fit neatly into the normative communal identity (Black Jews are a very clear but not sole example).[30] The socially committed critics who recognize the relations between these different forms of discrimination, some of them belonging to these communities, do not think all modern racisms are equal or that other racialized populations have not been implicated in discriminations in particular contexts. Shohat and Stam explain that the relation may include but goes beyond the recently heavily criticized "metaphoric analogy" and understand that the experiences of these multiple communities have been interwoven from the beginning and thus should be put in "productive relationality," a methodological opening that enables us to study entanglements, overlappings, manipulations, instrumentalizations, continuities, implications, spatial/temporal reclassifications, and border/hybrid forms beyond normativity and monopolies of representation.[31]

If the diverse models of non-Europeanness have been connected since the outset of modernity, genocidal projects in their altruism are also connected, and this can be seen with particular clarity in the second modernity. This period during the eighteenth and nineteenth centuries saw liberal programs engaged with the "Jewish Question." Proponents of these programs argued that European Jews should be "uplifted" from their "uncivilized nature" in the metropolis. This altruistic program advocated a double control over Jews, first because of their age-old "rebellious" nature and now because of the new requirements for "achieving modern humanity." Eurocentric readings may have problems in comprehending how "The Final Solution" was seeded during a time when Jews had allegedly achieved the most successful integration in western Europe. But looking at the Holocaust through the discourses of coloniality and the dictum "Civilize—for your own good—or I will kill you," we realize the genocide was not an interruption of a process. It was, on the contrary, one of continuation. The point is that even though every historical event has its particularities, this does not negate the existence of connections. This is why scholars such as Jürgen Zimmerer and the above-mentioned Rothberg continue to think through a relational integration. Zimmerer explores the connection of Holocaust history in Central and Eastern Europe with German genocides in Africa, and Rothberg challenges competitive models of memory by showing how historically the Holocaust was successfully mobilized beyond its insularity in Caribbean history and for Algerian struggles.[32]

We saw previously that this connection between coloniality and Jewish persecution existed since at least the Great Conspiracies of Peru and Mexico of early modernity. Intra-European hermetic readings of the Holocaust, however, limit this exploration. One of the tragic consequences is suffered by, for example, Palestinians and non-European Jews. The Jewish project of statehood known as political Zionism shortsightedly claims that the problem of modern antisemitism is a Jewish exceptional "abnormality." And as consequence, instead of objecting to the tropes of coloniality that deeply influenced antisemitic development, it reproduces them. The State of Israel defines itself as "culturally civilized," "technologically/economically developed," and "politically democratic" in contrast to the forcibly excluded Palestinians and the forcefully included Arab/African-Jews. This ultimately emphasizes its ideology as "an outpost of civilization against barbarism."[33] It remains to be seen whether, under future rearticulations of coloniality, this intention to join the ranks of western nations will be convincing in times of philosemitism and antisemitism in Europe and neo-Nazis shouting, "Jews will not replace us," in the United States. Or, departing from the analysis of Atalia Omer and Alana Lentin as to how to decolonize our understanding of antisemitism, we need further critical grassroots and intellectual work to stop the reinstrumentalization of racial hatred toward Jews when it is employed to support a western agenda, a staple of post-Holocaust geopolitics.[34]

The "altruistic" dynamics of coloniality also created a deep rupture between Arab/Berber-Jews and Arab/Berber-Muslims. Before the nineteenth century, Jews had found refuge from Christian persecution in Muslim-ruled lands. Europeans connected Jews rhetorically with Muslims through Orientalism. But the European colonial invasion of the Maghreb, starting in the late 1820s and lasting formally until the 1960s, was premised on "altruistically" saving not only Christians but also Jews from the "tyranny" of Muslim rule. This project of "liberation" was quickly supported and backed by the European Jewish communities, who saw a double opportunity to both demonstrate their allegiance to "civilized" Europe and "develop" non-European Jews. This was the beginning of a long nightmare for Arab/Berber/

non-European Jews. Altruistic European coloniality divorced them from their millenary local networks, right-wing settler coloniality permanently objected and limited their access, Nazi coloniality singled them out for actual genocide, and ultimately Zionist coloniality uprooted them from their lands and turned them into second-class citizens who needed to be "developed" and "civilized" to achieve humanity—embodied now by Israeli Euro-Judaism. The marriage of coloniality left Jews, the "eternal candidate for assimilation" for Tunisian Jew Albert Memmi, in an "impossible condition" that ultimately resulted in the exodus of hundreds of thousands of Jews from North Africa (and with some differences from the Middle East).[35]

Muslims have not been exempt from this rhetoric either. Since the 1990s until today, most of the invasions of the Middle East/North Africa (MENA) region have been justified with the most recent articulation of the dictum of coloniality, "Democratize—for your own good—or I will kill you." The narratives put forward about Muʻammar Muḥammad al-Gaddafi in Libya, Saddam Hussein in Iraq, or the former mujahideen in Afghanistan as regressive tyrants who needed to be defeated for the well-being of not only the security of "the west" but also of their own populations, who "ought" to have a western-style of democracy, became more of a normative rather than an exceptional portrayal. This is not to say that their ruling cannot and should not be impugned from within. But the historical support of dictatorships and extremisms by the west, especially but not limited to the Cold War, shows its hypocrisy and the failure to secure durable western democracies and the reproduction of the racist structure of dualism.[36] In these incursions, millions have been persecuted as "terrorists" or murdered as "collateral damage" of a "just war."

In Europe itself, liberal discourses have tolerated the presence of Muslims on the condition that they accept permanent state surveillance to secure their civilized/democratic status. Scholars of modern Islamophobia in Europe and the United States, such as Nadia Fadil (a contributor to this volume), Farid Hafez, and Nazia Kazi, have pointed out the configuration of programs of deradicalization and surveillance.[37] S. Sayyid, another contributor to this volume, has been one of the pioneers in presenting the role that Islamophobia plays as one of the "central vectors" of European self-constitution and the permanent interrogation of the possibility of assimilation as a way to limit the emergence of "a Muslim political consciousness."[38] As happened with Jews (again, the situations do not need to be "the same" in order to be relational and inform each other) more than a century ago, right-wing populism today seems to be encouraging a "Final Solution" (transfer or genocide) for the "uncivil/terrorist" Muslim placed under the surveillance of the liberal state. This time, they argue that they support diversity, even the "liberation" of Muslim sexual differences, to create epistemological blackmail. But a longer history of coloniality determines the current situation. From the beginning of modernity, Muslims (among others) were kidnapped in Africa, stripped of their religion, and reduced to the linked identity of Blackness and slavery. Western luminaries such as G. W. F. Hegel justified this as the only path for them to achieve their humanity.[39] And even before the Enlightenment, *Moriscos* who attempted to save their lives through conversion during times of the Spanish Inquisition were still expelled in the early seventeenth century, in a historical record that some Christian populisms may reclaim as a project. The constant among these versions of coloniality, from Iberian to Euro-American, is the marriage between liberal discourses of forced inclusion and right-wing genocidal discourses. These examples show how Islamophobia, antisemitism, and racism did not emerge from intra-European developments alone. This is why a hermetic comparative reading is misleading in attempting to understand the threats that millions suffer from today.

Opening Challenges

The objective of this chapter has been to explore old news. In other words, the central point has been to analyze systemic continuities veiled by the use of narrow epistemological lenses that overlook the historic role coloniality plays in wedding liberal discourses to "right-wing" genocidal populisms. I would like to interrogate the challenges that this argument poses to our geopolitical frameworks, our methodologies, and the role of discursive altruism.

The first challenge questions the consequences of analyzing the sociology of European thought (in this case "right-wing genocidal populisms") only through the lens of intra-European history. Brubaker's proposal is perhaps one of the most insightful and sophisticated examples of this epistemology that, though helpful in some regards, remains hermetic in its scope. Here, I want to recognize that studies such as Brubaker's have clearly identified a key element of the new populist movements, but I ask, What is being occluded and even erased by adopting a narrow geopolitical conception of the modern world? As a possible answer, I propose that we take seriously Césaire's words of caution. As we may remember, he mentioned that (what will be known as) the twentieth-century European phenomenon of antonomasia, the Holocaust, is misread when analyzed only according to European history. Instead, he ponders how many of the objectives, techniques, and programs that populations suffered from in Europe were direct consequences of centuries of developments in the colonies. If we apply Césaire's words of caution to other Euro-American phenomena, such as "right-wing populisms," we are able to see that their marriage to liberal ideas is far from new. On the contrary, it is a refashioning of old programs that have been practiced worldwide. As such, the geopolitical relocation of seemingly European phenomena (from the Holocaust to the liberal–populist marriage) serves to question instead of reaffirm the way our disciplines treat Euro-America as the pure origin, center, and theater of world history. I have responded to a challenge in order to probe how our disciplines can learn from Afro-Caribbean (and as an extension Muslim-Maghrebi in the reflections of Bouteldja) thought so that we can confront our misreading of the present.

Second, I would like to challenge the use of comparative analysis as our primary methodology. Here, instead of employing the voices of Afro-Caribbean thought, I would like to recall a proposal emerging from an Arab Jewish scholar. For the past decades, Iraqi Shohat (at times with Stam) has been delving into the transmission of conceptions of racism, Islamophobia, and antisemitism and philosemitism in the intersectional "rainbow Atlantic." Instead of setting a disenfranchised community to compete for primacy of victimhood, Shohat has demonstrated the usefulness of analyzing the transmission of racial categories, discourses, and techniques throughout the Atlantic. Her work questions the isolation of comparative area studies that remains one of the most enduring legacies of Cold War analysis in the United States and most of westernized academia. If we were to analyze the emergence of right-wing populisms in a relational framework instead of a comparative one by exploring how the conceptions are translated and/or travel beyond geopolitically constructed borders, we might realize that the current phenomena may be more intertwined than comparative analysis permits us to see. Consequently, our analysis and our political confrontation with the phenomena will require a broader coalition than what is imagined by traditional postwar social scientific methodology.

Shohat's proposal pushes us beyond hermetic understandings of European politics, like Brubaker's, because it forces us to think about the multidirectional roles of "traveling" ideas. While other insightful and erudite scholars, such as Bryan Cheyette, have already shown us the usefulness of exploring the traveling of concepts of governmentality that emerged from Europe and then traveled to the rest of the world,[40] for example, the segregation of communities, we can investigate the models, techniques, and ideologies that emerged in the context of the colony and have traveled in time and space even to the very centers of power and knowledge, namely, Europe and the United States. This is why exploring the above-mentioned contributions of Silverblatt, Perceval, Schorsch, Kandiyoti, and Martinez may break the hermeticism of European politics.

Finally, I would like us to pay special attention to the long-standing articulations of coloniality. When analyzing Islamophobia and the philosemitism and antisemitism of right-wing populisms, the emphasis is often placed on the exclusionary discourses and tactics of the new movements. In other words, the identitarian constructions seem to delineate clear borders of what is considered to constitute the community and what is seen as a threat when these borders are imagined. Yet I would like to challenge liberal binary conceptions that favor inclusion as the solution to confronting genocidal practices, and in doing so exclude an analysis of global neocolonialism from the equation. Drawing from the Latin American school of modernity/coloniality, and from Quijano in particular, I challenge us to explore the relationship between the altruism of forced inclusion and the virulence of forced exclusion as partners in the construction of hierarchies of populations. Altruistic projects are not a solution to exclusion but are many times the precursor to an imagined social order that will be employed simultaneously or a posteriori by so-called right-wing populisms to justify their superiority. As such, global neoliberalism is not the solution but rather the partner to what we have defined above as the relationship between evolutionism and dualism. So, pondering the role that "altruistic" projects of forced inclusion play in shaping the current political stage is as necessary as confronting exclusion.

Through this chapter, I am inviting the fields of political sociology and religious studies to challenge political frameworks, methodologies, and global discourses of altruism that obscure the geopolitics of the genocidal marriage between the liberal and "right-wing."[41] By reevaluating the role of Eurocentric epistemologies, comparative methodologies, and liberal frameworks, we can shed light on a more accurate reading of the current political stage and start a new conversation. Guided by Afro-Caribbean, Arab-Jewish, and Latinx-American thought, we can explore the forces behind an analytical misreading and offer an intellectual proposal that actively confronts the common genocidal forces behind not only right-wing populisms, but also liberal colonial altruism.

NOTES

1. Rogers Brubaker, "Between Nationalism and Civilizationism: The European Populist Movement in Comparative Perspective," *Ethnic and Racial Studies* 40, no. 8 (2018): 1191–1226.

2. For a challenging trajectory of texts offering a variety of rich proposals to decolonize European and global political sociology, see Immanuel Wallerstein, *Open the Social Sciences: Report of the Gulbenkian Commission on the Restructuring of the Social Sciences* (Stanford, CA: Stanford University Press, 1996); Edgardo Lander, ed., *La Colonialidad del Saber: Eurocentrismo y Ciencias Sociales* (Buenos Aires: CLACSO, 2000); Encarnación Gutiérrez Rodríguez, Manuela Boatcă, and Sergio Costa, eds., *Decolonizing European Sociology: Transdisciplinary Approaches* (New York: Routledge, 2010); Ramón Grosfoguel, "Decolonizing Post-Colonial Studies and Paradigms of Political Sociology," *Transmodernity* 1, no. 1 (2011): 1–38; Manuela Boatcă, *Global Inequalities beyond Occidentalism* (London: Routledge, 2016); Julian Go, "Decolonizing Sociology: Epistemic Inequality and Sociological Thought," *Social Problems* 64, no. 2 (2017): 194–99; and Ali Meghji, *Decolonizing Sociology: An Introduction* (London: Polity Press, 2021).

3. Aimé Césaire, *Discours sur le colonialisme* (Dakar: Présence africaine, 1955), 30–31; in English as Césaire, *Discourse on Colonialism*, trans. John Pinkham (New York: Monthly Review Press, 2001), 35–36.

4. Houria Bouteldja, *Les blancs, les juifs et nous* (Paris: La Fabrique éditions, 2016), 56–59; in English as Bouteldja, *Whites, Jews and Us*, trans. Rachel Valinsky (Boston: MIT Press, 2017), 58–62.

5. See Edward Said, "Michel Foucault, 1926–1984," in *After Foucault: Humanistic Knowledge, Postmodern Challenges*, ed. Jonathan Arac (New Brunswick, NJ: Rutgers University Press, 1998), 3–5.

6. See Robert Stam and Ella Shohat, *Race in Translation: Culture Wars around the Postcolonial Atlantic* (New York: NYU Press, 2012), xiii–xv.

7. Walter Mignolo, *Local Histories/Global Designs: Coloniality, Subaltern Knowledges, and Border Thinking* (Princeton, NJ: Princeton University Press, 2000), 95–110.

8. For an erudite explanation of the role that conspiracies played in the construction of early modernity, see Francoise Soyer, *Antisemitic Conspiracy Theories in the Early Modern Iberian World: Narratives of Fear and Hatred* (Leiden: Brill, 2019). The existence of forgeries, from the "Letter to Constantinople of 1489" (where allegedly Turkish Jews recommended European Jews under threat to convert and infiltrate Christianity to destroy it) to the Great Conspiracy in Peru and Mexico in the seventeenth century (where Jews were allegedly gathering slaves kidnapped in Africa and colonized Natives to expel Spaniards from the continent), show the relation between the construction of race and the creation of conspiracies from the very beginning of modernity.

9. These conceptions are largely based on the school of modernity/coloniality interpretation in such contributions, especially, as Sylvia Winter, "1492: A New World View," in *Race, Discourse and the Origins of the Americas*, ed. Vera Lawrence Hyatt and Rex Nettleford (Washington, DC: Smithsonian, 1994), 5–57. The most insightful and influential exploration of the implications of this structure for the study of religion can be found in Nelson Maldonado-Torres, "Religion, Conquest, and Race in the Foundations of the Modern Colonial World," *Journal of the American Academy of Religion* 83, no. 2 (2014): 636–65. A further exploration of this trajectory can be seen in the introduction to An Yountae and Eleanor Craig, eds., *Beyond Man: Race, Coloniality, and the Philosophy of Religion* (Durham, NC: Duke University Press, 2021), 1–31. I explored this issue in Santiago Slabodsky, "It is the Theology, Stupid! Coloniality, Anti-Blackness, and the Bounds of Humanity," in *Anti-Blackness and Christian Ethics*, ed. Andrew Prevot and Vincent Lloyd (Maryknoll, NY: Orbis Books, 2017), 19–40.

10. Anibal Quijano, "Coloniality of Power, Eurocentrism, and Latin America," *Nepantla: Views from the South* 1, no. 3 (2000): 533–80.

11. Ramón Grosfoguel, "The Structure of Knowledge in Westernized Universities: Epistemic Racism/Sexism and the Four Genocides/Epistemicides of the Long 16th Century," *Human Architecture* 11, no. 1 (2013): 73–90.

12. Max Horkheimer and Theodor Adorno, *Dialektik der Aufklärung* (Amsterdam: Fischer Verlag N.V., 1947), 15–18.

13. It is important to point out, for example, the role that some Jews played in the constitution of "western frontiers," especially in Dutch and English colonization (and to a limited extent French colonization, until they were formally expelled) in the Atlantic. See, for example, Paolo Bernardini and Norman Fiering, eds., *The Jews and the Expansion of Europe to the West, 1450–1800* (New York: Berghahn Books, 2001). If one wants to see this as a precursor of the normative Jewish relation with the west after World War II, this can be very helpful. See, for example, the work of Eli Rosenblatt, "Creole Exegesis: Jewish Theopolitics in Suriname, 1860–1960," *Studia Rosenthaliana* (forthcoming). But if one intends to generalize the role of a small minority to explain the portrayal of all Jews before this time across colonial experiences, its anachronism runs the risk of reproducing

antisemitic conspiracy stereotypes. Furthermore, it may naturalize a relatively recent narrative that constitutes a "Judeo-Christian tradition" that fails to account for the discourses about and status of the majority of Jews before 1945 and the diversity of colonial experiences, especially in the large part of the Americas under Spanish and Portuguese colonization where Jews were generally forbidden until the mid-nineteenth century and even those who were able overcome the purity of blood tests were under threat from an Inquisitorial society. If one were to analyze these largely Protestant spaces, it is interesting to see how paths have crossed, even in these unequal spaces, and yielded populations that will hold, for example, creole Jewish and African-descendent identities. See, for example, Aviva Ben Ur, *Jewish Autonomy in a Slave Society: Suriname in the Atlantic World, 1651–1825* (Philadelphia: University of Pennsylvania Press, 2020). A further exploration of entanglements beyond the Atlantic, especially in North Africa and southern Africa, can be found in Ethan Katz, Lisa Moses Leff, and Maud Mandel, *Colonialism and the Jews* (Bloomington: Indiana University Press, 2017); Mitchel Joffe Hunter, "Dirty Subjects: Shaping Jewish Colonial Subjectivities in Early Twentieth-Century South Africa," *Decolonial Horizons* 7, no. 1 (2021): 7–39; in terms of history, see Heidi Grunebaum, "Between Nakba, Shoah, and Apartheid: Notes on a Film from the Interstices," in *Memory and Genocide: On What Remains and the Possibility of Representation*, ed. Fazil Moradi, Ralph Buchenhorst, and Maria Six-Hohenbalken (London: Routledge, 2017), 122–37.

 14. Mignolo, *Local Histories/Global Design*, 57–65.

 15. Quijano, "Coloniality of Power, Eurocentrism and Latin America," 558.

 16. Walter Mignolo, "Dispensable Lives and Bare Lives: Coloniality and the Hidden Political/Economy Agenda of Modernity," *Human Architecture* 2, no. 7 (2009): 77–79.

 17. Javier García Fernández, *Descolonizar Europa: Ensayos para pensar históricamente desde el Sur* (Madrid: Editorial Burmaria, 2019), 47–96.

 18. Manuela Boatcă and Anca Parvulescu, "Creolizing Transylvania: Notes on Coloniality and Inter-imperiality," *History of the Present* 10, no. 1 (2020): 9–27. The authors repurpose Laura Doyle's term and show the entanglements with decolonial frameworks. See also Parvulescu and Boatcă, *Creolizing the Modern: Transylvania across Empire* (Ithaca, NY: Cornell University Press, 2022).

 19. Enrique Dussel, "World System and Transmodernity," *Nepantla: Views from the South* 3, no. 2 (2002): 222–44.

 20. This multidirectional and relational proposal, in addition, has the potential to enter into noncompetitive dialogue with multiple trends that explore the relation between religion and race from different geopolitical, disciplinary, and epistemological perspectives. This includes, for example, four provocative trajectories in scholarship today (some that are already in nourishing dialogue). One is the exploration of European protoracist and racist discourses and practices, the connection to coloniality of which still needs to be explored further. See, for

example, Geraldine Heng, *The Invention of Race in the Middle Ages* (Cambridge: Cambridge University Press, 2018); Matthea Westerduin, "Questioning Religio-secular Temporalities: Medieval Formations of Nation, Europe and Race," *Patterns of Prejudice* 54, no. 1–2 (2020): 136–49; and Jonathan Boyarin, *The Unconverted Self: Jews, Indians, and the Identity of Christian Europe* (Chicago: Chicago University Press, 2018). A second includes critical race studies outside the Americas that explore the "constellation" between religion and race, which emphasize the former while occluding the latter. See, for example, Anya Topolski, "The Dangerous Discourse of the 'Judeo-Christian' Myth: Masking the Race-Religion Constellation," *Patterns of Prejudice* 54, no. 1–2 (2020): 71–90, which discusses the European context that includes the usually occluded antiziganism or anti-Romani discrimination; and Josias Tembo, "Race-Religion Constellation: An Argument for a Trans-Atlantic Interactive Relational Approach," *Critical Research on Religion* 10, no. 2 (2022): 137–52. The latter extends the conversation to Africa. A third trend, which is interrelated with the Tembo article, is the exploration of features of premodern anti-Black racism in North Africa and the Middle East that were fully crystalized through the expansion of coloniality in the Americas. See Jesse Benjamin, "North Africa and the Origins of Epistemic Blackness," in *UNESCO History of Africa V.X* (University of California Press, forthcoming); and Iskander Abassi, "Anti-Blackness in the Muslim World: Beyond Apologetics and Orientalism," *Maydan*, October 14, 2020, https://themaydan.com/2020/10/anti-blackness-in-the-muslim-world-beyond-apologetics-and-orientalism/. The final trend is the theological exploration of the construction of race in the United States. See Willie James Jennings, *The Christian Imagination: Theology and the Origins of Race* (New Heaven, CT: Yale University Press, 2010); and J. Kameron Carter, *Race: A Theological Account* (Oxford: Oxford University Press, 2008).

    21. Irene Silverblatt, *Modern Inquisitions: Peru and the Colonial Origins of the Civilized World* (Durham, NC: Duke University Press, 2004), 141–86.

    22. Jonathan Schorsch, *Hidden Lives of Jews and Africans: Underground Societies in the Iberian World* (Princeton, NJ: Markus Wiener, 2019), 143–68.

    23. Dalia Kandiyoti, *The Converso's Return: Conversion and Sephardi History in Contemporary Literature and Culture* (Stanford, CA: Stanford University Press, 2020), 6–10. Interestingly, one parallel effort was recently made across borders to find alternatives to the current oppression of Palestinians in a Jewish state by Gil Hochberg in *Becoming Palestine: Toward an Archival Imagination of the Future* (Durham, NC: Duke University Press, 2021). This shows the fruitfulness of this novel approach.

    24. José María Perceval, "Animalitos del señor: Aproximación a una teoría de las animalizaciones propias y del otro, sea enemigo o siervo, en la España imperial (1550–1650)," *Areas: Revista de Ciencias Sociales* 14 (1992): 173–84.

    25. The term "New Christians" refers to those Jews and Muslims who were forced to convert to Christianity by the Spanish and Portuguese Empires. See

María Elena Martínez, *Limpieza de Sangre, Religion, and Gender in Colonial Mexico* (Stanford, CA: Stanford University Press, 2009).

26. María Lugones, "The Coloniality of Gender," *Worlds and Knowledges Otherwise* 2, dossier 2 (Spring 2008): 1–17; and Ann Stoler, *Carnal Knowledge and Imperial Power: Race and the Intimate in Colonial Rule* (Berkeley: University of California Press, 2002). See a superb proposal to integrate these distinctive trends for a decolonial understanding of revolutionary feminism in Nefertiti Takla, "Feminism and Revolution," in *The Routledge Global History of Feminism*, ed. Bonnie Smith and Nova Robinson (New York: Routledge, 2022), 339–413.

27. Ella Shohat, "Genealogies of Orientalism and Occidentalism: Sepharadi Jews, Muslims, and the Americas," *Studies in American Jewish Literature* 35, no. 1 (2016): 13–32.

28. Gil Anidjar, *The Jew, the Arab: History of an Enemy* (Stanford, CA: Stanford University Press, 2003); and Anidjar, *Blood: A Critique of Christianity* (New York: Columbia University Press, 2014).

29. I owe the interrogation of the purity of victimhood to discussions with Yonathan Listick. See Listick, "Barbaric Jewishness: Resistance to Anti-Semitism and Judeo-Christianity," *Decolonial Horizons* 8, no. 1 (2023): 7–52.

30. Lewis Gordon, "Rarely Kosher: Studying Jews of Color in North America," *American Jewish History* 100, no. 1 (2016): 105–16; and Walter Isaac, "Locating Afro-American Judaism: A Critique of White Normativity," in *A Companion to African-American Studies*, ed. Lewis Gordon and Jane Gordon (New York: Blackwell, 2006), 512–42.

31. Stam and Shohat, *Race in Translation*, 154. Here it is also important to notice the brilliant critique made by Sarah Phillips Casteel about the dangers of the generalization of the US case. Casteel points out that interrelations of, for example, "Jewish and Black relations" are many times interpreted according to the particular American experience "inflected by the persistent political tensions between African Americans and Jewish Americans." By recentering the discussion in other spaces such as the Caribbean, the authors she explores do not dismiss the power dynamics and implications developed for five centuries, but they show how communities have interwoven their experiences to understand what Paul Gilroy calls "knotted intersection of history," a clear example of multidirectional memories (Michael Rothberg's important framework is referenced in the next footnote). See Sarah Phillips Casteel, *Calypso Jews: Jewishness in the Caribbean Literary Imagination* (New York: Columbia University Press, 2016), 5–7. Building on Casteel, I would argue that many times the arguments about the clarity of Jewish participation in the colony is limited to the study of a late and reduced space occupied by Dutch, English, and to some extent French colonies (before they were expelled) since Jews (and Muslims) were forbidden in the great majority of the territories of the Americas occupied by Spaniards and Portuguese

and those who were able to circumvent the "purity of blood" laws lived under the threat (or actual repression) of the Inquisition independently of the service they provided to the colonial state. As an example, see Ronnie Perelis, *Blood and Faith: Family and Identity in the Early Modern Sephardic Atlantic* (Bloomington: Indiana University Press, 2016).

32. For historical studies, see Jürgen Zimmerer, *Von Windhuk nach Auschwitz? Beiträge zum Verhältnis von Kolonialismus und Holocaust* (Münster and Berlin: Lit Verlag, 2011); for memory studies, see Michael Rothberg, *Multidirectional Memories: Remembering the Holocaust in an Age of Decolonization* (Stanford, CA: Stanford University Press, 2009).

33. Theodor Herzl, *Der Judenstaat* (Berlin: Jüdische Verlag, 1920), 24; in English as Herzl, *The Jewish State*, trans. Jacob Alkow (New York: Dover, 1988), 86. I explore the role of western political Zionism in the integration of Jewish normativity into a western project in Santiago Slabodsky, *Decolonial Judaism: Triumphal Failures of Barbaric Thinking* (New York: Palgrave, 2015).

34. Atalia Omer, *Days of Awe: Re-Imagining Jewishness in Solidarity with Palestinians* (Chicago: University of Chicago Press, 2018), 212–45; and Alana Lentin, *Why Race Still Matters* (Cambridge: Polity, 2020), 131–71.

35. See Albert Memmi, *Portait d'un Juif* (Paris: Gallimard, 1962), 227–40; in English as Memmi *The Portrait of a Jew*, trans. Judy Hyun (New York: The Orion Press, 1962), 263–67.

36. The west's support for dictatorial regimes throughout the world and in North Africa and the Middle East in particular is well known. Today the most notorious case is Saudi Arabia. Yet, I point out especially the Cold War since this was an international strategy that can connect different experiences throughout the "tricontinental" Global South.

37. See, for example, Nadia Fadil et al., eds., *Radicalization in Belgium and the Netherlands: Critical Perspectives on Violence and Security* (London: I. B. Tauris, 2019); Naved Bakali and Farid Hafez, eds., *The Rise of Islamophobia in the War on Terror: Coloniality, Race, and Islam* (Manchester: Manchester University Press, 2022); and Nazia Kazi, *Islamophobia, Race, and Global Politics* (Lanham, MD: Rowman and Littlefield, 2018).

38. S. Sayyid, "Topographies of Hate: Islamophobia in Cyberia," *Journal of Cyberspace Studies* 2, no. 1 (2018): 55–73. See a further inquiry in Sayyid, *A Fundamental Fear: Eurocentrism and the Emergence of Islamism* (London: Zed Book, 1997).

39. G. W. F Hegel, *Vorlesungen über die Philosophie der Geschichte* (Berlin: Dunker and Humboldt, 1804), 116; Hegel, *Lectures on the Philosophy of World History*, trans. Hugh Nisbet (Cambridge: Cambridge University Press, 1975), 176.

40. Bryan Cheyette, *The Ghetto: A Very Short Introduction* (Oxford: Oxford University Press, 2020).

41. Given the scope of this chapter, I was not able to fully explore the different strategies in order to connect these two fields. But the suggestion of "critical caretaking" of Atalia Omer could provide the necessary orientation and tools to achieve this goal. See Omer, "Can a Critic Be a Caretaker Too? Religion, Conflict and Social Transformation," *Journal of the American Academy of Religion* 79, no. 2 (2011): 459–96; and Omer, *Days of Awe*, 122–42.

CHAPTER 2

Deradicalization as a Fetish

The Threat of Da'wa *and the Regulation of the Real*

NADIA FADIL

ABSTRACT

This chapter examines deradicalization policies in Europe as technologies of sovereign power that aim to provide languages, imaginaries, and affects to maintain the symbolic stability of the liberal and secular order. I draw on Achille Mbembe's concept of the fetish *to examine the operation of such policies. For although they are designed to bolster the secular and liberal political order, they also simultaneously reveal its fragility. This double movement, I want to suggest, is at the heart of the operation of deradicalization policies and is essential to account for why they continue to hold sway in the public sphere, despite their lack of empirical support. Through an examination of how practices of* da'wa *(Islamic proselytization) have been resignified by these deradicalization policies, I show the operations and ramifications of such policies and the politico-theological work of the state.*

> *A significant part of the Muslim community danced after the attacks. They threw stones and bottles at the police and the press after the arrest of Salah Abdeslam. That is the real problem. We can arrest terrorists, remove them from the society. But they are just the surface. There is a much more difficult to treat cancer below. We can deal with this, but not from one day to another.*
>
> —Jan Jambon, Belgian minister of interior, in De Standaard, April 16, 2016

A few weeks after the March 22, 2016, attacks in the Brussels International Airport in Zaventem and the Metro station in Maelbeek, Minister of the Interior Jan Jambon (NV-A) made these provocative comments in an interview with one of the leading Flemish dailies, *De Standaard*. The reactions to this interview were prompt. Several commentators responded furiously, arguing that these assertions were nothing more than fake news, and challenged Jambon to provide evidence to back his claims. Some politicians even called on him to apologize (which he refused to do) and called for his resignation.[1] Meanwhile, journalists inquired into the veracity of his claim, examining whether there were Muslims who were actually dancing in the streets in the days following the attacks.[2] Jambon's remarks, and the controversy they provoked, could be read as an illustration of how anti-Muslim racism has become institutionalized within the highest ranks of various European states, thus turning the "Muslim question" into an important instrument for regulating the population.[3] By explicitly targeting the "Muslim community" as sympathizers with the terrorist attacks, Jambon fed into a dominant narrative that links terrorism with Islam, and thus turns all its adherents into members of a suspect community.[4] Yet in addition to this, there is also a particular element in Jambon's statement that I want to briefly reflect upon, and that touches upon his assessment of threat. In the epigraph to this chapter, the Belgian minister of the interior not only warns about the terrorists, who are presented here as the "surface" threat, but also about what lies beneath this surface, "the cancer." It is this cancer, he suggests, that leads people, namely, Muslims, to dance after the attacks or throw bottles at the police. In evoking the metaphor of a cancer, Jambon imagines the social threat as a mortal pathology that infuses the social body slowly and threatens it from within. A cancer tends to develop in a rather imperceptible manner and is too often discovered at quite an advanced stage. It also remains difficult to cure because of its unpredictable spread. Chemotherapies might reduce the growth of the tumor, or even eradicate it, but the successful treatment depends on early detection of the tumor and its containment. Finally, even though cancers can be cured, one is only declared cancer-free after a few years of treatment and remission, and there is always a risk that the tumor might return. Its proliferating nature and its capacity to emerge at unexpected moments are two of the more endangering and destabilizing aspects. By comparing the dancing or stone-throwing Muslims with a tumor, Jambon warns of the presence of damaged cells within the social body, which may, at any time, reappear.

In capturing the danger of violent extremism, epidemiological metaphors have often been invoked by public officials, as has been noted by several scholars.[5] Radicalization is depicted, through the use of such metaphors, as an invisible, difficult to contain, yet always present potential, akin to what Carlos Caduff describes as a "cosmology of the mutant strains" in his account of the specific temporality epidemiological threats are seen to represent.[6] Accompanying the deployment of biopolitics, society is, on this account, understood through organic metaphors that assimilate it with a discourse of health. Crisis, conflict, and threat become, on the other hand, understood as diseases and are equally treated with the same medicalized lens.[7] In *Epidemic Empire*, Anjuli Fatima Raza Kolb analyzes how this epidemiological imaginary emerged in the nineteenth-century colonial context, whereby insurgencies were conceptualized through this medical lens and combatted through that same lens.[8] At the heart of this epidemiological metaphor lies, however, an inherent ontological fragility of the social body. And it is precisely this fragility of biopolitics that I want to explore.

In some of his well-known Collège de France lectures, posthumously gathered as *"Society Must Be Defended": Lectures at the Collège de France, 1975–1976*, Michel Foucault noted that the idea of "biopolitics," a term that he uses to define the specific power configuration of modernity, was premised upon a political-historical discourse that understood the social order as fundamentally contingent and continuously endangered by a subterranean level or a "fundamental and permanent irrationality."[9] Biopolitics, he contended, introduces the idea of the "social" as premised upon a series of conventions and agreements, with the understanding that the latter is always provisional, fragile, and at the risk of falling apart. The main threat that is imagined within a biopolitical regime is not a threat that comes from "outside," but is one that comes from inside. It is the precondition upon which the idea of a social order rests. And it is this perpetual anxiety over those unruly parts of the social body that he uniquely describes as "race": "The other race is basically not the race that came from elsewhere or that was, for a time, triumphant and dominant, but that is a race that is permanently, ceaselessly, infiltrating the social body, or which is, rather, constantly being re-created in and by the social fabric."[10] One of the remarkable aspects in the diagnosis made by Foucault lies in the interdependence he highlights between the idea of "race" and "order."[11] Race emerges as a hidden subtext that is continuously threatening and "infiltrating" the social body. It is part and parcel of those dimensions of the social body that remain unknown, untamed, and uncontrolled, but of which one knows and is aware that they exists. It is threatening by virtue of the impossibility of fully identifying with, being domesticated within, and being contained by the social order. It is a threat that is equally manifested at an ontological level, and thus poses the possibility of questioning the existing social order. It is precisely this same analogy that we read in Jambon's assertion that a community (i.e., Muslims) represents a threat at a subterranean level.

In this chapter, this ostensible ontological fragility of the social body figures as the starting point for a reflection on contemporary security regimes through the lens of deradicalization policies. More particularly, I show how the perceived threat of "radical Islam" evokes the fragility of the liberal and secular social body. I explore how this biopolitical concern with Muslim life, as expressed through these security policies, equally reflects what Falguni Sheth calls an *ontopolitical* concern with secular modernity by looking at how deradicalization operates as a technology that seeks to attenuate ontological insecurities and restore the symbolic "health" of the liberal secular order.[12] "Ontopolitical" refers here to the capacity to define the world as we come to understand it and apprehend it. My argument is that the policies of deradicalization need to be read as the latest Orientalist effort at containing Muslim "otherness," not solely in their biopolitical but equally in their ontopolitical potential.[13] Yet these attempts are always insufficient, for a perpetual awareness of their incomplete reach will continuously animate and disturb their deployment. This results, therefore, in an incessant movement between reassurance and disturbance, containment and fragmentation, security and insecurity. To grasp this double movement, I want to resort to an analytical language that moves away from a functionalist and pragmatic account of these policies and rather attends to the elusive and contradictory dimensions of these policies. Therefore, I define deradicalization policies as a *fetish*, in the sense given to the term by Achille Mbembe.

DERADICALIZATION, POLITICAL POWER, AND THE FETISH

"The commandment aspires to act as a total cosmology for its subjects—yet, owing to the very oddity of this cosmology, popular humor causes it, often quite unintentionally, to capsize."[14]

Introduced in the early 2000s in the Netherlands, and since adopted by various Western European countries, the *dispositif* of deradicalization has become one of the most influential preventive public policy measures in the aftermath of the various terrorist attacks since 2015 in Europe.[15] At the heart of this discourse is the idea that a timely and correct identification of potential "signs" of radicalization, and the subjection of the concerned subjects to deradicalization programs, can enable the prevention of violence. Since their introduction, however, these policies have consistently been challenged on their efficacy, value-neutrality, and the way in which they selectively target and securitize ethnic and religious minorities, including Muslims in particular.[16] Nevertheless, these policies have continued to flourish and circulate as public policy, both on the European continent and outside of it.

In trying to account for the persistence of these public policies, several authors have examined their central role in the regulation of the population through the logic of race. Deradicalization policies, scholars have noted, collapse the distinction between those who are at risk and those who are seen to represent a risk. This collapsing enabled new forms of policing and control and has been informed by racialized grammars concerning religious and cultural difference, in particular with reference to Muslimness through the securitization of indexes of Islamic piety (such as having a beard, wearing face-veils, etc.).[17] Additionally, authors have also investigated the political-theological dimensions that are entailed in these security policies. Building upon the work of Talal Asad, they have approached these security policies as part and parcel of secularism, which is understood here as a *regime of truth* that draws on a discrete set of concepts, affects, and sensibilities.[18] Luca Mavelli, for instance, has argued that the securitization of Muslims in Europe "should be understood as part of the long-term process of securitization of religion which is one of the dimensions of the process of secularisation."[19] The formation of the Westphalian nation-state is premised, he contends, on "the securitisation of religion, that is, the perception of religion in the public sphere as a threat and its confinement to the private sphere. This securitization is characterized by a double movement: firstly, the 'downgrading' of religion from sources of knowledge to private systems of belief; and, secondly, its functional subordination to sovereign power."[20] Today's new threats, ranging from the "war on terror" to the securitization of Muslims in Europe, is therefore primarily read by Mavelli as a continuation of a secular imaginary that considers the public manifestation of religion (i.e., Islam) as an inherent danger to public order. A similar perspective can also be found in the work of Stacey Gutkowski, who has attended to how secular sensibilities—or what she describes as a *secular habitus*—informs British security strategists', public officials', and officers' views on the war on terror. Drawing on Bourdieu's notion of *hysteresis*, she suggests that "secular, liberal habits and myths about religion and violence conditioned the perception of Jihadism and Islam more generally," thus resulting in an ambivalent relationship to religion, and Islam in particular.[21] Security and surveillance policies, such as counter-radicalization policies, should therefore be understood as a continuation of the process of secularizing religious difference.

Whereas these latter studies shed an important light on how contemporary regimes of security draw upon and sustain a certain politico-theological imaginary (that is Christian and secular), which is equally racialized (i.e., Muslim otherness as the epitome of religious difference), they also assume that the security language produces, enhances, and highlights a perceived instability in the regulation of religious "otherness" that is concomitant with secularism. The language of insecurity and its convergence with secularism comes, in other words, to *produce* Muslim difference as intangible and uncontrollable. In what follows, I want to make the reverse argument: security policies, such as deradicalization policies, need to be read as attempts at *stabilizing* the idea of a secular order in confrontation with Muslim alterity. Within this perspective, Muslim otherness does not so much appear as a fantasy of the secular order, but rather exists as an ontological "other" that challenges the hegemonic contours of this liberal and secular order. In making this point, I draw heavily on the work of S. Sayyid, who has examined how languages of fundamentalism and extremism emerge in response to the affirmation of Muslim lifeforms that challenge a hegemonic liberal-secular nexus.[22] Rather than simply viewing them as a projection, they need to be understood as disciplinary strategies and languages that seek to mitigate and curtail the possible influence and expansion of such movements. Consequently, and building upon those insights, I view deradicalization policies as technologies of power that aim to provide languages, imaginaries, and affects that seek to maintain the symbolic stability of the liberal and secular order (understood both as a political order of rights, but equally as a regime of truth) in the face of alterity.[23] This is accomplished through the containment and redefinition of "religious" difference. Yet these aspirational attempts are always fragile, and the capacity to achieve ontological stability and control are never completely achieved. In looking for an appropriate language to qualify the status of these public policies and the relentless attempts at "deradicalizing" Muslim otherness, I now turn to Mbembe's concept of the *fetish*.

In *On the Postcolony*, Mbembe uses the notion of the fetish to reflect on the specific ways in which state power works in postcolonial Africa. The concept of the fetish has been critiqued for its colonial ramifications (as it was introduced by Marx and Freud), but it has recently gained renewed attention as an analytical concept that can help account for social formations, objects, or practices with a high symbolic and emotional charge and that hold together a complex relation of actors and objects.[24] Mbembe introduces the concept of the fetish to account for the operations of postcolonial state power, in particular its ontological incapacity to define "the real" or the world. In the African postcolonial context, an "economy of signs" that is "chaotically pluralistic" lies at the heart of this political space, which makes it impossible to create a unified system of representation.[25] The nation-state can propose a particular perspective and outlook on the world, but it is consciously challenged by religious and/or ethnic accounts of time and history. This results in what Mbembe describes as a condition of ontological doubleness or multiplicity, or what Ruth Marshall, in her discussion of the spiritual warfare of Pentecostal movements in Nigeria, has described as an "epistemological instability of representation."[26] Within this perspective, different worldviews and perspectives of time and space compete, thus challenging the unitary, state-centric, and modernist model of the political sphere as defined by the nation-state. This ultimately creates several public spaces that operate according to their own meaning structure, but that can also be entangled with one another. This leads Mbembe to describe the postcolonial subject as someone who "has had to learn to bargain in this conceptual marketplace."[27]

To compensate for this failure to contain a unitary political sphere, a distinct style of commandment is deployed, which is characterized by exaggeration and the grotesque, or what Mbembe describes as a "surplus of meanings that are non-negotiable and that one is officially forbidden to depart from or challenge."[28] An example is the omnipresence of presidential pictures, flags, or national discourses that reflect attempts to exert the commandment of the sovereign while at the same time being unsuccessful in holding power over the definition of the real.[29] This inability to capture the national imaginary thus becomes compensated for through an exaggerated display of the state's ornaments. Hence, the state's semiotic overcharging and investment into objects or rituals simultaneously signals, for Mbembe, its impotence. And these ornaments are what Mbembe designates as a fetish. Yet the fetish here is understood not only as an object that compels a degree of reference but also as a signal of the fragility of power. For it is because of this absence of hegemony that a semiotic overinvestment in objects or symbols is required. The fetish, for this reason, signals a double condition of strength and fragility, of attempts to control and the impossibility to achieve such aims. It is a style of power that is grotesque and never entirely successful.[30] The fetish is, thus, at once overpowering and unstable, serious and false. And it operates by virtue of its intermediate position between knowledge and belief, reality, and fiction, as has been suggested by Cecile Bishop.[31] Consequently, its capacity to contain and capture the real is never completed, for the relationship between the commandment and the subject is not one of subjection, but a simulacrum thereof.[32] The ingredients for its subversion are, therefore, always manifestly included in its deployment. I thus employ the fetish here as an analytical concept to understand how sovereign power is exerted through fixation onto objects, concepts, and ideas, but at the same time exposes the arbitrariness of this operation.

I want to argue that the logic of the fetish can help us to understand the ideological investment in, and deployment of, deradicalization (and security) policies. This perspective becomes particularly clear when we examine the way deradicalization policies are implemented and treated, both in everyday life and in scholarly literature. These policies have come to be considered as essential for global security, but their legitimacy and efficacy is continuously interrogated, among scholars, policymakers, and social workers who study their effective implementation in everyday life.[33] If deradicalization exists by virtue of a powerful promise—that is, the capacity to penetrate through the impermeable, to guide us through rough waters, to decipher indecipherable signs—it is also the object of constant ridicule and mocking, starting with a wide range of experts and professionals (including deradicalization experts). A large degree of satire and mocking characterizes the deployment and effective implementation of these policies among security experts. Didier Bigo, for instance, has argued that the labor of prevention and profiling entails "astrological dimensions" akin to a job of science fiction: "The will to control time and space, present and future, here and there, has an effect that goes beyond antiterrorist policies; it creates a powerful mixture of fiction and reality, of virtual and actual, which merge their boundaries and introduce fiction into the reality for profiling as well as de-realizing the violence of the state and of the clandestine organizations."[34] Charlotte Heath-Kelly, in turn, has argued that magical-realist components inform the PREVENT program, referring to how the "knowledge of radicalization indicators" invokes the idea of a powerful world of the unseen and the occult, which is recognizable through "signs" in a way that is comparable to witchcraft: "The supernatural discourse of the contemporary era [found in radicalization indicators] invokes possession by unseen evil, as in the old, and both fantasies revolve around the notion that a secret society exists within, and threatens, the greater society—a feature noted of witchcraft discourse in the Middle Ages by Norman Cohn."[35]

The language invoked by Bigo and Heath-Kelly—that of "astrology," "science fiction," "magical realism," "the supernatural"—can be read as an analytical attempt to capture the intermediary zone that these policies occupy. Not fully penetrable, the existence of these policies becomes justified by virtue of their attempts to alleviate our anxieties and control future outcomes, a functionalist goal already diagnosed by Malinowski as central for the operation of magic.[36] Yet by qualifying the indefinite nature of these policies primarily through the modernist language of "belief," they become equally relegated to the domain of the unreal. One of my aims here is to take this intermediary zone of deradicalization policies seriously, as policies that have a sustenance in time and place and are largely supported by policymakers, but that are also continuously questioned and sidelined. By using the language of the fetish, I inquire into how deradicalization policies seek to overrule the "chaotic pluralism" that characterizes the social world (i.e., the presence of Muslims as social and political actors and carriers of meaning) through a process of resignifying Muslim otherness, which then becomes juxtaposed to a secular and liberal ontological order. I will document this process by attending to one angle in this process: the semiotic overinvestment into and redefinition of Islamic vocabularies and political imaginaries. More particularly, I will pause at one iteration: how the European security services have been concerned with *da'wa*—Islamic proselytization—by carefully transforming it into an object of surveillance. I will argue that this discursive overinvestment in *da'wa* can be read as an attempt to contain Muslim otherness in two ways: in a biopolitical and an ontopolitical fashion.[37] The material I will examine draws on the yearly security reports of the Dutch intelligence services to counter radicalization, but it is not restricted to it. The Netherlands served an important role as a laboratory in the deployment of the first deradicalization policies, but other European countries have followed suit.

I will also address how the anxiety with *da'wa* emerges in the context of a concern with social integration, which is centered around the existence of liberal subjects with a free will. *Da'wa* becomes, from this perspective, perceived as an obstruction to the subject's free will, and thus to the capacity of creating an integrated social order. Deradicalization policies emerge, in this context, as instruments or techniques that seek to track the circulation of *da'wa* and their influencing activities. I will then turn to the critical awareness of the impossibility of these stated aims. For although deradicalization policies aim to track these influencing activities, there is also an understanding that the latter is impossible to achieve because of the anatomy of *da'wa* as opaque and untransparent. This double movement of identifying and tracking, though also maintaining an awareness of the impossibility of doing so, is what characterizes deradicalization policies and leads me to qualify them as a fetish.

From *Da'wa* to *Jihad*:
The Problem of "Radical Islam"

The development of the policies of deradicalization in the Netherlands in 2001 occurred against the background of an important restructuring of Dutch security services. This restructuring regrouped the international and domestic intelligence services under one office and resulted in the rebranding of the former BVD (*Binnenlandse Veiligheidsdiensten*) into the AIVD (*Algemene Inlichtingen- en Veiligheidsdienst*).[38] This restructuring also coincided with a changing scope in the surveillance practices of the Dutch security agencies. The first change was related to the growing concern with international terrorism, the latter being understood as an intrinsically unpredictable hazard with potentially devastating effects, but that could be prevented if properly anticipated. This change, furthermore, also converged with a new diagnosis and analysis of what was understood to represent a new threat in a post–Cold War context, namely, (Islamic) terrorism. In addition to this first concern emerged a second, interrelated concern: the problem of integration of ethnic-cultural (in particular, Muslim) minorities into Dutch society. In the 1990s, this concern was manifested through growing public debates in the Netherlands about the increasing visibility and inclusion of Muslim minorities.[39] This debate led to a series of governmental measures and a changing tone on multiculturalism, which also deeply influenced the surveillance practices of the Dutch security services.[40] This double movement, a growing attention to changing global dynamics around terrorism and their interrelation with domestic preoccupations with integration, was at the heart of what came to be known as the *brede benadering*, the "comprehensive approach" to security.

The term *brede benadering* was first introduced in the Dutch security report of 2001.[41] At the heart of this shift was a gradual securitization of the "problem of integration," which would come to play a pivotal role in the further deployment of the security policies. Whereas this question hardly figured as a point of inquiry in the previous years, it became an important source of concern in the late 1990s and around the year 2000. In the reports of 1999 and 2000, the question of sociocultural minorities was explicitly framed and rebranded as a generic challenge for society, and an important preoccupation for the security services.[42] And in their 1999 annual report, the security services redefined their tasks and functions as follows: "signal and [help] counter threats to the integration process at an early stage."[43] Whereas the target of such failed integration remained unspecified in this initial phase, it became more explicit in the subsequent years and in particular with the publication of the influential report, *From Da'wa to Jihad: The Various Threats of Radical Islam against the Democratic Legal Order.*[44] The explicit mentioning of Islamic organizations as a potential threat was not new, because they had already been subjected to monitoring in the previous reports. But in this report, a new connection was drawn, that between radicalization, which could lead to violence, and Islamic proselytism, understood here as *da'wa*.

Da'wa refers more broadly to the testimony of Islam, and figures as an inherent part of the Islamic tradition, but it becomes redefined in these deradicalization policies as a hallmark of "radical Islam." *Da'wa* is understood as a privileged technique of puritan movements to propagate a millenarian view of the world, understood here as a struggle between *dar-al-islam* and *dar-al-harb*, which is translated in the report as the struggle between "the sons of light" and the "sons of darkness," and which contrasts with classical Islamist groups that openly strive for practical political changes (through legitimate and illegitimate means).[45] From the different variants of radical Islam, the radical puritan groups were seen to represent a more serious threat because of their apocalyptic worldview and the insidious and erosive work that they seek to achieve through the practice of *da'wa*. Their nonviolence is therefore not seen as an absence of danger. AIVD continues: "The choice of such *dawa*-oriented groups for non-violent means doesn't imply a principled non-violent stance. Often, they simply do not consider *jihad* to be opportune at this stage."[46]

It is important to briefly pause to reflect on the continuum that is assumed between *da'wa* and *jihad*, and how *da'wa* becomes conceptualized as a social threat in these policies. *Da'wa* is defined here as an "influencing activity" (*beïnvloedingsactiviteit*) that openly and/or covertly affects the relationship between the citizen and society.[47] This occurs, first, through a redefinition of the term "integration" and a broadening of the scope of competences of the security services. The term "integration" is defined through a horizontal axis (i.e., *horizontale integratie*), which refers to the problem of social cohesion, and a vertical axis (i.e., *vertical integratie*), which refers to the relationship to the state and the potential use of violence. Whereas the vertical axis has traditionally figured as a competence of the security services, by adding a horizontal axis to it social cohesion became a new target. The latter was tied to the very basic premise that is at the heart of this comprehensive approach: the idea that social fragmentation is a precursor to violence. Hence, a new continuum became established between the problem of social disintegration (which is enabled through *da'wa*) and the problem of political violence. The question of integration is no longer perceived as a problem of social alienation only (i.e., poverty, marginality, etc.), but becomes here securitized through a connection with proselytizing activities. The way this occurs is, however, by not only attending to the failing "process" of integration as such (for this is still seen as a competence of the integration policies), but by also identifying and monitoring the carriers who are understood to hinder this integration process.

This potential social threat of *da'wa* is, second, also articulated through the hold it was seen to exert over people's minds and the mental reorientation it can produce. Proselytism—*da'wa*—is not treated as an infraction upon one's freedom of conscience, understood here as negative freedom, but rather as a manipulation of one's consciousness.[48] This points toward a deeper concern with the psychology of religious freedom, which attends to the subconscious dimensions of the Self, hence suggesting that the corruption of one's free will primarily occurs at that level. What seems to be at stake here is the concern with a possible corruption of one's capacity to think, even without one realizing it. The state appears, in this context, as the protector of this (sub)conscious mind.[49] This psychological concern with the (sub)conscious mind is neither new nor unique in the operation of the liberal security state, but echoes older and preexisting concerns with brainwashing that have consistently been expressed in western security policies since the second half of the twentieth century, and that assume a disjuncture between one's actual thought and action and one's real desire. We find this articulated in the securitization of religious sects throughout the 1980s and 90s for instance, but also in the treatment of the communist threat during the Cold War in the United States.[50] In *The Covert Sphere*, Timothy Melley describes how this concern with brainwashing figured as a powerful part of the anticommunist propaganda promoted by the U.S. intelligence services during the Cold War.[51] This fear of brainwashing was initially invented as a CIA propaganda instrument but led to actual experiments in mind control and the development of interrogation techniques that were refined during the "war on terror."[52] A similar concern with brainwashing has also emerged as a recurrent theme in some contemporary theories of radicalization.[53] French sociologist Fahrad Khosrokhavar, for instance, defines the phenomenon of radicalization as sectarian movement that deploys a strong inner/outer group logic, and a kind of movement that ruptures one's individuality.[54] In the Netherlands, Peter Prudon and Bertjan Doosje have also argued that the analytical concept of sect could be useful for understanding the process of deradicalization.[55] Central, in these different perspectives, is the view that one's free will can be threatened not only at a conscious level but also at a subconscious level. This concern is not unconnected with how Muslims have historically been racialized within liberal modernity. As also noted by Melley, the idea of total submission, and absence of free will, propagated during the Cold War echoed preexisting Orientalist tropes that were projected onto the communist regime, and that presupposed the idea of a controllable and malleable mind that stood at odds with the liberal (enlightened) self.[56]

The Muslim thus emerges here as malleable and fragile, for she is continuously threatened by the corrosive and manipulative forces of *da'wa*, and thus needs to be protected by the liberal state. Deradicalization policies emerge as instruments and techniques that can safeguard the fragile Muslim mind from these "influencing activities," which can corrode the settled liberal social order. This is most explicitly expressed in another influential report published around the same period, *Saudi Invloeden in Nederland: Verbanden tussen Salafistische Missie, Radicaliseringsprocessen en Islamitisch Terrorisme* (2004) (Saudi Influences in the Netherlands: The Relationship between Salafi Missioning, Radicalization Processes, and Islamic Terrorism).[57] In this report, the Dutch security services warn of the "attraction" Salafism might represent for young Muslims in western countries since they might "offer apparently easy solutions to the identity problems many of them are struggling with."[58] One of the central tasks of the deradicalization policies of the liberal security state is, thus, to restore the resilience and discernment capacity of Muslims by offering identity trainings to young people, investing in positive role models, or in emancipating women.[59] Arun Kundnani describes such actions when discussing similar examples in the PREVENT program in the UK. He describes these as attempts to recapture "hearts and minds."[60] This alludes—as has also been noted by Gutkowski—to the pastoral power of the state.[61]

Yet these perplexities around the captivating power of *da'wa* are linked, I want to suggest, not only with the imagined fragility of Muslim mind, but also with a particular anatomy of *da'wa* and its operating force. Differently than the secular power that is imagined as *transparent*, *da'wa* emerges here as opaque and not immediately traceable. It is represented as a hidden underworld that needs continuous policing, deciphering, and tracking. This produces a perpetual insecurity, suspicion, and anxiety within the liberal order. It is this difficulty with tracking the circulation of *da'wa* that I now want to turn to, as it confronts us with the ontological dimensions, or what Melley calls the "covert sphere," of deradicalization policies.[62]

The Elusive Nature of *Da'wa*

In the previous section, I discussed the concern around the "influencing activities," which drew on a particular resignification of *da'wa* and an anthropology of the Muslim mind as easily manipulable. In addition to that, however, the danger of *da'wa* is also entailed in a second set of characteristics, that is, its elusive nature. In this section, I want to look more closely at this concern. More particularly, I want to show how this concern with the circulation of *da'wa* reflects the inherent doubleness of these deradicalization policies: even in expressing an ostensible attempt to contain *da'wa*, they equally articulate anxiety over the impotency of the state and an impossibility to contain *da'wa*.

This becomes particularly clear as we consider how the Dutch security services understood the danger of *da'wa* in the 2005 report, *From Da'wa to Jihad*. In discussing the different forms of threat posed by radical Islam, the AIVD distinguishes between a horizontal and vertical dimension, immediate and long-term threats, and open or covert activities.[63] Covert *da'wa* (*heimlijke dawa*) is identified as one of the shapes *da'wa* can take and is seen in the report as important for some types of radical Islam that strive for deep societal change through the long-term use of pacific means. This makes them particularly threatening:

> This concerns types of radical Islam that try to undermine the structures of the democratic constitutional state through covert *da'wa*. There are indications at the international level that, more specifically, the

> nonviolent branches of the Muslim Brotherhood make use of stealthy *da'wa* strategies. In employing such strategies, the choice is made to avoid a direct violent confrontation with the state, and to undermine its operation rather gradually through an indirect and eventual takeover of the civil service, the judiciary, the education institutions, the local authorities, and so on. In addition to covert entry politics, covert *da'wa* can also focus on bringing Muslim minorities to civil disobedience, promoting parallel power structures, or even incite Muslim masses to revolt.[64] (my translation)

Differently from the other organizations that openly defy law and order, the groups that perform covert *da'wa* are understood to use legitimate means by remaining within the confines of the law and acting in ways congruent with the democratic state. Yet their overt actions are only a façade, for the threat resides in what lies behind those actions: an intentional striving for a different social order.

The idea that Muslim radicalism—and in some cases Islam—represents an "unknown" threat to western societies is not uncommon. Far-right politicians and pundits have routinely thematized the notion of *taqiyya* (the practice of concealing one's faith) to stress the incapacity of the state to obtain full transparency over the motivations of Muslims and their continuous deceit.[65] They thus warn of a slow and gradual replacement of European societies by (radical) Muslims.[66] Such conspiracy theories are, however, not solely a property of far-right movements, but form an extension—as has been observed by several analysts—of the epistemological and ontological insecurity at the heart of modernity.[67] "Radical Muslims" are seen to exacerbate this insecurity by critically challenging established regimes of truth—that is, the idea of a multireligious and multicultural society as embodied by the liberal state. In this instance, however, it is not so much nonstate actors, but rather the state that is the carrier of a discourse of deception by Muslims.[68] Radical Muslim groups are accused of using "stealthy" *da'wa* strategies against the state. Their ostensible engagement with liberal democracy appears as a mere façade, and behind it lies a continued attempt at eroding the liberal tenets assumed to form the cement of the social order. We thus see how distrust and suspicion emerges as major themes here. These attitudes structure the relationship of the state toward these movements.

In a piece on the matter, Hussein Ali Agrama has argued that a "structure of suspicion" figures as an essential hallmark of modern secular power.[69] He links this with a contradiction that he views to be inherent to the modern and secular semiotic ideology or discursive construction of religion: in defining religion as a symbolic system, it equally assumes a separation between (inner) belief and (outer) religious expression, which thus "leads one to see the act [of religious conduct] as a *sign* of belief." Simultaneously, however, there is also an understanding of religious conduct's unique capacity to shape one's interiority, as there is a "recognition of the *causal efficacy* of acts, that they can constitute or powerfully shape belief and thus the values that people hold—a recognition that erodes the divide between 'inner belief' and 'outer act.'" In other words, religious conduct and symbols (exteriority), such as a cross or the headscarf, are seen as capable of instilling and inciting religious sentiment and belief (interiority). This entanglement, he continues, "lends itself to an ever more pronounced vigilance against the potential power of religious beliefs and acts," which must be seen as the flip side of the principle of religious freedom.[70] Thus religious freedom as articulated in the modern secular structure does not only lie in the protection *of* one's freedom of consciousness (positive freedom), but also in the protection *from* the intrusive power of religious discourse and practice (negative freedom). The structure of suspicion is thus tied, Agrama contends, with this concern over the overpowering effects of religious discourse and practice—as also explored in the previous section.

Yet to understand the distrust toward *da'wa*, it is also important to consider another aspect of its manifestation: its form. *Da'wa* not only poses a threat because of the potential influence it can have, but also because of its ability to evade the regulatory and classificatory power of the state. Its indecipherability is often mentioned as a problem in the various reports by the state. Different from the headscarf or the beard, which are embodied acts of otherness, *da'wa* distinguishes itself through this absence of a corporeal or material manifestation. Its lethalness does not (only) lie in the potential threat it poses to a Kantian "autonomy of the will," but in its long-term capacity to circulate in and erode the civil order in a disembodied manner. *Da'wa* can circulate in the "civil service, the judiciary, the education institutions, the local authorities." These are central aspects of the modern secular state. And one is never sure whether Muslims' political activities are not also an expression of their religious ideologies. As already noted by Sayyid and Tyer, this incorporeality, or "the difficulties of correctly identifying the incorporated unreal/unracial presence of the deathly Muslim other," generates governmental panic and concern.[71] Anything Muslims do can function as *da'wa*, whether it is praying, fasting, engaging in public life, or working. There is a perpetual inability to contain *da'wa* by marking it distinctly as religious, as Muslim, as "other."

Hence, what seems to be at stake here are the politico-theological capacities of the state. In making this point, I am inspired by the work of Falguni Sheth, who seeks to complement Foucault's analytical model of biopolitics through a sustained focus on ontology. She suggests that contemporary events following 9/11, and the sweeping Islamophobia that has accompanied it, force us to consider the functionality of what she calls the "onto-politics of sovereign power."

> We need to refocus and expand our investigation to include an analysis of how (sovereign) power collaborates with regulatory power to produce ontological divides and resorts to a moral plane to legitimate those divides. . . . Ontopolitics can consistently operate alongside biopolitics; however, its scope of (political) management refers to non-biopolitical, indeed moral, cultural, social, ontological categories that are recalled by Foucault in *Abnormal*, among other writings.[72]

Sheth's aim is to complicate the notion of "productivity of life" that lies at the heart of Foucault's notion of biopower by going beyond its strictly biological meaning. She seeks to also include "the cultural, religious, ideological" components through which segments of the population are marked as "threats to the existence of the prevailing sovereign regime."[73] This preoccupation is understood as a product of sovereign power, which she conceptualizes as a "direct force" aimed at inscribing subdivisions within the political body.[74] For Sheth, the question of sovereign power thus exceeds the territorial and disciplinary mode, but also includes a capacity to organize and classify the world, or what she describes here as "onto-power."

Coming back to the perceived threat of *da'wa* and the necessity to act upon it, one notes that it is precisely its disincarnated nature and the impossibility of classifying it that poses a problem. This allows for a circulation that curtails the ontological (or politico-theological) capacities of the secular state (i.e., its capacity to define the real through a liberal-secular nexus). Furthermore, attempts at containing the circulation of *da'wa* are continuously troubled because of its undefined form. Even a legion of security experts seem unable to withhold its theological force, for it is precisely its banality and ordinariness that make it a formidable contender with the state. It is not so much the "otherness" of *da'wa* (or Muslimness) that represents a threat to the symbolic unity of secularism, but rather its "commonness" and porosity, and, thus, impossibility to be bounded as other. Deradicalization policies thus emerge as attempts to mediate this challenged ontological order by restoring new boundaries, by deciphering the presence of this Islamic otherness, by recognizing its "signs" (which, in turn, generate a perpetual fear and anxiety). With grand claims and promises, deradicalization policies appear as desperate attempts at restoring a secular coherence and liberal order, but these are nevertheless understood as hopeless and always fraught.

Conclusion

This chapter has been an attempt to reflect on the policies of deradicalization in western Europe through a political-theological lens. In recent years, these preventive policies have gained an unprecedented expansion as public policies both in Europe and also across the world. A key aim of this contribution has been to understand the continued mobilization of these policies despite the continuous critiques to which they have been subjected. For, since their deployment, attempts at preventing radicalization have often been met with disqualification and ridicule—both by scholars and experts on the ground. Yet, simultaneously, states have continued to reinforce their investment in the idea of preventing radicalization and in tools to recognize the signs of radicalization. This combined feature of belief in the need for prevention and disbelief in the efficacy of these measures has formed the starting point for a broader reflection that aims to account for the cultural and political-theological role of these public policies. To grasp the inherently contradictory status of the deradicalization policies, I have relied on Mbembe's notion of *fetish*. This concept has been introduced to reveal the double movement of investment and symbolic overcharging and also the continuous boundedness and fragility of the postcolonial state. By applying this concept to the public policies of deradicalization and outside the African context, I have sought to grasp the vexed and unsettled relationship Western European, in this case Dutch, security states entertain with the presence of Islam in its public sphere. The securitization of Islam appears here as a fetish, that is, as a desperate attempt to trace the manifestations of "radical Islam"—through the reification of *da'wa*. By clothing *da'wa* with an "aura of factuality," it becomes objectified into a powerful political contender, and thus constructed into a legitimate target of surveillance.[75] At the same time, however, the impossibility of settling the form of *da'wa* exposes the state's limited interpretative reach. As such, the fetishization of *da'wa* expresses both the state's attempt at stabilizing a liberal-secular order and its inability to do so. For the threat of *da'wa* persists, and its unique manifestations continue to haunt the ontological integrity of the liberal and secular state.

I want to briefly reflect on this attempt to make use of the concept of the fetish to discern the cultural function and operation of deradicalization policies, and on the usage of a conceptual language theorized for the African context to grasp a reality in Europe. Ongoing critical examinations of security policies have consistently sought to undo these policies by either highlighting their stigmatizing, criminalizing, and overpowering effects, or by underscoring their lack of efficacy and the various forms of "magical thinking" informing them. Additionally, scholars have also increasingly sought to demystify the "black box" of security (and the state) by ethnographically detailing its routines, internal contradictions, banality, and contingencies.[76] Instead of dismissing these esoteric components of the state, I have rather sought to find the appropriate language to restore this aspect of mystery and evasiveness in the workings of the secular state. In doing so, my intention has not been to resuscitate the idea of an overpowering agent or to demonstrate the irrationality of these endeavors, but rather to enable the usage of a particular analytical language that is not bounded by the logics of functionalism or pragmatism. This analytical language tries to grasp and assess moments of elusiveness and contemplation that escape one's control. Through the documents examined in this chapter we are witnesses of furtive attempts by security agents to speculate, to develop theologies and apocalyptic views, and to expose vulnerabilities. But these are enveloped in harnesses of discipline and expertise that are deemed essential for the performance of a secular state. This is where the language of the *fetish* becomes useful, for it enables us to examine how this contingency of social life becomes displaced onto the "other." "Radical

Islam," or in this case *da'wa*, comes to stand in for both the threat of and the necessity to affirm a coherent social order. Whereas anthropologists have traditionally examined the importance of state rituals and ceremonies, security policies have less often been examined through this lens. Yet they appear as a realm full of potential, but also of risk, which allow us to observe the state in all its splendor and ostensible certitude, and in its weakness and its impotency. Addressing deradicalization policies through a different lens—as a ritual performance of the state, as a fetish—serves to not only enhance the anthropology of security, but also to understand the theology of the state.

Finally, using a conceptual language that has been developed to account for the realities of African postcolonial states is an unusual move, but one I understand to fit the effort and exercise to decolonize our scholarly imaginaries and vocabularies. Using a conceptual language developed in the west and for the west to address realities across the globe is rarely questioned—that is, the concept of "religion" or "secularism"; however, utilizing the notion of the fetish is not only an effort at provincializing Europe, but also one of rendering empirical insights grasped and theorized from the Global South onto the Global North.[77] It allows us to capture the relationalities between these different contexts—as suggested by Slabodsky in his contribution (chapter 1). The condition of the postcolony, as described by Mbembe, equally concerns Europe.

NOTES

I am grateful to all the participants of the Contending Modernities workshop organized in March 2019 at the University of Notre Dame for their stimulating reflections and comments on the first draft of this chapter. Since that workshop, this chapter has been substantially revised, and I owe much gratitude to Atalia Omer for initiating this project and her careful reading of the different drafts. Also, a special thanks to Miriyam Aouragh, Mieke Groeninck, and Hamza Esmili for their comments on previous versions, and to Joshua Lupo for his editing work and important comments on the final version of the draft. (Reference code project funding FWO G0D8521N)

    1. See Nora Khaleefeh, "'Des musulmans ont dansé après les attentats,' Jambon provoque la polémique," RTBF Info, April 17, 2016, https://www.rtbf.be/article/des-musulmans-ont-danse-apres-les-attentats-jambon-provoque-la-polemique-9272001; and Roel Wauters and Jonas Muylaert, "De Storm over

'Dansende Moslims' Uitspraak van Jambon Gaat Niet Liggen," *De Morgen*, April 19, 2019, https://www.demorgen.be/nieuws/storm-over-dansende-moslims-uitspraak-van-jambon-gaat-niet-liggen~bfba3ceb/.

2. Bram Vandeputte, "Factcheck: Feestende Moslims na de Aanslagen?," VRTnws, April 4, 2016, https://www.vrt.be/vrtnws/nl/2016/04/18/fact_check_feestendemoslimsnadeaanslagen-1-2632801/.

3. Abdellali Hajjat and Marwan Mohammed, *Islamophobie: Comment les Élites Françaises Fabriquent le "Problème Musulman"* (Paris: La Découverte, 2013).

4. Christina Pantazis and Simon Pemberton, "From the 'Old' to the 'New' Suspect Community," *British Journal of Criminology* 49, no. 5 (2009): 646–66.

5. Christopher Baker-Beall, Charlotte Heath-Kelly, and Lee Jarvis, *Counter-Radicalisation: Critical Perspectives* (Abingdon: Routledge, 2015), 20; Arun Kundnani, *The Muslims Are Coming: Islamophobia, Extremism, and the Domestic War on Terror* (London: Verso Books, 2014), 17.

6. Carlos Caduff, *The Pandemic Perhaps: Dramatic Events in a Public Culture of Danger* (Oakland: University of California Press, 2015). The cosmology of the mutant strains refers to the ever-changing and ever-evolving nature of the virus (77), thus making it impossible to make definite claims and producing a type of medical discourse that he describes as "pandemic prophecy." He describes the latter as an indeterminate form of scientific speech that is centered on the unknown and draws on the production of anxieties and anticipation, yet which is never fully realized.

7. Michael Dillon, *Biopolitics of Security. A Political Analytic of Finitude* (London: Routledge, 2015).

8. Anjuli Fatima Raza Kolb, *Epidemic Empire: Colonialism, Contagion, and Terror, 1817–2020* (Chicago: University of Chicago Press, 2021).

9. Michel Foucault, *"Society Must Be Defended": Lectures at the Collège de France, 1975–1976* (London: Penguin, 2004[1997]), 55.

10. Ibid., 61.

11. See also Dillon, *Biopolitics of Security*, 151.

12. Falguni A. Sheth, "The War on Terror and Ontopolitics: Concerns with Foucault's Account of Race, Power Sovereignty," *Foucault Studies* 12 (October 2011): 51–76.

13. I thank Atalia Omer for the precise formulation of this sentence.

14. Achille Mbembe, *On the Postcolony* (Berkeley: University of California Press, 2001).

15. Nadia Fadil and Martijn de Koning, "Turning 'Radicalization' into Science: Ambivalent Translations into the Dutch (Speaking) Academic Field," in *Radicalization in Belgium and the Netherlands: Critical Perspectives on Violence and Security*, ed. Nadia Fadil, Martijn de Koning, and Francesco Ragazzi (London: I. B. Tauris, 2019), 53–79; Arun Kundnani and Ben Hayes, *The Globalisation of Countering Violent Extremism Policies: Undermining Human*

Rights, Instrumentalising Civil Society (Amsterdam: Transnational Institute [TNI] Amsterdam, 2019).

16. Baker-Beall, Heath-Kelly, and Jarvis, *Counter-Radicalisation*; Kundani, *The Muslims Are Coming*; Mark Sedgwick, "The Concept of Radicalization as a Source of Confusion," *Terrorism and Political Violence* 22 (2010): 479–94; Paul Thomas, *Responding to the Threat of Violent Extremism: Failing to Prevent* (New York: Bloomsbury Academic, 2012).

17. Tufyal Choudhury, "The Radicalisation of Citizenship Deprivation," *Critical Social Policy* 37, no. 2 (2017): 225–44; Nisha Kapoor, *Deport, Deprive, Extradite: 21st Century State Extremism* (London: Verso, 2018); Kundani, *The Muslims Are Coming*.

18. Talal Asad, *Formations of the Secular: Christianity, Islam, and Modernity* (Stanford, CA: Stanford University Press, 2003); Monique Scheer, Nadia Fadil, and Brigitte Schepelern Johansen, eds., *Secular Bodies, Affects and Emotions: European Configurations* (London: Bloomsbury, 2019)

19. Luca Mavelli, "Between Normalisation and Exception: The Securitisation of Islam and the Construction of the Secular Subject," *Millennium* 41, no. 2 (2013): 159–81.

20. Ibid., 167.

21. Stacey Gutkowski, *Secular War: Myths of Religion, Politics and Violence* (London: I. B. Tauris, 2014), 121.

22. S. Sayyid, *A Fundamental Fear: Eurocentrism and the Emergence of Islamism* (London: Zed, 1997); Sayyid, "Islamophobia and the Europeanness of the Other Europe," *Patterns of Prejudice* 52, no. 5 (2018): 420–35; David Tyrer and S. Sayyid, "Governing Ghosts: Race, Incorporeality and Difference in Post-Political Times," *Current Sociology* 60, no. 3 (2012): 353–67.

23. I understand liberalism and secularism as normative political orders that revolve respectively around the (assumed) protection of individual rights through the privatization of religion, but equally as epistemological and ontological perspectives that rely on a set of assembled categories that are constitutive for how "life" and/or "reality" are conceived and apprehended (e.g., the individual, self, religion, and freedom are more than normative categories, they operate as relevant units of existence).

24. J. Lorand Matory, *The Fetish Revisited: Marx, Freud, and the Gods Black People Make* (Durham, NC: Duke University Press, 2018); Sónia Silva, "Reification and Fetishism: Processes of Transformation," *Theory, Culture & Society* 30, no. 1 (2013): 79–98. Within anthropological scholarship, the work of Michael Taussig stands out as an early example of the use of fetish in his well-known *The Devil and Commodity Fetishism in South America* (Chapel Hill: University of North Carolina Press, 1980). Yet in this work, he relies on a Marxist take on the concept to attend to how the transformation from traditional to capitalist forms of production (dominated by the exchange value system) went along

with new forms of folk belief around money and crops. His later book, *The Magic of the State* (London: Routlegde, 1997), comes closer to the objective of this chapter, as he examines how both spirits and the state emerge as fetishes surrounded by their paraphernalia.

25. Mbembe, *On the Postcolony*, 108.

26. Ruth Marshall, *Political Spiritualities: The Pentecostal Revolution in Nigeria* (Chicago: Chicago University Press, 2009), 104.

27. Mbembe, *On the Postcolony*, 104.

28. Ibid., 103.

29. Ibid., 108.

30. Judith Butler, "Mbembe's Extravagant Power," *Public Culture* 5, no. 1 (1992): 67–74. Butler draws the analogy with the parody in a discussion of Mbembe's concept of the fetish. The travesty is a semblance of performance that is neither entirely successful or "real" but also not entirely false.

31. Cecile Bishop, *Postcolonial Criticism and Representation of African Dictatorship: The Aesthetics of Tyranny* (London: Routledge, 2014), 98.

32. Mbembe uses the term "conviviality" rather than "resistance/subordination" to refer to the simultaneous display of seriousness of the manifestation authority and its downplaying in everyday life. See Mbembe, *On the Postcolony*, 112.

33. Silke Jaminé and Nadia Fadil, "(De-)Radicalization as a Negotiated Practice: An Ethnographic Case Study in Flanders," in Fadil, de Koning, and Ragazzi, eds., *Radicalization in Belgium and the Netherlands*, 169–93; Francesco Ragazzi and Lili-Anne de Jongh, "Countering Radicalization: Hijacking Trust? Dilemmas of Street-Level Bureaucrats in the Netherlands," in Fadil, de Koning, and Ragazzi, eds., *Radicalization in Belgium and the Netherlands*, 147–68.

34. Didier Bigo, "Security, Exception, Ban and Surveillance," in *Theorizing Surveillance*, ed. David Lyon (London: Taylor & Francis, 2006), 46–68.

35. Charlotte Heath-Kelly, "Can We Laugh Yet? Reading Post-9/11 Counterterrorism Policy as Magical Realism and Opening a Third-Space of Resistance," *European Journal of Criminal Policy and Research* 18 (2012): 343–60; Francesco Ragazzi, "La lutte contra la Radicalisation ou Deux Formes de Pensées Magique," *Mouvements* 4, no. 88 (2016): 151–58.

36. Bronislaw Malinowski, *Magic, Science and Religion and Other Essays* (London: Profile Books, 1982[1925]). Malinowski introduces a functionalist account of magic, which he views as a practice that is performed when "scientific" and rationally accountable methods and techniques prove insufficient. Magic thus becomes the substitute of science, which comes to fill the gaps that remain incomplete and unaccounted for. This account has the merit of suspending the idea that the use of magic is simply "irrational," but it remains indebted to the idea that it comes to compensate for an absence or failure of rationality, rather than considering its function for its own sake (29). Hence, an evolutionary account becomes tacitly reproduced, which considers the presence of magic as a presence by

default. Furthermore, and as has also been documented by Randall Styers, the category of magic is introduced in European language to demarcate it from religion. Magic is understood as the smaller brother of the more advanced "religion" (with Protestantism as the most purified version), and a remaining signpost of primitiveness within western societies. See Randall G. Styers, *Making Magic: Religion, Magic, and Science in the Modern World* (Oxford: Oxford University Press, 2004).

37. Falguni A. Sheth, "The War on Terror and Ontopolitics: Concerns with Foucault's Account of Race, Power Sovereignty," *Foucault Studies* 12 (October 2011): 51–76.

38. For a further and more detailed discussion of the way radicalization was introduced among the Dutch security services, see Fadil and de Koning, "Turning 'Radicalization' into Science," 53–79. The following short historical reconstruction in this section largely builds on that chapter.

39. Rinus Penninx, Henk Münstermann, and Han Entzinger, *Etnische Minderheden en de Multiculturele Samenleving* (Amsterdam: IMES, 1998); Johann Rath, *Minorisering: De Sociale Constructie van "Etnische Minderheden"* (Amsterdam: Sua, 1991).

40. Baukje Prins, *Voorbij de Onschuld: Het Debat over de Multiculturele Samenleving* (Amsterdam: Van Gennep, 2000); Willem Schinkel, *Denken in een Tijd van Sociale Hypochondrie: Aanzet tot een Theorie Voorbij de Maatschappij* (Kampen: Klement, 2007).

41. See Fadil, de Koning, and Ragazzi, eds., *Radicalization in Belgium and the Netherlands.*

42. See Martijn de Koning, Carmen Becker, Ineke Roex, and Pim Aarns, "Eilanden In een Zee van Ongeloof: Het Verzet van de Activistische Da'wa-Netwerken in België, Nederland en Duitsland," in *IMES Report Series* (Nijmegen; Amsterdam, 2014).

43. Binnenlandse Veiligheidsdiensten, *Jaarverslag 1999* (Den Haag 2000), 15.

44. Published as *Van Dawa tot Jihad: De Diverse Dreigingen van de Radicale Islam tegen de Democratische Rechtsorde* (Algemene Inlichtingen en Veiligheidsdiensten: Den Haag, December 2004).

45. Ibid., 27.

46. Ibid., 28.

47. Ibid., 33.

48. Isaiah Berlin, "Two Concepts of Liberty," in *Four Essays on Liberty*, ed. Isaiah Berlin (Oxford: Oxford University Press, 1969[1958]), 118–72. Several scholars have attended to the way in which the very idea of religious freedom is premised upon a scripted notion of religion (as belief), a particular view on religious agency, and an expression of state power. Elizabeth Shakman Hurd has argued, in this respect, that the notion of religious freedom draws upon a "religious psychology that relies on the notion of an autonomous subject who chooses beliefs and then enacts them freely," thereby excluding alternative notions and/or views on

religious traditions that stress the communal or relational dimensions. See Hurd, "Believing in Religious Freedom," in *Politics of Religious Freedom*, ed. Winnifred Fallers Sullivan, Elizabeth Shakman Hurd, Saba Mahmood, and Peter G. Danchin (Chicago: The University of Chicago Press, 2015), 48–49.

49. And in so doing, it goes further than a Kantian concern with "free will" as expressed in the classical concerns with religious freedom.

50. Annette P. Hampshire and James A Beckford, "Religious Sects and the Concept of Deviance: The Mormons and the Moonies," *British Journal of Sociology* 34, no. 2 (1983): 208–29.

51. Timothy Melley, *The Covert Sphere: Secrecy, Fiction, and the National Security State* (Ithaca, NY: Cornell University Press, 2012).

52. Ibid., 61.

53. Analogies between radicalization and sectarian movements are routinely made in the public debate in the Netherlands, Belgium, and France, and occasionally even turned into an analytical model. French sociologist Fahrad Khosrokhavar, for instance, defines the phenomenon of radicalization as a sectarian movement through the deployment of a strong inner/outer-group logic, and through the rupture it produces in one's individuality. See Khosrokhavar, *Radicalisation* (Paris: Editions de la Maison des Sciences de l'homme, 2014). In the Netherlands, the chairholder of radicalization studies at the University of Amsterdam, Bertjan Doosje, has also argued that the analogy with sects is useful for understanding the process of deradicalization. See, for instance, Doosje, "Radicalisering: Een Analyse in Termen van Sekten," *Tijdschrift de Psycholoog* (2015), https://www.tijdschriftdepsycholoog.nl/artikelen/radicalisering/.

54. Farhad Khosrokhavarm, *Radicalization: Why Some People Choose the Path of Violence* (New York: The New Press, 2016).

55. Peter Prudon and Bertjan Doosje, "Radicalisering: Een Analyse in Termen van Sekten," *De Psycholoog* (February 2015): 44–51.

56. The obsessional concern with this question drew on an Orientalist representation of communist regimes suspected of programming their subjects into absolute obedience ("the search for a new slave race") through new psychological and cognitive techniques. This idea would, however, find expansion, Melley notes, through the further theorization by influential psychologists, such as Joost Meerloo, who warned about "techniques of mass submission" that could operate through subtle techniques, often unknowingly (cited in Melley, *The Covert Sphere*, 52). Anidjar reminds us of how this idea of "absolute submission" operated as a central theological-political marker in the Enlightenment through the racialization of the Muslim as "other." See Gil Anidjar, *The Jew, the Arab: A History of the Enemy* (Stanford, CA: Stanford University Press, 2003); Alberto Toscano, *Fanaticism: On the Uses of an Idea* (London: Verso, 2010). Discussing the work of Kant and Montesquieu, Anidjar describes how the Muslim appeared as essentially submissive, and how his submission was thematized together with the notion of despotism

that was primarily theorized with reference to the Ottoman sultanate: "Indeed, if the privileged, if not exclusive example of despotism was the Ottoman sultan, its structurally opposed pole, the privileged example of the submitted became, therefore, the Muslim" (Anidjar, *The Jew, the Arab*, 126).

57. For a further discussion of this report, see Fadil and de Koning, "Turning 'Radicalization' into Science." See the report of AIVD, *Saudi Invloeden in Nederland: Verbanden tussen Salafitische Missie, Radicaliseringsprocessen en Islamitisch Terrorisme* (2004), https://www.aivd.nl/documenten/publicaties/2004/06/09/rapport-saoedische-invloeden-in-nederland.

58. Ibid., 5.

59. Grewal, *Saving the Security State*; AIVD, *Saudi Invloeden in Nederland*, 55.

60. Kundani, *The Muslims Are Coming*, 153.

61. Gutkowski, *Secular War*.

62. Melley, *The Covert Sphere*.

63. AIVD, *Saudi Invloeden in Nederland*, 37.

64. Ibid., 44. Original text: "Hier betreft het vormen van de radicale islam die via heimelijke dawa de structuren van de democratische rechtsstaat trachten te ondermijnen. Er zijn, op internationaal niveau, aanwijzingen dat met name de niet direct gewelddadige takken van de Moslim Broederschap heimelijke dawa-strategieën hanteren. Bij deze strategieën wordt gekozen om niet tot een direct gewelddadige confrontatie met de staatsmacht te komen maar deze stilaan te ondermijnen door een indirecte in en uiteindelijke overname van de ambtenarenapparaat, de rechtelijke macht, de onderwijsinstellingen, de lokale overheden enzovoort. Naast op heimelijke intredepolitiek kan heimelijke dawa ook gericht zijn op het brengen van moslimminderheden tot burgerlijke ongehoorzaamheid, het bevorderen van parallelle machtsstructurern of zelfs het aanzetten van moslimmassa's tot revolte."

65. Maryam El-Shall, "From Risk to Terror: Islamist Conspiracies and the Paradoxes of Post-9/11 Government," *Open Cultural Studies* 2, no. 1 (2018): 39–49; Yasemin Shooman, "Between Everyday Racism and Conspiracy Theories: Islamophobia on the German-Language Internet," in *Media and Minorities: Questions on Representation from an International Perspective*, ed. Georg Ruhrmann, Yasemin Shooman, and Peter Widmann (Göttingen: Vandenhoeck and Ruprecht, 2016), 135–55.

66. For a discussion, see Sarah Bracke and Luis Manuel Hernández Aguilar, "'They Love Death as We Love Life': The 'Muslim Question' and the Biopolitics of Replacement," *British Journal of Sociology* 71, no. 4 (2020): 1–22.

67. Stef Aupers, "'Trust No One': Modernization, Paranoia and Conspiracy Culture," *European Journal of Communication* 27, no. 1 (2012): 22–34; Asbjørn Dyrendal, David G. Robertson, and Egil Asprem, eds., *Handbook of Conspiracy Theory and Contemporary Religion* (Leiden: Brill, 2018); Ulrich Beck, *Risk Society: Towards a New Modernity* (London: Sage, 1998[1992]).

68. The accusations of *taqiyya* (dissimulation) are routinely articulated in far-right milieus, but the concept has also been picked up by security experts in Europe in recent years. See, for instance, this article on the French security service's use of the word: Anne-Diandra Louarn, "Taqiyya, or the Terrorist Art of 'Deception,'" France24, March 3, 2013, https://www.france24.com/en/20130313-taqiya-france-islam-deception-favoured-terrorists-jihad.

69. Hussein Ali Agrama, "Religious Freedom and the Bind of Suspicion in Contemporary Secularity," in Sullivan et al., eds., *Politics of Religious Freedom*, 305.

70. Ibid., 306 (Agrama's emphasis). This structure of suspicion has equally been observed by Brigitte Schepelern Johansen and Riem Spielhaus, "Quantitative Knowledge Production on Muslims in Europe as a Practice of 'Secular Suspicion,'" in Scheer, Fadil, and Johansen, eds., *Secular Bodies, Affects and Emotions*, 171–84. They discuss how quantitative surveys on Muslims in Europe interpellated Muslims as theologico-political outsiders to the secular body (172). Several authors have, furthermore, noted how questions of transparency are inherent to modern power in a way that is not restricted to religious, or esoteric, movements. See Lilith Mahmud, *The Brotherhood of Freemason Sisters: Gender, Secrecy, and Fraternity in Italian Masonic Lodges* (Chicago: University of Chicago Press, 2014); Mathijs Pelkmans, "The 'Transparency' of Christian Proselytizing in Kyrgyzstan," *Anthropological Quarterly* 82, no. 2 (2009): 429–52.

71. Tyrer and Sayyid, "Governing Ghosts," 357.

72. Sheth, "The War on Terror and Ontopolitics," 55.

73. Ibid., 75.

74. Ibid., 69.

75. Clifford Geertz, *The Interpretations of Cultures* (New York: Basic Books 1973[1966]), 90.

76. Didier Bigo, "Globalized (In)Security: The Field and the Ban-Opticon," in *Terror, Insecurity and Liberty: Illiberal Practices of Liberal Regimes after 9/11*, ed. Didier Bigo and Anastassia Tsoukala (Abingdon: Routledge, 2008), 10–48; Mark Maguire, Catarina Frois, and Nils Zurawski, eds., *The Anthropology of Security* (London: Pluto Press, 2014).

77. Dipesh Chakrabarty, *Provincializing Europe: Postcolonial Thought and Historical Difference* (Princeton, NJ: Princeton University Press, 2000).

CHAPTER 3

Afrofuturism, Islamofuturism, and Post-Western Modernity

S. SAYYID

ABSTRACT

Multiple modernities can represent either the continuation of Eurocentrism or its critique. The critique of Eurocentrism opens the possibility of imagining a post-western future. Decolonial thinkers have theorized modernity as being intrinsically entangled with the colonial-racial order of things. This raises the question of what a post-western future would look like if the modern and the colonial relationship no longer existed. Articulating the modern as distinct from the west and the colonial in the language of westernese presents a profound philosophical challenge. The author draws on two recent films, Black Panther *(2018) and* Dune *(2021), to explore tensions in dreams of modernity not contained by the ideological boundaries of the west and not contaminated by the colonial. These films gesture toward what a modernity not defined by the west might look like and make clear the challenge of what such post-western imaging entails. One of the principal challenges of imagining the post-western is the way in which the liberal-secular-democratic assemblage is mobilized to foreclose any possibility of a future without the hegemony of the floating signifier of the west.*

World Gone Wrong

The country of Wakanda as depicted in *Black Panther* (2018), and the universe, as portrayed in the recent adaptation of Frank Herbert's novel *Dune* (2021), are two contemporary representations of an imaginary future in which modernity has a distinctly non-western flavor.[1] The concoction of imaginary worlds as mirrors of the "actually existing world" have been the hallmark of satirical, speculative, and escapist fiction in many kinds of literature. One way to look at the Contending Modernities project is to see it as an exceptionally insightful series of exercises in speculative fiction in the form of counterfactual histories. What if modernity was not one but many? What if the constitutive rupture between modernity and tradition was reinscribed as a series of divisions between different modernities? Modernity, however, is, among other things, the origin story of the west. Modernity turns the western peninsula of the Asian landmass into a continent that molds all other continents. It is modernity that turns the west into a cartographic gauge, an epistemological center, and a maker of the world in which we all live. If the hegemonic narrative of modernity is disrupted, the result is a change in the origin story and, thus, the very identity of the west.[2] The question of modernity is so tied to western identity that any addition of pathways toward it implies contention over what constitutes the west. Therefore, imaginaries such as *Black Panther* and *Dune*, which suggest a break in the axiomatic association between modernity and the west, raise fundamental questions about the western order of things.

In *Black Panther*, Wakanda is depicted as one of the most technologically advanced countries in the world. *Black Panther* is the superhero alter ego of T'Challa, the heir and eventual ruler of Wakanda, a rare example of an African country that has escaped the European "scramble for Africa."[3] Thus, Wakanda gestures toward the possibility that Africa could have become modern if it had not been colonized. This possibility is represented on the screen by an Afrofuturistic sensibility signified by its cast, costumes, architecture, female agency, and Africana art.[4] The Afrofuturism of *Black Panther* feeds the decolonial imagination by displacing two key tenets of racist narratives: Africa could not have technology and it could not modernize without colonialism.[5] *Black Panther* seems to provide speculative confirmation of recent academic literature, which argues that colonization derailed possibilities of non-European autochthonous developments that would have led to the emergence of "Indigenous" technologies. Wakanda, therefore, demonstrates that the relationship between modernity and colonialism is contingent rather than historically necessary. This conception of what Africa might have been like if it had not been colonized appears to open up the possibility of imagining multiple modernities.

Black Panther is set in an indeterminate temporality, but it appears similar to the contemporary world, and therefore its representations of coloniality/modernity resonate directly. In contrast, *Dune* takes place in a distant future, and its relationship to the world of multiple modernities seems more indirect. It depicts a future not based on the infinite expansion of western history. It does so by drawing on Islamicate terminologies (e.g., *fedaykin/fedayeen, hajj, hajr/hijria, Jihad*, padishah emperor, Mahdi, etc.) and thematic analogies.[6] *Dune* is primarily set on a desert planet named Arrakis, which is the only source of a natural material—called "melange" (spice)—that makes space travel possible. The planet is controlled by outsiders who extract its resources, exploit its Indigenous population, and ruin its ecology. The inhabitants of Arrakis are mainly desert dwellers with mysterious customs and of unknown numbers who are awaiting a messiah who will end their exploitation and break the chains of their subjugation. The *Dune* novels are often compared to epic fantasy works such as *Lord of the Rings*, but their story is told not in a European but rather in an Islamicate register. *Dune* translates and projects Islamicate vocabularies and history far into the future—apparently 10,000 years. In many ways, the *Dune* mythos, as a global phenomenon marked by the release of a two-part movie series, presents a similar spectacle to *Black Panther*. Despite its reliance on the circulation of familiar Oriental tropes (despots, fanaticism, and desert landscapes), *Dune* remains a rare example of a mass cultural experience that imagines a future by drawing on the Islamicate.

It is the case, however, that *Dune* is more ambiguous in its celebration of Muslimness than *Black Panther* is in the emancipatory joy of Blackness. This is partly because of *Black Panther*'s debt to Afrofuturism, which not only has a definite cultural aesthetic (literature, music, visual arts, fashion), but enjoys a broader influence rooted as it is in the Black radical tradition, civil rights struggle, and the Black Atlantic. Afrofuturism combines cultural production and critical reflection that help make it a recognizable genre that transcends the regions and circumstances of its production.[7]

What I am describing as Islamofuturism is a nascent enterprise, it is not a synonym for Muslim futurism or Islamicate sci-fi, nor is it a translation of Afrofuturism into an Islamicate medium, assuming that the figure of the Muslim in the age of Islamophobia can be an analogue for the Black subject. Islamofuturism has to be more than just the ostensive appearance of Muslims in the future or other settings of speculative fiction. Islamofuturism cannot be limited to the science fiction crafted by a Muslim diaspora primarily located in the plutocracies of the Global North. Nor is it the creative output in a range of aesthetic forms (graphic novels, art, music, film, literature) by authors and artists who identify as Muslim. Nor is it reducible to the science fiction produced in what could be described not unproblematically as Islamicate languages, whether it be Indonesian, Kiswahili, Arabic, Bengali, Turkish, or Urdu. Islamofuturism has to be more than the reference to Islam, Islamic, and Islamicate motifs and tropes in an anti-Orientalist key. It cannot emerge by replacing Orientalism with its epistemological mirror: anti-Orientalism. This is because anti-Orientalism remains within the bounds of Orientalism, substituting an essentialism of the whole with an essentialism of the parts.[8] The profound affinity between Afrofuturism and Islamofuturism primarily lies in both discourses' attempts to craft a counterhistory of the world as counterhistories of the future. It is these counterhistories that support efforts to interrogate the historiographies that insist on the convergence between modernity and western destiny. These counterhistories stand in opposition to hegemonic historiographies rooted in liberal epistemologies and methodological nationalism. History-making requires a theory of power that understands it as not only repressive but also constitutive.

Only by theoretically fleshing out Islamofuturism beyond the prism of the liberal episteme, with its focus on the national and dreams of a politics without power, can we feed a radical imagination of the future. Islamofuturism must locate itself downstream of Critical Muslim Studies before it can envision a social world beyond the present. Put another way, the theoretical insights generated by Critical Muslim Studies affirm a conception of Islamofuturism, at its most radically transformative, as a series of cultural expressions and aesthetic algorithms that are not conventionally diasporic but automatically Ummatic.

Despite the differences in social significance and conceptual depth between Afrofuturism and Islamofuturism, both *Black Panther* and

Dune present examples of cultural comportments commonly marked as external to the west as "modern" and modernizing. Wakanda and Arrakis, therefore, act as counterfactuals and imply that in the absence of violent colonial-racial modernization, multiple modernities could be possible. The horizon of multiple modernities thus seems to have reached the level of mass culture, building on academic accounts and activist interventions that seek to banalize the telos of the west. In other words, both mass cultural products (primarily targeting an Anglophonic, internationally connected audience) can bear a decolonial reading. It could be argued that such flights of fantasy have always been a possibility in literature, where writers can imagine what social scientists dare not theorize, let alone quantify. The current cultural moment reveals not only speculation about the future but a wary anticipation of the post-western. For implicit in the public imaginings fostered by *Black Panther* and *Dune* is the suggestion of a post-western future built upon a pre-western past. A future that is unsullied by colonial-racial-modern world-making because it is forged from a past where the Age of Europe never really took off, thus enabling diverse communities of humans to become modern in their own way. If the future cannot be western, then what does it mean to be western? The inability to represent a world without the west means we lack a horizon that helps us make sense of a world seemingly gone wrong. The absence of such an overarching image is what I mean by "the crisis of representation." Examples of this crisis can be found in the debates surrounding the production of both films (e.g., issues about the cast's ethnicity and the metaphoricity of the narratives in relation to the global politics of racialization). White revanchists expressed unease with how the banality of Eurocentrism seemed to be challenged in depictions of the film in which cultural forms associated with people of color are seen as being agentic or at least involved in the production of history. One could be forgiven for believing or hoping that *Black Panther* and *Dune* signify a break with the monolingualism of westernese and teach a world audience a new language of the future, in which diverse and different expressions of humanity are at least whispered if not fully enunciated.[9] These films point to a pre-western possibility that enables a different way of world-making to be projected forward. A precolonial possibility names not a nostalgic attempt to restore a past but rather the potential to generate "other ways of being that are not enframed by formations of coloniality/modernity."[10] This radically decolonial version of historical transformation would lead to multiple modernities different from those envisaged by Shmuel N. Eisenstadt and other types of Eurocentric narratives that see multiple modernities as ultimately being exclusively "invented" in Europe and then being globally diffused from there.[11]

Beginning this chapter with an excursion into fictional depictions of alternative futures in mass cultural productions may seem odd. This might seem so, especially in light of the invitation that my chapter should reflect on the perceptive and provocative contributions curated here, finding family resemblances that constitute the unity of our endeavor—not clusters of common features but series of similarities and dissimilarities—and picking up threads along the way, untying these if they become knotted. There is, however, a reason to preface reflections on this Contending Modernities volume with a meditation on how cultural configurations represent what may come as a way of understanding what has gone before. Wakanda and Arrakis remind us that the discussions around contending modernities—the questions raised, addressed, and deflected—have salience beyond the academy in broader culture and society. Thus, attempts to understand the ties that bind modernity, coloniality, and western supremacy are not only found in academic debate but also inform the culture itself. The question of what is modern is also a question of what is coloniality? What is the west? And what metaphors do we have to apprehend our world? Before exploring the relationship between modernity, colonialism, and post-western possibilities in the context of multiple modernities, we must be clear about what modernity *is* and how it came to be.

Modern Times

Dominant explanations of modernity are divided over which processes they consider central features of the phenomenon. However, they agree that modernity is uniform and that this uniformity becomes more explicit the more modern one becomes.[12] Modernity is theorized as unidirectional, uniform, and universal. In other words, even though the blended factors that lead toward modernization vary somewhat, the modern society that results looks and is experienced similarly. However, some skepticism about the "European miracle" as the crucible for modernity characterizes recent scholarship. Shifting from an overt Eurocentric focus on this "miracle" facilitates a decolonial reading, suggesting that many features considered unique to it can be found in other historical formations, such as the Sinosphere and the Islamicate world system.[13] Such accounts plot the emergence of modernity from different temporalities, spaces, and admixtures of the western and non-western.

In standard narratives of modernity, modern societies are prosperous, peaceful, and tolerant, having shorn themselves of the irrational beliefs and practices that in the past led to violence and cruelty. The template for this modernity is provided by the historiographies of western European and Anglo-American societies. Modernity and western identity are thus assumed to be synonymous. The equivalence of modernization with westernization is not incidental but intrinsic to the vision of the modern and the construction of western identity. A society that is modern would be liberal-democratic, economically advanced, and philosophically rational; it would be exactly how Eurocentric historiography likes to present the history of the west.

The apparent opposition to this standard script of unitary modernity is in arguments for multiple modernities. These appear to break the relationship between the western and modern by envisaging multiple forms that modernity can take. As Eisenstadt, an early proponent of multiple modernities, suggests, there are three crucibles for producing different kinds of modernity: nation-states, "ethnic and cultural groups," and social movements.[14] The multiplicity of modernity depends on the prior existence of these social containers. The diversity of formations that make up the modern allows us to imagine a version that is no longer unilinear or universal. Eisenstadt writes:

> The idea of multiple modernities presumes that the best way to understand the contemporary world—indeed to explain the history of modernity—is to see it as a story of continual constitution and reconstitution of a multiplicity of cultural programs. These ongoing reconstructions of multiple institutional and ideological patterns are carried forward by specific social actors in close connection with social, political, and intellectual activists, and also by social movements pursuing different programs of modernity, holding very different views on what makes societies modern. Through the engagement of these actors with broader sectors of their respective societies, unique expressions of modernity are realised. These activities have not been

confined to any single society or state, though certain societies and states proved to be the major arenas where social activists were able to implement their programs and pursue their goals.[15]

The evidence for multiple modernities comes from rapid industrialization of what are deemed to be non-western societies: Japan, the Asian Tigers (Hong Kong, Singapore, South Korea, and Taiwan), and, most significantly, China. This industrialization has led to a shift in the distribution of world GDP away from the established economies of the west.[16] Multiple modernity theories have been criticized for being confused and confusing about their unit of analysis: Is it a region, a country, or a "civilization" where modernity is enacted?[17] Does the existence of the Dubai skyline—with more than 200 skyscrapers—necessarily announce a distinct Emirati modernity? Is the multiplication of modernity simply a geographical matter without philosophical significance?

Addressing these questions requires a theorization of multiple modernities rather than just an empirical expansion of the sites to which we apply the label of "modern." If we were able to theorize multiple forms of the modern, this would create the conceptual space to turn the speculations associated with post-western futurologies, such as Afrofuturism and Islamofuturism, into socioeconomic and epistemic horizons. Modernity, however, signifies not only socioeconomic and epistemic arrangements; it also has a cultural and political form. The relationships between these aspects of modernity are not inherent, but contingent.[18] What would need to be in place for us to conclude that there is a form of modernity outside its conventional locations? Imagining an Afrofuturist or Islamofuturist society is then part of the process by which the emergence of the modern in non-western locales appears organic rather than imposed or imported. But if modernity becomes multiple, what would constitute its identity? Eisenstadt again: "In acknowledging a multiplicity of continually evolving modernities, one confronts the problem of just what constitutes the common core of modernity. This problem is exacerbated and indeed transformed with the contemporary deconstruction or decomposition of many of the components of 'classical' models of the nation and of revolutionary states, particularly as a consequence of globalization."[19] The question around the "common core" of modernity has intensified in light of the decolonial insistence on the essential relationship between modernity and colonialism. Previously, there was an acceptance that colonialism was the harbinger of capitalism or that atavistic premodern motivations caused it.[20] In other words, colonialism was the antipode of modernity. Despite the idea of multiple modernities not being identical to westernization, it is very difficult to sustain a non-western modernity, for—as Eisenstaedt understands—multiple modernities is nothing more than the local adoption of the modern imposed through colonial conquest.

A contemporary approach to understanding modernity, aligned with and expanding on decolonial thinking (as a name for broad epistemological critique of Eurocentrism and the elision of the colonial from the modern) could consider its constitutive exterior in the place of a detailed enumeration of its systematically dispersed elements. This means that what we identify as modernity is not a list of its main objective features but rather the articulation of its contrast with what is considered external to it. Positing such an exterior would provide an understanding of modernity's identity as relational and contrastive rather than objective and substantive. The identity of modernity, like all identities, is purely negative, that is, contrastive. Articulating an exterior that provides the frontier by which identity can be formulated is a move into undecidability.[21] The articulation of a constitutive exterior both threatens and makes possible (constitutes) modernity. The borders of modernity are both its making and its unmaking. These effects can be seen in the various categories (many of them found in this volume) deployed in meditations considered external to modernity: religion, tradition, and non-Europeanness; these "externalities" are an affair of frontiers.

And once we talk of frontiers, we are in the space of the political. The political arises when a frontier is drawn between those considered to be our friends and those considered to be our enemies.[22] The political designates an antagonism constitutive of collective identities. Politics is a culturally and historically specific provisional arrangement that attempts to domesticate the political by transforming fights into games (however, the possibility of a game becoming a fight remains).[23] The political, by definition, seeks to draw a line between those with whom we agree and those with whom we disagree. It is this process of differentiation by which collective wills are formed.

Time out of Mind

To understand the effects of contending modernities on the political, I turn to the contributions of Nadia Fadil (chapter 2) and Santiago Slabodsky (chapter 1) in this volume. Both chapters, in their way, gesture toward what Schirin Amir-Moazami describes as "the liberal-secular matrix of state power."[24] She notes that the "liberal-secular matrix operates with specific modes of inclusion and exclusion, and it is productive of normality and deviations. These modes are neither fixed or homogenous but contingent and dynamic."[25] Amir-Moazami's departure point is an analysis of integration polices in regard to Muslims in Germany. The idea of the liberal-secular matrix of state power, however, transcends the particularity of the German case. In what follows I want to focus on this matrix of state power and sketch out some of its modes of exclusion and inclusion by drawing on its conventional description as a liberal democracy.

Liberal democracies are tied tightly to modernity, so being modern means being liberal and democratic. Put another way, liberal democracy is the expression of the politics of modernity.[26] The "modern" means of taming the political has been hegemonized by intertwining liberalism and democracy. Liberal democracies include many variants in terms of electoral systems, constitutions, and state–civil relations. Despite the variety of these arrangements, for the purposes of my argument, it is possible to summarize liberalism as characterized by an individualist and rationalist approach to politics.[27] Liberalism attempts to erase the political by asserting that the application of reason will resolve disagreements. In liberal democracies, the political (that is, the dimension of antagonism and foundation) is evacuated from politics. This evacuation increasingly invites the explosion of decolonial writings; it inscribes liberalism in the critique of modernity, it reprises in faint echoes the Enlightenment as an antidote, not one of the main causes of colonialism. By recuperating liberalism, we risk undoing the deep imbrications between modernity and coloniality. In this section, I explore the relationship between liberalism and coloniality/modernity using Fadil and Slabodsky as my guides and traveling companions.

The founding claim of decolonial thinking is that modernity and colonialism are two sides of the same European coin. If modernities are multiple, does it not follow that colonialities must be too? If modernities and colonialities are multiple, one might believe that liberal democracies can be liberated from modernity/coloniality. Fadil and Slabodsky, however, clearly show the continued and contemporary complicity between liberalism and the logics of coloniality and modernity.[28] The relational approach that Slabodsky explicitly deploys, and Fadil shows the practical ramifications of, demonstrate the reach of Eurocentric currency, not only in university brochures and academic gestures toward decoloniality but also in the tentacles of protocols, practices, and algorithms that connect an ensemble of social relations. They displace the conventional ways of thinking about multiple modernities and defend the central claim of decolonial thinking from being debased when multiple modernities point toward multiple colonialities.

At first sight, Fadil examines deradicalization policies in the Netherlands, beginning with the operationalization of counterviolent extremism programs there. However, she quickly takes the imaginaries and technologies of sovereign power beyond the geopolitical limits of the Netherlands. Fadil reports on how policies countering violent extremism are based on disciplining Muslimness through an ideological overinvestment in Islamic theological languages and practices—that is, by reference to the category of religion (see p. 58 of this volume). There are two distinct moves at play in her argument. First is the opposition between religious and modern/secular logic. Second is the identification of religion with Islam, and thus an assertion of the western character of the modern. In the context of the global institution of Islamophobia, deradicalization policies predicated on the necessity of defending society perversely destabilize secular modernity.

Juxtaposing Fadil with Slabodsky, it is possible to see what is at stake in Fadil's argument. In old Europe (defending liberalism and a post-Nasrani secularity), older India (defending the Hindu character of the nation), and still older China (defending the Chinese Dream), counterradicalization is a defense against the threat of unruly expressions of Muslimness, which problematize the consummation of modernity.[29] Counterradicalization programs, in the current conjuncture, have as a primary focus the domestication, marginalization, or elimination of Muslimness. These programs enable Islamophobia to travel all around the world, even to places forsaken by Muslims. They are translated in established liberal democracies as a necessary protection for guarantors of secularity, freedom of expression, gender equality, and liberal values. At a prosaic level, it is possible to see how the U.S.-led "War on Terror" (with its attendant deradicalization programs) became the medium for establishing Islamophobia on a planetary scale and expanding the category of terrorism to contain almost any autonomous expression of Muslimness. The logic of a global "War on Terror," its protocols and practices, has instrumentally transformed the civil rights struggles of the Uyghurs into a "terrorist" threat for the administration of Xi Jinping.[30] In India, the expansion of the pogrom system (shadowing "the largest democracy in the world") has been able, under the aegis of the "global War on Terror," to install a Jim Crow-esque system directed at Muslims—replete with lynching and collaboration between state authorities and local communities in the production of exemplary violence against expressions of Muslimness.[31] Fadil describes, using the concept of the fetish drawn from Achille Mbembe's work, how policies of deradicalization that aim to uphold the liberal secular order simultaneously reveal the fragility of that same order. As the examples from India and China show, this logic has been expanded beyond Europe.

The liberal order is contained not only within Europe. It is defined not by its contents but as a synecdoche for the status quo.[32] A status quo that, in the current conjuncture, needs to be defended by deradicalization policies with their echoes of colonial governance. The contemporary international order and its various repertoires of institutions, cultural comportments, and subject positions continue to be shaped by the legacy of European-colonial world-making.[33] Slabodsky reminds us of Aimé Césaire's warning of the epistemological risks in relying on a Eurocentric episteme in which European history is explained within the confines of a Europe drawn by European cartographers.

Slabodsky is explicit about the primal baptism of this world-making that occurred in the wake of Columbus sailing the oceans. His reading signals the global dimension of the current liberal/secular order, plotting out the seventeenth-century theological division of the world along lines we would now unproblematically call "religion": people with religion, people with false religion, and people with no religion. These divisions positioned Muslims and Jews as those with false religions conspiring together to bring down Christendom, which was claimed to be the only true religion. This is interesting from our current vantage point, where the prefix "Judeo-" has been attached to "Christian(ity)" and naturalized as a transhistorical reality about these groups. The *Oxford English Dictionary* records the first use of "Judeo-Christian" in 1821 in reference to Jews who became Christian. It records 1881 as the first use of the expression to describe a formation that unites values common to Jews and Christians. Such theologically inspired mapping of the world was reoccupied by post-Christian logics, which are too quickly and too often described as simply secular. From today's perspective, it is difficult to recall that there was a period when the dominant representations of Muslims and Jews were through the prism of Semites.[34] The prefix "Judeo-" was more likely to belong to the family of Muslimness, and Muslimness itself was an elaboration of the Semitic.

Highlighting what Slabodsky calls the "liberal–populist marriage" and its continuities with coloniality demonstrates the impossibility of reading the development of politics as internal to Europe and the west.[35] Slabodsky also captures the way populism occupies a problematic position in liberal political thought, and he describes circumstances in which democratic demands produce outcomes considered to be outside the pale of liberalism.[36] What is compelling about Slabodsky's argument is its recognition that one of the central features of modernity/coloniality/the west is its accepted political form: liberalism. Belief in the intrinsic relationship between modernity as economic prosperity and liberal democracy is part of its hegemonic cultural discourse. Prosperity and liberal democracy are not often associated with what are considered to be characteristic of colonies. Yet, the teleology of modernity establishes a relationship between economic development and the eventual political-cultural form: that of liberal democracy.

Liberalism has an exclusionary logic that has historically been compatible with racialized dispossessions, imperial expansions, and the imposition of white sovereignty.[37] This means it is the exemplar of coloniality also. Coloniality is summarized by Slabodsky as a pattern of hierarchies that structure relations of power through vectors of race, gender, sexualities, labor, disability, and so on. Liberal democracies are dependent on liberalism's claim to transcend power itself. Thus, the hierarchies of, for instance, labor, gender, race, disability, and sexuality become social, economic, or cultural relations rather than political ones. The compatibility between coloniality/modernity and liberal democracies was perhaps more apparent when the Netherlands, France, Britain, or even the United States, to name the most prominent examples, considered themselves to be both liberal democracies and empires.[38] With the overt dismantling of European empires, liberal democracies were more likely to be seen as incompatible with imperialism. Thus, the idea of the European empires being racial states was lost, thus helping restore a perceived innocence to liberal democracies. The postcolonial in metropoles is very often marked by a nostalgic refashioning of the white person's burden as a gallant attempt to bring liberalism and democracy to the world. In the process there is a forgetting of the continuities of colonial rule, for example, in the illiberal legislation in the colonies used to undermine liberalism and democracy. This has happened, for example, in countries such as Malaysia, where measures were taken to curtail "freedom of expression" by drawing on British colonial laws. We might also consider how heteronormative constructions of sexuality are reinforced by colonial legislation in the former colony of Uganda. A whitewashed liberal democracy remains central to the construction of notions of white/western identity. This has philosophical, geopolitical, and affective consequences for attempts to disarticulate the modern from the liberal-democratic.

Imagining multiple or contending modernities as only epistemological standpoints evades affective investment in the liberal democratic assemblage, which is the background of most academic practices. A project that engages contending modernities without considering the possibilities of a broadening imaginary of political forms or considering how academic subjectivities formed by modernity are embedded in the planetary archipelago of westernized universities risks transforming decolonial energies into an exclusively epistemological and methodological enterprise. Decoloniality and decolonization, however, are not always synonyms. Decolonization was a struggle for countervailing power to undo colonial rule. On the other hand, decoloniality's focus on academic space has succeeded, for example, in South African student mobilizations, which has led many universities to adopt programs to decolonize their curriculum. This often means tweaking curriculum (broadening reading lists), but rarely translates into a project of transforming the institution of the university itself. This is not necessarily because of the bad faith of university leaders and administrators, many of whom are enthusiastic about the possibilities of decolonizing. Instead, it reflects how the contemporary university was forged in the smithy of colonial/modern world-making projects. The university's contribution to the European colonial enterprise was to train servants of empire, to accumulate data that helped measure and master the planet, and to help imagine the world as being centered around Europe.[39] To furnish imaginations for the post-western requires not only the elaboration of critiques based on experiential determined standpoints but the possibility of protocols of power and statecraft that can translate such imaginations into institutions and embedded practices.

In the present conjuncture, multiple modernities are rarely discussed in a space outside of liberal-democratic sensibilities. Today we only seem to have a liberal-democratic way of telling the story of the challenges to modernity, and in these narratives, the colonial is too often marked by an absence. To the extent that literature on multiple modernities is a means to loosen the relationship between the west and modernity, it stands in opposition to the founding project of decoloniality, with its insistence on coloniality/modernity being a unified phenomenon. The evocation of contentious, multiple modernities can be another pathway to restoring the link between the modern and the universal by disaggregating coloniality from modernity. If we accept that there are multiple modernities, can we find examples of modernity disarticulated from coloniality, and examples of "non-western modernities" that display "non-western colonialities"? Such a possibility exists in literature of varied intents and scopes, for example in the arguments asserting that sub-Saharan slave systems are an analogue to transatlantic slavery, or make the case for the cartographically informed colonialism of Qing China, or propose the notion of polyracism. Other interventions put forward a set of propositions that would group Islam and Christianity in an equivalential relationship in opposition to African religions (see Lynch, chapter 5 in this volume).[40] The colonial/modern refashioning of the planet becomes not a rupture but an extension or expansion of particular formations. This dilutes the colonial category and replaces it with an amorphous postcolonial, as in the description of the contemporary Global South, where the reconstitution of various cultural programs is apparently taking place. It allows us to maintain the unevenness of power relations, which affects the ability of distinct cultural programs to be realized. The assertion that cultural programs offer alternatives to the colonial paradigm fails to consider the dynamics of global power relations. The logic of this position, however, is to make impossible any project of cultural and political transformation that involves a critique of the current ordering of modernity. This subverts the project of decolonization in the name of the decolonial. The idea that the purpose of decoloniality is not only to "dismantle" the Western colonial matrix of power but all matrices of power—because all power is colonial/racial/modern—has become the default position of many who labor under the flag of decoloniality. Expanding the category of "decolonial critique" beyond a specific historical process raises a series of fundamental questions. If power itself needs to be decolonized, what happens to subjectivity? If the distinction between enmity and amity has to be decolonized, what happens to the political?

The liberal dream of a world without power—without antagonism—is delivered by decaffeinated decolonial mobilizations and, in the process, elides the foundational violence of modernity through the cultivation of historical amnesia about its role in constituting a specific order. The signifier "liberal democracies" circulates not only among a familiar institutional array but also more diffusely as a marker of legitimate international society. It is possible to make the case that many countries could be deemed, based on governmental practices, incompatible with liberal democracies, but they are still considered to be members of international society.[41] In this way, liberal democracies are "superhard."[42] Historians have shown how genocide, enslavement, and dispossession are not incompatible with liberal democracies. Slabodsky and Fadil remind us of the complicity between liberal democracies and forms of rule that are racialized and repressive. This reminder also alerts us to the superhard nature of liberal democracy and allows its hollowing out. One key mechanism for this hollowing out is the globalization of countering violent extremism policies and practices. Whether the securocrats are from China, India, Myanmar, Tel Aviv, France, Austria, Egypt, the United States, or Britain, their language and the policies they implement have a family resemblance. The regulation and disciplining of Muslimness, with reference to a modernizing horizon, is enabled by the way religion is constructed as a symbol of something antimodern. Islam is seen as a signifier of religion itself.

The antimodern description of the Islamicate is a familiar Orientalist trope often played out in Islamophobic practices and interventions. In the context of multiple modernities/colonialities, Muslimness becomes both a marker of antimodernity and a form of colonialism. To the extent that decolonial projects of reconstruction depend on the recovery of cultural resources before the global imposition of the colonial matrix of power, it becomes necessary to identify this "before." One way of representing the "before" is to focus on two dimensions: the premodern and precolonial. The prefix "pre-," like the prefix "post-," should be read not simply as a marker of temporality but rather as the description of a condition.

The premodern can be found occupying subject positions in the various contrasts by which categories constitutive of modernity are spatially and temporally fixed: tradition (versus modern), rural (versus urban) and, of course, the focus of the contributions to this volume: religion (versus secular). These conceptual contrasts, floating signifiers of the discourse of modernity, are put in place as part of the assemblage of the current world order in its epistemological, socioeconomic, and geopolitical impositions. The subordinate terms of these contrasting concepts (tradition, religion, etc.) are found on the other side of modernity but not outside the discourse of modernity. What is compelling about the interventions by Slabodsky and Fadil is how—in different ways—they refuse the temptation to find, in subordinated categories, modernity's discourse of authentic premodern "reality." Religion may seem premodern, but this is a historiographical convention betraying its Enlightenment formation; religion is no less modern than the secular.

The precolonial is the second representation of the "before." The precolonial is synonymous with the autochthonous, what was before coloniality. For instance, if we consider "Africa" before European colonization and accept the idea that colonialism can exist independently of modernity, this would mean parts of "Africa" were colonized by Muslims and, by extension, other political societies, such as the Romans, Macedonians, Persians, and Assyrians. Furthermore, this approach would prompt inquiries into the external or internal nature of Ethiopian and Coptic Christianity. What is this "Africa"? This is not a question of whether "Africa" is a cohesive entity or not. As Lynch (chapter 5) points out, treating "Africa" as a unified and taken-for-granted unit is just as problematic as describing the Global North or the west in a similar way. The problem is not one that can be resolved by placing all grand formations *sous rature*, or pointing to complex etymologies by which we describe these formations. If "colonial" is not a specific historical enterprise but refers to any displacement of the autochthonous, one can advance arguments contained within, for example, Hindutva ideologies; these narrate a timeless lineage of India/Bharat previous to colonial interruption, not before the British conquest of the Mughal Empire, but rather before the Muslim invasions of eighth century CE.[43] The Muslim subject in contemporary India then becomes an immigrant or invader; they are denied autochthonous status. Similarly, one could take examples from the meager resources of Afropessimist thought, which posit an essential Africanity in which Islam, or Christianity, is external to Africa rather than constitutive of it.[44] An essentialist reading of Africa is not only a feature of Afropessimist or Afrocentric writing. This way of thinking continues to enjoy a broader cultural appeal and academic respectability. What I describe as positivist approaches to knowledge formation erase the genealogical. Thus, paradoxically, in the act of recovering Africanity, such modes of writing reinscribe Africa as being a historical land for a people without history. The invention of Africa cannot be a recovery of pristine practices (religious, social, economic), for such practices do not signify authenticity outside anthropological discourses, which insert them in particular classificatory schemes (see Lynch, again). Rather the invention of Africa is an anticolonial achievement, a product of a struggle to end the colonial-racial rule, and in so doing create an Africanity that is deconstructive of a western episteme.

Given the intimate relationship between anthropology and colonialism, is there any reason for assuming that authenticity can be found before colonialism? However, if we say that there is no precolonial authenticity, on what grounds could we mount a critique of colonialism? Is authenticity not necessary for anticolonialism? Indeed, part of the anticolonial armory has been the claim, especially against settlers, that there were real claimants to the land/space before colonial settlement. We could cite many historical examples in which previous claims of ownership are used to justify political struggles and conflict. This seems to suggest that there is some purchase in the idea of authenticity that cannot easily be abandoned on the altar of high theory. The repeated use of a claim or description, however, does not mean that such a description is not socially constructed, or politically constituted. The construction of authenticity is ultimately a function of successful hegemonic struggles, as much as the denial of authenticity is a hegemonic project. Fanon comments on how "colonialism is not simply content to impose its rule upon the present and the future of a dominated country. Colonialism is not satisfied merely with holding a people in its grip and emptying the native's brain of all form and content. By a kind of perverse logic, it turns to the past of the oppressed people and distorts it, disfigures, and destroys it."[45]

The destruction of the past can take the form of a dehistoricization and retreat into presentism.[46] Annexing the observation made by Wittgenstein, "A picture held us captive. And we could not get outside it, for it lay in our language and language seemed to repeat it to us inexorably," allows us to see the challenge of reading modernity on its own terms and the complexity of trying to simply will ourselves to transcend it. The interventions in this volume help show the relation between a captivating picture and a language that promises liberation, but itself is part of the picture that has us trapped. This raises questions that haunt the epistemological: Can we use the logic of modern subjectivities to present the past without dehistoricizing? Or can we assume that one cartographic expression is exterior to another when both formulations are the expression of the same cartography? This is a cartography underwritten by the gradual enframing of the planet through imperial racial-colonial logics. Modern/colonial epistemologies and liberal democracies are where critiques of modernity become possible and simultaneously contentious.

Love and Theft

In the opening scene of *Black Panther*, Wakanda, as a manifestation of multiple modernities, is mobilized to extend the hegemonic discourses of modernity rather than deconstruct them. In this scene, the eponymous hero of *Black Panther* confronts an allegorical Boko Haram, drawing a frontier not only between justice and cruelty but also between Africanity and the Islamicate. This structures an opposition in which Boko Haram proxies are marked as being non-African, as opposed to those being captured and their rescuer, who are marked by Africanity. Such opposition is a confirmation of what Sherman Jackson has described as "Black Orientalism."[47] At the end of *Black Panther*, Wakanda becomes a western ally, with T'Challa channeling the role of an enlightened autocrat who brings (western) modernity to his non-western society and turns Wakanda from a nonaligned country splendid in its isolation to a member of an American-led colonial-racial liberal international order.[48]

The assumption is that the inclusion of a strong independent Black polity in the international system would not suffer the fate of Haiti or Ethiopia or the Sokato state, nor would it become a superpowered Liberia reproducing American racial order in Africa. Ultimately, *Black Panther* offers a postracial fantasy, not a decolonial vision. This is a postracial fantasy that assumes that racism has been banished from established liberal democracies and is no longer a problem. Boko Haram surrogates are not represented as belonging to Africa but as a radical exteriority marked by the signs of Muslimness.[49] The question is not whether Muslims can be modern or not, but whether modernity and Muslimness are compatible. In other words, how much of their Muslimness must Muslims surrender to be considered modern.

It could be argued that there is a degree of irony about the production of both *Black Panther* and *Dune*. The original creators of these imaginaries are not exclusively Black Muslims, or Muslims, or Black. Stan Lee and Jack Kirby are credited with the origin of *Black Panther* (unconnectedly but serendipitously, the Black Panther Party was announced a few months after the first issue of the comic was published). Similarly, neither Frank Herbert nor subsequent writers, directors, and producers of the various iterations of *Dune* can be described as being invested in or inhabiting Muslimness. Their familiarity with the Islamicate does not extend beyond the anthropological. *Dune* is saddled not only with a white savior, but fundamentally it is a meditation on fatalism, fanaticism, and the allure of oriental despotism. The rebellion of desert dwellers is predicated on reactivation by an external (white) elite figure, disenfranchised and outcast. Rebellion leads not to liberation but to the imposition of even greater despotism. *Dune* offers a fantasy not of Muslimness as decolonization but as a reoccupation of colonial-racial logics in a ministrelized non-western register. This affirms the present by warning about a post-western future: the present condemned as the worst age, except for any other age to come. What could be more liberal than a cynicism toward power, sitting alongside joys and fruits of the exercise of that power?

Despite these caveats and limitations, both *Black Panther* and *Dune* gesture (hesitantly, half-heartedly, superficially) toward a future no longer represented by the signifier of the west. In a process of perhaps unintended irony, these cultural imaginings unsettle the explanations that assert the case for the west's unique trajectory and destiny. These cultural imaginings fix the Islamicate and Africanity in the past, present, and future—hinting at multiple modernities and problematizing the account of the future as westernization. Notwithstanding that Wakanda and Arrakis are shot through Orientalist imaginaries, these two episodes of world-making are open to decolonial readings, which do not simply reproduce the enunciative essentialism of many such interpretations.[50] If the future is what modernity produces, then a future signified without reference to (the signifier of) the west could only be the product of imagination beyond the distortions of colonial-racial world-making, which defer rather than derail alternative conceptions of what it is to be modern. In the absence of the hegemonic referent, visions of modernity contend as the struggle for a better world is joined. The post-western futurologies of Afrofuturism, or the development of Islamofuturism, brings forth a possibility, not of a true universal west to come, but of a west that is passing.

NOTES

Atalia Omer's and Joshua Lupo's patience and insightful commentary on previous versions of this chapter were very much appreciated. I would also like to thank Sophia Steel and Shvetal Vyas for their assistance in the preparation of this manuscript. Barnor Hesse and Abdoolkarim Vakil were both generous with their time and helpful with their comments.

1. This chapter does not discuss at any great length *Wakanda Forever*, the sequel to *Black Panther*.

2. Martin Bernal's distinction between the ancient model and Aryan model of history and the place of non-Greek influences on ancient Greece generated great controversy because it was seen as an attempt to contaminate the purity of the western telos. This episode is just one example that shows how embedded the conventional origin story of modernity and its relationship with the west is. See Bernal, *Black Athena: The Afroasiatic Roots of Classical Civilization*, Vol. 3, *The Linguistic Evidence* (New Brunswick, NJ: Rutgers University Press, 2020). For an analysis of the modern discipline of classical studies as the origin story of the west, see Mathura Umachandran and Marchella Ward, eds., *Critical Ancient World Studies: The Case for Forgetting Classics* (London: Routledge, 2024).

3. Elisabeth Abena Osei describes Wakanda as a "modernized African superpower" and recognizes *Black Panther* as "a significant blueprint of Afrofuturism." See Osei, "Wakanda Africa Do You See? Reading *Black Panther* as a Decolonial Film through the Lens of the Sankofa Theory," *Critical Studies in Media Communication* 37, no. 4 (2020): 389.

4. For a decolonial reading that traces precolonial African thought as a critical element in the construction of Wakanda, see ibid.

5. For an introduction to Afrofuturism, see Ytasha L. Womack, *Afrofuturism: The World of Black Sci-Fi and Fantasy Culture* (Chicago: Chicago Review Press, 2013); and Lisa Yaszek, "Afrofuturism, Science Fiction, and the History of the Future," *Socialism and Democracy* 20, no. 3 (2006): 41–60. Ryan Coogler, director of *Black Panther*, described Afrofuturism as a bridge between traditional African cultures and the future that disrupts the dominant stereotypes of Africa. See Clarisse Loughrey, "*Black Panther* Brings Afrofuturism into the Mainstream: Director

Ryan Coogler Shares His Definition of the Genre and Philosophical Outlook," *The Independent*, June 13, 2018, https://www.independent.co.uk/arts-entertainment/films/features/black-panther-afrofuturism-ryan-coogler-definition-explainer-watch-release-date-a8209776.html.

6. The concept of the "Islamicate" was introduced by Marshall G. S. Hodgson. It refers to "the social and cultural complex historically associated with Islam and the Muslims" and non-Muslims. See Marshall G. S. Hodgson, *The Venture of Islam: Conscience and History in a World Civilization* (Chicago: University of Chicago Press, 1974), 1:59. It could be argued that the distinction between Islam and the Islamicate replays the divide between religion and society, which is fundamental to post-Nasrani (i.e., post-Christian) secularity. Such a reductive reading, however, forecloses an interpretation that is consistent with most expressions of Muslimness, in which Islam is a horizon and the Islamicate refers to the post-Prophetic collective efforts to actualize Islam. The failure to distinguish between Islam and the Islamicate has the effect of making Islam ontic, whereas for Muslims it is ontological. See S. Sayyid, *A Fundamental Fear* (London: Zed Press, 2003), 54–56.

7. See Yaszek, "Afrofuturism, Science Fiction, and the History of the Future," 41–42, for a discussion of the work of critical theory performed by Afrofuturism allied to its cultural production. One illustration of how Afrofuturism has expanded globally can be seen in the fact that in 2022 the Royal Shakespeare Company put on a production of *Much Ado about Nothing* based on Afrofuturist motifs. See https://www.rsc.org.uk/news/what-is-afrofuturism.

8. For a development of this argument, see Sayyid, *A Fundamental Fear*, 36–40.

9. "Westernese" is a play on the idea of a global *lingua franca*, a common conceptual vocabulary by which past, present, and future are represented and constructed. See S. Sayyid, *Recalling the Caliphate: Decolonization and World Order* (London: C. Hurst & Co., 2022).

10. Walter D. Mignolo and Catherine E. Walsh, *On Decoloniality: Concepts, Analytics, Praxis* (Durham, NC: Duke University Press, 2018), 81.

11. Shmuel N. Eisenstadt, "Multiple Modernities," *Daedalus* 129, no. 1 (2000): 1–29. The arguments for multiple modernities are not exclusive to Eisenstadt, and my focus on his version of multiple modernities is pragmatic and illustrative. The argument that I am advancing is not dependent or fixed to Eisenstadt.

12. This includes embodying such features as industrialization, rationalization, democratization, and secularization.

13. Two of the prominent representations of this literature are Kenneth Pomeranz, *The Great Divergence: China, Europe, and the Making of the Modern World Economy* (Princeton, NJ: Princeton University Press, 2021); and Janet L. Abu-Lughod, *Before European Hegemony: The World System A.D. 1250–1350* (Oxford: Oxford University Press, 1989). These texts focus on a world system that began

in the thirteenth century with the Mongol conquests. See also John Obert Voll, "Islam as a Special World-System," *Journal of World History* 5, no. 2 (1994): 213–26; and Francis Robinson, "The Islamic World: World System to 'Religious International,'" in *Religious Internationals in the Modern World: Globalization and Faith Communities since 1750*, ed. Abigail Green and Vincent Viaene (London: Palgrave Macmillan, 2012), 111–35. They focus on the existence of what they describe as the Islamic world system.

14. Eisenstadt, "Multiple Modernities," 2.

15. Ibid.

16. The economist Gustav Cassel coined the term "purchasing power parity" (PPP) in 1918. An overview of his theory can be found in Cassel, *The Theory of Social Economy* (New York: Harcourt, Brace, and Co., 1967[1928]). The adoption of PPP in GDP calculations and its popularization (e.g., Big Mac Index or iPad Index) reshaped views of the global economy. This highlights the shift toward populous Global South nations. For example, PPP places China's economy above that of the United States, unlike other nominal measures.

17. Elsje Fourie, "A Future for the Theory of Multiple Modernities: Insights from the New Modernization Theory," *Social Science Information* 51, no. 1 (2012): 52–69.

18. There are versions that reduce modernity to a material condition determined by specific mixes of geology, economics, and historical development. In this modernization literature, modernity can be captured by focusing on equipment, technology, and the replacement of muscle power with fossil energy. The place of multiplicity in such schemes would be constrained because it would for the most part see the development of modernity as being a ruptural moment in human history. Such accounts would seem to be favored by a positivist epistemology that would be able to mark out a shift in the history of the world when modernity emerges, expands, and confronts what was before it both temporarily and spatially.

19. Eisenstadt, "Multiple Modernities," 3.

20. For example, in the Marxist lexicon, see Bill Warren, *Imperialism: Pioneer of Capitalism* (London: NLB, 1980).

21. Ernesto Laclau and Chantal Mouffe, *Hegemony and Socialist Strategy: Towards a Radical Democratic Politics* (London: Verso, 1985), 93–148.

22. Carl Schmitt, *The Concept of the Political*, exp. ed., trans. George Schwab (Chicago: University of Chicago Press, 2008[1932]), 27–37; Chantal Mouffe, *On the Political* (London: Verso, 2005), 10–14.

23. For the distinction between games and fights, see Frederick George Bailey, *Stratagems and Spoils: A Social Anthropology of Politics* (New York: Routledge, 2018), 1–18.

24. See Schirin Amir-Moazami, *Interrogating Muslims: The Liberal-Secular Matrix of Integration* (London: Bloomsbury, 2022).

25. Ibid., 22.

26. The politics of modernity has included absolutist monarchies, National Socialism, Soviet-style modernization, imperial-nationalism of European colonial empires, and the racialized nationalism of European settler states. It is only with the end of the Cold War that one could make the case for the hegemony of liberal democracies over modernity despite the attempt to articulate an authoritarian modernization associated with China or Singapore. It is worth remembering that in 1930s the politics of modernity included those of fascist Italy, Nazi Germany, and the Soviet Union. See Mark Mazower, *Dark Continent: Europe's Twentieth Century* (London: Penguin, 1999).

27. Mouffe, *On the Political*, 10. These characteristics do not exhaust liberalism. As is often pointed out, the repertoire of liberalism is extensive, and it has been suggested it might be more useful to think of liberalism in the "plural." See Michael Freeden, *Liberalism: A Very Short Introduction* (Oxford: Oxford University Press, 2015), 3.

28. There are, of course, question marks in regard to regimes in places such as Russia, Hungary, and others, as Slabodsky notes in his contribution (chapter 1).

29. In 2013, Xi Jinping, the ruler of the People's Republic of China, introduced the concept of the Chinese Dream as the centerpiece of his revised ideological framework for the country. The Chinese Dream promotes national rejuvenation, cultural revitalization, and China's global influence.

30. Sean R. Roberts, *The War on the Uyghurs: China's Internal Campaign against a Muslim Minority* (Princeton, NJ: Princeton University Press, 2020), 63–94.

31. Paul Brass has documented the persistence of an institutionalized system of pogroms and communal riots in India since partition in 1947. The production of Hindu-Muslim violence is most often directed at eliminating the perceived threat of "mini-Pakistans" (the pockets of Muslim population found in Indian cities and towns) to the destiny of India as a great power. See Paul R. Brass, *The Production of Hindu-Muslim Violence in Contemporary India* (Seattle: University of Washington Press, 2003), 384.

32. What I am arguing is that what determines whether a particular regime is considered liberal is not an objective exercise measured by seemingly neutral international organizations (e.g., Freedom House). Instead, it hinges on whether the regime in question is perceived to align with or deviate from the international liberal order. In simpler terms, a regime that is not considered to be challenging the core practices of the prevailing world order is considered liberal. Liberal in this context refers to a historic bloc or settlement, not a philosophy or system of beliefs and values. See Sayyid, *Recalling the Caliphate*, 63–83.

33. For example, nation-states, neoliberal horizons, capitalist-technological constructions of value, governmentality, realist geopolitics, and consumerist notions of citizenship.

34. According to Gil Anidjar, the category of "Semite" emerged as inclusive of the figure of the Jew and the Muslim. It was in relation to the category of Semites that a Europe secularized by the Enlightenment was able to maintain its identity. See Anidjar, *Semites: Race, Religion, Literature* (Stanford, CA: Stanford University Press, 2007).

35. Fadil's positioning of counterradicalization policies in the context of western hauntologies of Muslimness hints at a similar reading of the impossibility of a purely European account of the current juncture.

36. Sayyid, *A Fundamental Fear*, 92.

37. For an elaboration of the concept of white sovereignty, see Barnor Hesse, "Black Populism," *South Atlantic Quarterly* 121, no. 3 (2022): 561–92.

38. There is lengthy debate about the degree to which the United States considered itself an empire. To some extent, such historiography belongs to the genre of "absent-minded" imperialism. That is, the view that European powers (Great Britain being the paradigmatic case) became empires without an intention or consciousness of doing so in a series of ad hoc steps without an overall plan or design. An account of U.S. interventions around the world between the end of the Civil War and World War II suggests that the American republic's transformation into an empire (bracketing for a moment its conquest of Indigenous polities in Turtle Island) is perhaps more an act of forgetting than is easily admitted by conventional narratives that deny the existence of a U.S. empire. The "colorful" career of Smedley Butler is an apt illustration of U.S. global interventions from 1898 to 1940. See Jonathan M. Katz, *Gangsters of Capitalism: Smedley Butler, the Marines, and the Making and Breaking of America's Empire* (New York: St. Martin's Press, 2022).

39. See Isaac Kamola, *Making the World Global: U.S. Universities and the Production of Global Imaginary* (Durham, NC: Duke University Press, 2019). Kamola investigates the way in which U.S. universities helped not only to produce knowledge, which was linked to U.S. imperial projects from the Cold War to the War on Terror, but also helped to reimagine the world. What is true of the United States also applies to other westernized universities, which are key centers in world-making.

40. See Ian Law, with Anna Jacobs, Nisreen Kaj, Simona Pagano, and Bozena Sojka-Koirala, "Postface: Theorizing Polyracism," in *Mediterranean Racisms: Connections and Complexities in the Racialization of the Mediterranean Region* (London: Palgrave Macmillan, 2014), 161–62; Laura Hostetler, *Qing Colonial Enterprise: Ethnography and Cartography in Early Modern China* (Chicago: University of Chicago Press, 2001); and Ronald Segal, *Islam's Black Slaves: The Other Black Diaspora* (London: Palgrave Macmillan, 2001).

41. For example, countries that engage in torture, extraordinary killings, thwarting of popular will, and suppressing civil war and minorities are not necessarily excluded from international society. Rather there is tendency to view such actions as being different depending on whether a particular regime is considered to

be inside or outside international society—in other words, if it is considered to be aligned with the western-led liberal order. There are many examples that illustrate this point. For example, the contrast between the installation of the brutal de facto martial regime following the overthrow of democratically elected Imran Khan in Pakistan and the overthrow of pro-western president Mohamed Bazoum in Niger. The latter has been condemned by the United States and its allies, and international efforts have been mobilized to restore Bazoum to power. In the former case, there has been an official silence that has been reinforced by western media outlets. See "Niger Coup: Will the West Change Its Security Approach to the Sahel?," Al Jazeera, August 15, 2023, https://www.aljazeera.com/opinions/2023/8/15/niger-coup-will-the-west-change-its-security-approach-to-the-sahel; and Peter Oborne, "Pakistan: Imran Khan—Why the US Hates a Politician with Principles," *Middle East Eye*, August 8, 2023, https://www.middleeasteye.net/opinion/pakistan-imran-khan-us-hates-politician-principled.

 42. Wittgenstein in his *Lectures and Conversations on Aesthetics, and Religious Belief* gives the example of "a geometrical lever that cannot be bent because it is harder than any lever can be. This superhardness is a function of logical necessity." For an elaboration of this point, see Henry Staten, *Wittgenstein and Derrida* (Lincoln: University of Nebraska Press, 1984), 151–52.

 43. Hindutva is, as others have shown, premised on Indological reading of South Asia in which the essential characteristic of South Asia is Hindu and the Islamicate is an invasion that disfigures this true and authentic nature of India. As has been pointed out, the very translation of Hinduism into a religion is part of the colonial matrix of power. See Ronald Inden, *Imagining India* (Oxford: Blackwell, 1990), for an elaboration of the category of Indology.

 44. Afropessimism is an interpretative framework that uses Blackness to interrogate the assumptions and logics of theories that are associated with Marxism, psychoanalysis, feminism, and postcolonialism. See Frank B. Wilderson III, *Afropessimism* (New York: Liveright Publishing, 2020), 14. Afropessimism refuses the "ruse of analogy" to postulate the singularity of a world that has been anti-Black since 622 CE. It is an emerging body of writing in which American exceptionalism is translated into an African American register. The central tenet of Afropessimism is the claim that Blackness emerges as what is excluded from the human. The genealogy of anti-Blackness that Afropessimists champion is inconsistent, as it links Blackness with slavery (highlighting the Atlantic formations of early modern period) and sees it as a perennial condition that goes beyond the Atlantic both spatially and temporally and is hardwired in the formation of the "anti-Black world" beginning in 622 CE.

 45. Frantz Fanon, *The Wretched of the Earth*, trans. Richard Philcox (New York: Grove/Atlantic, 2007[1961]), 37.

 46. By "presentism," I refer to a broader cultural tendency to consider only recent social phenomena to be relevant. A sociological imagination is problematic if it is not attuned to history.

47. Jackson develops the concept of Black Orientalism as a way of describing the circulation and distribution of a particular set of Orientalist tropes within "Blackamerican" society. Jackson builds on Ali Mazuri's polemic against Henry Gates Jr.'s depiction of Africa and its relationship to the Islamicate. See Sherman Jackson, *Islam and the Blackamerican* (Oxford: Oxford University Press, 2005), 99–130.

48. The "Third Worldization" of Wakanda continues apace in the sequel to *Black Panther*, *Wakanda Forever*. Wakanda's power is reduced to a possession of mineral wealth. It has a ruling elite increasingly integrated with the United States, with its members attending universities there.

49 See Haroon Bashir, "Black Excellence and the Curse of Ham," *ReOrient* 5, no. 1 (2019): 92–116.

50. Reading "positionality" in enunciation is itself an interpretive exercise the turbulence of which cannot be calmed by reference to standard litanies of subject positions (class, gender, sexual orientations, race).

CHAPTER 4

The Neoliberal Rationality of Secularism

LUCA MAVELLI AND EDMUND FRETTINGHAM

ABSTRACT

This chapter explores how the principles of neoliberalism have shaped the ideological landscape of secularism and religion. In contrast to comparative approaches that treat the secular via its iterations in different national contexts, we show how neoliberalism has become the governing logic of secularism and performed a colonialism internal to the western episteme. In this "self-colonialism," neoliberalism has progressively transcended the economic domain and colonized all other spheres of human existence. By rewriting other imaginaries and systems of value, we suggest, neoliberalism has become a kind of religion. Through a close comparative reading of the work of Ludwig von Mises and Friedrich Hayek, we explore how the two prominent neoliberal economists (and Hayek in particular) laid the foundation for this worldview.

INTRODUCTION

Recent work on comparative secularisms has prioritized the nation-state as the primary context for understanding the plurality of secularisms in world politics. We argue that in an age when the nation-state is "rolled back" to create space for new markets or reconstituted as a "market state," secularism needs to be problematized as an expression of transnational neoliberal rationalities. Accordingly, we explore the largely neglected relation between neoliberalism and secularism by showing how the principles and values of the market have become the governing logics of secularism. Focusing on the treatment of religion by neoliberal founding fathers Ludwig von Mises and Friedrich Hayek, we argue that neoliberalism advances a distinctive understanding of secularism as a discourse that polices the boundaries of religion by positing the market society as foundational for peaceful and prosperous communities. This discussion aims to contribute to existing debates on religion and modernity by developing a critique of neoliberal secularism as a regime that colonizes all domains of existence. Two main arguments are advanced. First, neoliberal economic rationalities are increasingly employed as conceptual foundations for constructing and evaluating religion. Second, neoliberal secularism has performed a remarkable co-optation of religion to the effect that, in a neoliberal age, the relation between religion and modernity is not one of expulsion/subordination of the former from/to the latter, but one in which logics of belief are constructed from the perspective of neoliberal secularism and constitutive of its very meanings and functions.

The relationship between religion and economic rationalities has long been a topic of interest in the social sciences. Until recently, most debates revolved around either the Marxist thesis that religion is essentially an ideological legitimation for economic exploitation, or the Weberian thesis that Calvinism played an important role in the development of capitalism.[1] In an age characterized by both the globalization of neoliberal capitalism and the generalization of neoliberal discourses and policies beyond the economic sphere, the questions have changed and taken on a renewed urgency. Some have explored how religion is mobilized to resist the worst social effects of neoliberalism;[2] others have investigated the idea that neoliberal capitalism itself may be considered a religious phenomenon.[3]

Another group of scholars has focused on how contemporary neoliberal capitalism may be shaping more conventional forms of religious belief and practice. National churches with close links to states are in decline, while adaptable and deterritorialized forms of religion such as Pentecostalism are thriving, as are traditions with transnational institutional structures, such as Catholicism.[4] The values of religious movements increasingly reflect those of capitalism, such as individualism, consumerism, and materialism.[5] An even closer fusion of capitalism and religion is evident in the "prosperity gospel" (the doctrine shared by some Protestant Christians that economic success is the will of God[6]), the notion of "neoliberal piety" (the idea that neoliberalism and Islamic practice may be fused and support each other[7]), and in phenomena such as "workplace spirituality" and "corporate religion."[8]

These studies offer important insights into the appeal and social effects of religious movements that have affinities with contemporary neoliberal capitalism. However, for the most part, they conceive of the neoliberalization of religion as a *process* rather than a *project*, namely, as the outcome of relatively impersonal structural forces operating "behind the backs" of social actors, while nonetheless transforming the conditions of their existence. Alternatively, in this chapter, we focus on how religion is interpreted and transformed by neoliberalism and argue that the neoliberalization of religion is not merely the spillover of neoliberal economic rationalities into the societal sphere of religion, but part of a broader process of economization in which the reconstitution of religions according to economic rationalities is instrumental to advancing the neoliberal project.

This analysis is taken up from the perspective that the neoliberal worldview—the ideological driver of capitalist globalization over the last forty years—cannot be reduced to a widespread and penetrating dynamic of commodification of all domains of human existence or a project of economic reform aimed at "the restoration of class power."[9] Neoliberalism, instead, is a broader project that entails "normalizing and disciplining society on the basis of the market value and form."[10] It extends market logics of competition and inequality to all spheres of human existence, thus performing most fundamentally an *economization* of state and society that "disseminates the model of the market to all domains and activities—even where money is not an issue."[11]

To investigate how religion has been progressively "economized," we focus on the "constitutive other" of religion, that is, secularism, and build on the critique of secularism as a regime of coloniality that has constructed religion as a universal, disembodied, and cognitive category. We concentrate on the distinctively neoliberal dimension of what has been described as the "coloniality of secularism": a discourse, ideology, and logic of power that in its "mode of knowing and being . . . claims universality for itself."[12] This approach draws on the famous concept of the "coloniality of power" as the regimes that govern "the distribution of epistemic, moral, and aesthetic resources in a way that both reflects and reproduces empire."[13] Our focus, however, is not on the traditional, external projection of the colonial logic—the "coloniality of power" as "the hegemony of Eurocentrism as epistemological perspective"[14]—but on its internal European/western introjection or, paraphrasing Étienne Balibar, on its internal "reduplication" and deployment.[15]

Our starting point is Giorgio Agamben's observation (inspired by Walter Benjamin[16]) that "[neoliberal] capitalism" desacralizes or profanes "everything that is done, produced, or experienced, even the human body, even sexuality."[17] By colonizing all domains of human existence, neoliberalism performs "an absolute profanation without remainder," which ultimately "coincides with an equally vacuous and total consecration."[18] The paradoxical effect is that neoliberalism establishes the market as "absolutely unprofanable," that is, as a sacred entity.[19] We are interested in this process of internal colonization whereby neoliberalism shapes the power-knowledge regime of secularism by grounding its hegemonic pretensions on the supposedly natural and universal logics of the market. Hence, rather than investigating how the "global design" of secularism has shaped "local histories," we problematize how neoliberalism has shaped the "global design" of secularism in a movement of internal reduplication of the logic of coloniality.[20] This is a colonialism internal to the western episteme; a *self-colonialism* in which neoliberalism transcends the economic domain and colonizes all other spheres of human existence.

Neoliberalism is thus approached as the epistemic, moral, and aesthetic framework that gives meaning to and saturates contemporary understandings of secularism and, accordingly, establishes desirable and legitimate modes of religious belief and practice. We ask how religion is interpreted from the standpoint of neoliberal secularism, what place and role religious traditions have in a world in which secularism is increasingly shaped by neoliberal rationalities, and to what extent neoliberal rationalities have been turned into the ultimate sacred foundations of the existing secular order. This analysis challenges the idea that religion is either expunged from modernity or subordinated to the latter's secular rationality. Rather, modernity has been transformed by the incorporation of religion in the form of capitalism to the effect that neoliberal secularism has become itself a religion.

We develop this argument against the background of comparative studies of secularism, which show secularisms to be contingent and plural. Secularisms are plural in the sense that there is no paradigmatic "secularism as such"; there are instead only assemblages of secularism, shaped by different intellectual and material backgrounds, and developed in response to different historical circumstances. The varieties of secularism—or different secularisms—are contingent because they draw their power from secular ontologies, which are the product of particular historical ideas and practices.[21] In marking the boundary between the secular and the religious, they presuppose and reinforce particular conceptions of what it means to be secular. Hence, secularisms are colonial epistemic regimes that construct "the religious" as a universal, transcultural, and transhistorical dimension, thus concealing their contingent western-centric historical situatedness.[22] Secularisms are colonial epistemic regimes, we contend, that have been themselves colonized by neoliberal rationalities.

The discussion proceeds in three steps. In the first section, we consider how recent comparative studies of secularisms have prioritized the nation-state as the primary context for understanding the plurality of secularisms in world politics. We propose a complementary framework that deems the differentiation of societal spheres as equally if not more relevant for grasping the most fundamental differences among contemporary secularisms. Instead of thinking primarily in terms of French, Indian, Turkish, and American secularisms, we contend, it is necessary to distinguish between political, economic, scientific, and even religious secularisms.

In the second and third sections, we argue that economic neoliberal rationalities have become the dominating force crucially shaping existing forms of secular life. We do so by exploring how Ludwig von Mises and most of all Friedrich Hayek, two of the most influential architects of neoliberalism, understood the place and role of religion in society. In a telling illustration of the coloniality of power, not only did they understand religion through the universalist prism of the Eurocentric Christian experience, but they rewrote it in light of the higher order of the market. We advance two main arguments. First, the neoliberal secular order is one in which religion is evaluated as normal or deviant based on whether it respects the integrity of market relations and legitimizes the moral principles that sustain them. Second, neoliberal secularism goes beyond the external policing of deviant belief. Religion is colonized to the point that logics of belief are not just constructed from the standpoint of neoliberal secularism but become constitutive of the latter's very meanings and functions.

UNDERSTANDING SECULARISMS: FROM NATIONAL TO SOCIETAL DIFFERENTIATION

"We speak of distinct models of secularism in national contexts, such as French, American, Indian, and Turkish secularisms. The story of secularism can hardly be told independent of the history of nation-state building," writes Nilüfer Göle.[23] This statement summarizes the major framework within which secularist plurality has been understood in recent literature. The primary perspective for interpreting the diversity of secularisms assumes that the western discourse of secularism has been both produced and universalized through the colonial expansion of European power. As western ideals of secularism were universalized, they were consciously and unconsciously reshaped when newly interpreted against the background of non-Christian religious practices and the particular historical circumstances of state formation around the world.[24]

In these accounts, primacy is ascribed to state-led projects of secularist nation-building, even though it is acknowledged that these have been increasingly challenged by the transnationalization of the public sphere and the new political assertiveness of religious movements seeking to remake the boundaries between the secular and the religious.[25] Similarly, a number of studies of secularism have pursued an investigation of the distinctive influence of religious traditions by mainly focusing on the constitutional arrangements and political norms of states.[26] State involvement in the governance of religion has been equated with nation-building projects of secularism.[27]

This scholarship has been valuable in showing how country-specific differences in "state–society relations, discourses of democratization, gender relations, nationalist projects and politics, religious and theological imperatives, and colonial and postcolonial interactions" have played a crucial role in shaping the contemporary landscape of secularisms and instituting different "varieties of secularism in a secular age."[28] However, as David Lyon observes, these lines of inquiry have largely neglected how "some of the long-term changes in the [manifestations of secularism and] conditions of belief are today accentuated and inflected by their association with the consumer phase of capitalism."[29] Neoliberal capitalism, in particular, is eroding the categories and identities constitutive of national models of secularism.

According to Talal Asad, models of secularism revolving around the nation-state attempt to construct citizenship as a primary identity that can transcend and subordinate class, gender, and religious identities, thus relativizing the social divisions that these particularizing identities produce.[30] However, we increasingly live in an age in which states are being reconstructed and reoriented either as institutions for creating, maintaining, and regulating markets, or for protecting the commercial interests of the nation, now reimagined as a competitive firm in the global economy.[31] Wendy Brown observes that "the state's table of purposes and priorities has become indistinguishable from that of modern firms" to the effect that the notion of citizenship has also evolved.[32] Citizens are now "consumers," "labor force," and even "stockholders"[33] who partake in the life of the country not just and primarily through political participation, but through their inscription in those economic activities deemed essential for boosting the country's "value."[34] The postpolitical economic rationalities of neoliberal citizenship are transnational in character and yet crucially prompted and shaped by the nation-state. They reveal an internal introjection of the coloniality of neoliberal power that is increasingly shaping the nation-state from within.

This transformation can be observed in the fact that the nation-state has progressively relinquished its duty "to care for its citizens 'from cradle to grave': to provide education, pensions, medical services, and public utilities, and to hold out a safety net for the less fortunate so that they [have] food, shelter, and the other necessities of life."[35] Its primary focus is to promote a favorable business climate capable of attracting investments and capital by improving infrastructure, lowering taxes and the cost of labor, reducing bureaucracy and regulations, and augmenting the stock of human capital.[36]

The parallel transformation of state and citizenship according to transnational economic rationalities points to the limits of conceptualizing secularism primarily in national terms. National variations in secularism must be understood against a broader background in which the global forces of neoliberalism act as a market-based coloniality of power, knowledge, and being. We propose that the significance and novelty of neoliberal rationalities of secularism can be usefully understood in relation to the differentiation of societal spheres that is constitutive of modern western secularity. The values and logics constitutive of these different spheres of life—particularly those concerning the economic sphere—provide a range of diverse standpoints from which different secularist projects are articulated.

The characterization of secular modernity as a condition of societal differentiation was originally proposed by Weber, for whom secularization (which he calls "disenchantment") is a process of fragmentation of life into contending value spheres.[37] The intellectual sphere, the moral sphere, the economic sphere, the political sphere, the legal sphere, and the aesthetic sphere once fell under the unifying framework of faith. According to Weber, with the modern process of secularization, these spheres began to function according to their own immanent laws, such as profit for the economic sphere and power for the political sphere. In addition, a new sphere was created, that of religion.[38]

Peter Beyer argues that the differentiation of autonomous societal spheres with their logics, institutions, and principles of operation has led to the creation of a range of perspectives from which to observe, evaluate, and construct religion in modernity.[39] Science, politics, the economy, law, education, health, and mass media all provide "ways of seeing" that have generated different conceptions of religion. These encompass those who conceive of religion as involving a human experience of, or encounter with, transcendence, and those who argue instead for a naturalistic, social scientific study of religion as a this-worldly phenomenon.

For Beyer, these disputes are rooted in different societal spheres: the religious and the scientific. Science defines religion in a way that accords with the purposes of scientific research. On this account, religion is a category created by scholars to delimit a phenomenon and thus to enable comparison and generalization.[40] Theological conceptions of religion, by contrast, are shaped by the scriptural content and hermeneutical methodologies of religious communities, primarily, the relation between persons and the transcendent or spiritual realm. On this account, "true" religion is that which involves an authentic connection with the transcendent, but "bad" religion is heresy, idolatry, and superstition.[41]

Science and theology are not the only standpoints from which religion is conceptualized and evaluated. Beyer points out that the nature and purpose of religion is also defined and described by other centers of institutional power, such as governments, courts, media, and schools. He argues that the political, legal, media, and educational systems may work with conceptions of religion influenced by theological or scientific conceptions, but that this may not always be the case. Such definitions and representations of religion may also be determined by political expediency, for instance, even if they draw on religious or scientific experts for legitimation.

The usefulness of Beyer's argument for our project is limited by the fact that he deliberately maximizes the independence of the social in his analysis. He does so on the grounds that the core properties of the emergent social systems of global society have an impersonal quality, abstracted from, yet working through, individual human beings.[42] This approach leads to an explanation of change in societal systems that downplays the ability of human beings to respond creatively to their social environment by developing new self-understandings and practices. It is a "process" of understanding that has trouble capturing the contingent "project" nature of many of the movements of thought and practice through which societal differentiation came about.

Nevertheless, the insight that societal differentiation has provided a set of differentiated standpoints and rationalities from which religion is shaped, transformed, and disciplined offers a very productive starting point for understanding contemporary secularisms. It is especially useful in qualifying the methodological nationalism that has characterized much of the discussions of secularism. The division of humanity into groups— families, tribes, nations, civilizations—remains a significant form of social division in modernity. Territorial divisions, principally the state, also remain very significant. However, territorial and group divisions are not the only way to understand modernity. Cutting across (and partially displacing and remodeling) these divisions are those constituted by societal differentiation, which creates ways of seeing, rationalities for action, institutional imperatives, and social roles—ways of thinking and acting politically, economically, and scientifically—that mobilize powerful configurations of power and knowledge in existing understandings of secularism and religion.[43]

These considerations open the way for understanding diversity in secularism as a feature that is generated as much by the division of modern societies into distinct societal spheres as by the division of the world into nation-states. Alongside French, Indian, and American secularisms, we suggest, there are political, economic, and scientific conceptions of secularism. From this perspective, it can be argued that the national organization of secular power reflects the modern primacy of the political rationalities of secularism. These political rationalities have as their primary goal the creation of strong, stable, and peaceful states through the subordination of religion to the ethos and identity of citizenship. In this nationhood model of secularism, religion is judged and managed according to what is expedient for the good of the political community. "Good" religion is that which is compatible with civil peace and the duties and responsibilities of citizenship; "bad" religion is that which prioritizes religious beliefs and practices that are incompatible with civil peace and citizenship.[44]

Religion is also conceptualized through the contending rationalities that are constitutive of the political sphere. Liberal political secularisms, for instance, conceptualize the practice of religion as a right to be protected, thus reflecting liberal conceptions of citizenship as a legal status that protects individuals' freedoms from interference by other people or the state.[45] In contrast, the republican political tradition, with its emphasis on the unity of the active body of citizens, evaluates religion according to whether it is unifying or divisive.[46] It follows that the secularism of republican-influenced polities has often involved employing "civil religion" as a condition of societal unity.[47]

Similar points can be made about the secularisms constituted by other societal spheres. Science has its own criteria for what can count as legitimate knowledge about religion and legitimate knowledge in the public sphere. The authority of science as founded on rational, evidence-based procedures, grounds authoritative claims about the true nature and significance of religion that can inform public policy and attitudes toward religious communities. At the same time, religious interventions in political life can be delegitimized by contrasting irrational religious faith with scientific reason, a contrast that depends on a narrow, scientistic view of reason as reducible to logical coherence and reliant upon empirical claims about material realities.[48]

It is more complex but not paradoxical to say that there are religious conceptions of secularism that in turn inform distinctive understandings of religion. This is simply the claim that the identity and proper limits of religion may be defined from a differentiated societal sphere in modernity that is concerned with transcendent or spiritual realities beyond the immanent concerns of nonreligious spheres. This process of codification draws on bodies of knowledge and practices that are interpreted and received as "religious" in society from a secular standpoint; it may also mean that the ensuing views of the relationship between faith and the realities of more mundane aspects of contemporary society implicitly reflects the transformation of religion in modernity. For example, fundamentalists claim possession of a timeless and pristine truth, untouched and uncorrupted by the political, economic, and social forces of modernity. Yet this self-understanding has been constituted in part by the modern secular construction of religion as a thing apart. In seeking to reorder political and social life according to this vision, they are renegotiating the boundaries of religion from a standpoint shaped by a prior constitution of religion as an autonomous and yet all-encompassing societal domain.

In line with the above illustrations, neoliberalism can be understood as a rationality of secularism that positions and defines religion in relation to a vision of sociality that draws on economic logics and values to an unprecedented extent. It imagines the secular in terms of the division of labor, competitive markets, and self-interested, utility-seeking actors. The primary goal of neoliberal secularism is to promote the creation and maintenance of competitive markets. To this end, it advocates the subordination of religion to a role that is simultaneously marginal—religion cannot legitimately question the basic principles of market society—and ancillary, religion provides the mythology required for the social acceptance of the moral values necessary for market society. "Good" religion is that which is compatible with the competitive ethos of the market; "bad" religion is that which challenges or undermines it.

This fundamentally "economic" standpoint of neoliberal secularism differs from secularisms that draw primarily on political, religious, or scientific rationalities to construct, define, and contest the boundaries between the religious and the secular. At the same time, it should not be supposed that neoliberalism is a purely economic rationality of secularism. As we shall consider in the next two sections through a discussion of neoliberal founding fathers Mises and Hayek, economic rationalities are not the only ones mobilized in the neoliberal secular construction and evaluation of religion. In particular, we argue that the question raised by societal differentiation accounts of contemporary secularisms is not simply one of how to classify secularisms as political, economic, and scientific, but also one of how to understand the way discourses from different spheres are combined in particular historical projects of secularism.

Neoliberalism is one such historical project that transcends the economic sphere and, as such, acts as a hegemonic framework that molds distinctive understandings of the political, the economic, and scientific, which in turn colonize and shape existing dominant versions of secularism and, by extension, of religion. As will become clearer in the next section, this argument challenges and expands existing theoretical approaches to religion and modernity in two main ways. First, modern conceptualizations of religion cannot be understood independently of the coloniality of power of neoliberal secularism. Second, the latter has not expunged religion from modernity, but rather rewritten, colonized, and ultimately embedded religion in its very foundations.

The Modern Neoliberalization of Secularism

Neoliberalism emerged in opposition to the Keynesianism of the mid-twentieth century. Keynesian policies aimed to create a more equitable and sustainable social order, and favored active government, higher taxes for the rich, the regulation of finance and industry, and welfare provisions. Many of the key ideas of the later neoliberal project were developed during the 1930s and 1940s, but it was not until the mid-1970s that they began to have any substantive influence on policy. As a response to the economic crises of that decade, economists influenced by the first generation of neoliberals argued for abolishing barriers to trade and financial flows, greater regional and global economic integration, deregulation of industry, deunionization and casualization of labor, cuts to government spending, privatization of state-run services, and generous tax regimes for capital.

Neoliberalism was more than an economic theory, though. It was also an "economism." Its proponents believed that the policies, institutions, and rationalities of governance they advocated for in economic affairs were appropriate for all areas of life. The self-regulating free market became the model for human sociality as such, and commercial values such as competitiveness, entrepreneurship, self-interest, and efficiency were celebrated as desirable individual dispositions.

The sources and development of neoliberalism are complex. It emerged from a "thought collective" rather than the mind of a single thinker, and it has been altered, reinterpreted, and embedded in different historical contexts.⁴⁹ Yet some thinkers were especially influential in providing a theoretical grounding for later intellectual and practical developments. Ludwig von Mises and Friedrich Hayek in particular played a crucial role in defining the shape and direction of the emergent neoliberal project from the 1920s onward. Hayek, Nobel Prize winner and "perhaps the single most important neoliberal economist," founded the Mont Pèlerin Society, the neoliberal think tank that was the epicenter for collective discussions of neoliberal ideas before they became influential in political and economic circles.⁵⁰ Although less celebrated, Mises had a deep influence on Hayek and other members of the Mont Pèlerin Society, in which he was also involved.⁵¹

In the remainder of this section, we focus on Mises and discuss how he lays the foundations for a distinctive neoliberal secularism that polices the boundaries of religion—its functions, remits, and possibilities—in his argument that market society is the foundation of peaceful and prosperous human communities. As it will become clear by the end of this section, this neoliberal account rests on a distinctive "modern" understanding of science and knowledge that can be contrasted with Hayek's "postmodern" account. We lay out these contrasting views in the third section to show a different and, arguably, ever-more prominent variation of neoliberal secularism.

According to Mises, a basic premise of neoliberalism is that individuals' self-interested pursuit of their own well-being in the market is the foundation not only of the economy but also of society in general. The market as an institution for social cooperation through the division of labor is "the foremost social body."⁵² The market does not exist alongside or arise out of society, but social solidarity is a product of market relations rather than something that exists prior to them: "In striving after his own—rightly understood—interests the individual works toward an intensification of social cooperation and peaceful intercourse. Society is a product of human action, i.e., the human urge to remove uneasiness as far as possible."⁵³ Feelings of friendship, mutual sympathy, and collective belonging are the product, not the origin, of cooperation in the market.⁵⁴ The market is self-regulating, and any attempt to intervene or reorganize the economy and society according to dangerous heteronomous blueprints is not only an unjustified restriction on individual freedom but a practice that will result in the destruction of society.

The dangerous blueprints Mises had in mind were primarily socialism and fascism, but he also included forms of religion that sought to reorganize society according to a divinely ordained plan. Indeed, he regarded socialism and fascism as analogous to religion, as they ascribed to "the people" or "society" the qualities of omniscience, omnipotence, omnipresence, eternity, and infinite goodness that are traditionally ascribed to religion.[55] Centrally planned projects for the reorganization of society according to a collectivist or heteronomous moral vision would inevitably make theological or metaphysical claims. This is because they cannot rationally demonstrate that their moral intuitions or social ideals are legitimate and true. They demand credulous acceptance of their authority.[56]

In contrast to such irrationalism, Mises argues that liberalism, as a political doctrine, can claim rational authority. It is based on social scientific theories developed to understand specific problems of human action in society. It contends, as an empirical fact, that most people want material well-being, and adds to this the results of scientific study of the most suitable means to this goal: the division of labor in a market society.[57] The laws, moral codes, and institutions that sustain market society are designed by humans for their own benefit, rather than by God, and "the only yardstick that must be applied to them is that of expediency with regard to human welfare."[58]

The liberal insistence on scientific and individual authority, rather than theological or mystical authority, to create social organization does not need to exclude religion; liberalism is not hostile to religion as such, but religion must know its place. Its place is in the private, personal sphere of individual commitment: "Liberalism limits its concern entirely and exclusively to earthly life and earthly endeavour. The kingdom of religion, on the other hand, is not of this world."[59] Religion, for Mises, is a set of feelings or beliefs about a divine creator that are not open to examination by reason or logic.[60] It is "a purely personal and individual relation between man and a holy, mysterious, and awe-inspiring divine Reality. It enjoins upon man a certain mode of individual conduct. But it does not assert anything with regard to the problems of social organization."[61]

Religion may have a role in regulating a person's private affairs, but it problematically becomes "theocracy" when it is mobilized as a social project. For Mises, "theocracy is a social system which lays claim to a super-human title for its legitimation. The fundamental law of a theocratic regime is an insight not open to examination by reason and to demonstration by logical methods."[62] All religions have historically shown theocratic tendencies, Mises maintains, but there is an important difference between religion as an individual and private commitment, on the one hand, and theocracy, which includes both religio-political projects along with fascism, nationalism, communism, and socialism, on the other.

Mises regards "theocracy" as a problem for three reasons. First, any heteronomous ideological, moral, or religious rules that seek to bend social and economic behavior away from the principles of social cooperation laid down by the market will disrupt the increase in human welfare markets promise. For Mises, Christian social reforms that sought to regulate the market with ideas about just wages and just prices would leave everyone worse off.[63] Second, any effort to interfere with market principles would have to be dogmatically imposed because "no deviation from the unhampered market economy is thinkable without authoritarian regimentation."[64] Third, a society in which social and economic policy was determined by ideological or religious beliefs rather than the rational, instrumental pursuit of material well-being would be prone to war. This is because there is no other way of deciding between rival visions of the good society. Any attempt to impose on society a claim to knowledge of the true laws of God or absolute values will result in violence because

> each party is prepared to make its own tenets prevail. But as logical argumentation cannot decide between various dissenting creeds, there is no means left for the settlement of such disputes other than armed conflict. The nonrationalist, nonutilitarian, and nonliberal social doctrines must beget wars and civil wars until one of the adversaries is annihilated or subdued. The history of the world's great religions is a record of battles and wars, as is the history of the present-day counterfeit religions, socialism, statolatry, and nationalism.[65]

Mises thus contrasts religion with a secularism grounded in the scientific political doctrine of liberalism and evaluates religion from the standpoint of a neoliberal understanding of society. "Good" religion is that which accepts the division between public liberal science and private religious faith; "bad" religion is that which escapes its proper sphere and interferes with the legal, moral, and scientific codes of society, which are meant to sustain the natural human pursuit of material well-being in the market:

> In the liberal opinion the aim of the moral law is to impel individuals to adjust their conduct to the requirements of life in society, to abstain from all acts detrimental to the preservation of peaceful social co-operation and to the improvement of interhuman relations. Liberals welcome the support which religious teachings may give to those moral precepts of which they themselves approve, but they are opposed to all those norms which are bound to bring about social disintegration from whatever source they may stem.[66]

True religion, for Mises, is the recognition that "God's magnificence does not manifest itself in busy interference with sundry affairs of princes and politicians, but in endowing his creatures with reason and the urge toward the pursuit of happiness."[67] Mises thus makes a strong distinction between a public liberal reason concerned with the instrumental pursuit of material well-being and private religious experiences and intuitions concerned with harmonious relations between individuals and a transcendent or spiritual reality. He argues that there should be no difficulties with this doctrine because "even religious zealots must concede that liberalism takes nothing from faith of what belongs to its proper sphere."[68] Moreover, churches and religious organizations that have involved themselves in social life have invariably abandoned the pure, otherworldly principles of religion as such. By involving themselves in social affairs, they are compelled to take account of the rational desire for material well-being and the necessity for some form of social cooperation that is necessary to secure it. There is therefore no ultimate dispute about ends when it comes to political and social questions. The only questions left concern the means employed to answer them, and these questions can be answered through scientific study and reasonable discussion.[69]

Hence, from Mises's perspective, any religious group that does not accept human, material well-being as the only possible end of social and political life—for example, those who argue that there are goods beyond and not entirely reducible to material wealth[70]—would put themselves beyond the pale of acceptable rationality, and presumably call up all the disastrous social consequences Mises associated with "theocracy." But

Mises believed that the battle to roll back the church had been decisively won by liberalism, so much so that it seemed incredible that the church could ever have had pretensions to regulate matters of this world in addition to humans' relationship with the world to come.[71]

This brief overview of Mises's thoughts on religion suggests two important considerations. First, for Mises the economic sphere and specifically the neoliberal outlook is the standpoint from which acceptable modes of religiosity should be evaluated. From the perspective outlined in this chapter, then, his neoliberal secularism can be critiqued as a colonial epistemic regime that establishes the functions and limits of religion by decreeing that religious movements that challenge market values and institutions are a threat to society and therefore should be opposed. Second, this coloniality of power performs what we previously described as a movement of internal reduplication with neoliberalism colonizing other spheres of human existence. This means that Mises's view of neoliberal secularism transcends the mere economic sphere. It encapsulates and molds distinctive neoliberal understandings of politics, science, and morality. Indeed, Mises draws on an idea of science that reflects the differentiated construction of the scientific sphere, on an ontology of natural causation, and on an epistemology centered on reason, logic, and empirical observation. Accordingly, his account reflects the modern invention of religions as private, cognitive, and otherworldly. For Mises, it is a personal system of belief that should not challenge the secular order of neoliberalism.

Seemingly sharing Mises's outlook, Hayek departs from his modernist approach. Hayek's view rests on a postmodern epistemology of limited knowledge that is skeptical of any claim that our modern social order may be the product of rational action and human design. Accordingly, he advocates a social and collective role for religious ideas and beliefs as the very condition of possibility for modern societies. Hayek does not disavow the idea that religion should be private, cognitive, and otherworldly, but he emphasizes the importance of nonrational beliefs and practices as conditions of possibility for a prosperous market order. The paradoxical result is that his neoliberal secularism does not simply colonize the religious domain but is itself colonized by logics of faith. The resulting sacralization of the market order—a *self-colonialism* in which neoliberalism colonizes all domains of human existence—suggests an understanding of the relationship between religion and modernity beyond the paradigms of expulsion or subordination.

Secular modernity has been transformed by the colonization of religion to the point that neoliberal secularism has become itself a form of religiosity.

THE POSTMODERN NEOLIBERALIZATION OF SECULARISM

At first sight, the remarks on religion scattered through Hayek's work appear consistent with the themes emphasized by Mises. For Hayek, the principles offered by religion are too general and disputed to provide a substantive social philosophy that could win general acceptance.[72] He concurs with Mises's insistence that liberalism is not opposed to religion, only to the imposition of religion on other people and to the blurring of boundaries between spiritual and temporal affairs.[73] He agrees that communism is most usefully understood as a religion.[74]

Hayek, however, differs from Mises in his concern with the moral and cultural foundations of a market society. In his later work, he increasingly emphasized the significance of tradition, morality, and religion as necessary cultural practices for sustaining market exchange. He also saw them developing according to the same principles of competition and spontaneous order that made the market a self-regulating domain. Whereas Mises's primary concern was the restriction of religion to its proper domain, Hayek was more positive about religion, believing that it had a valuable social role, and a distinct wisdom, which allowed it to contribute to the success of a market society in ways that secular rationalism could not. This in turn provided a rationale for limiting the interference of government in religious practices.

This argument is most systematically developed in Hayek's final book, *The Fatal Conceit: The Errors of Socialism*, which offers an account of the role of religion in the emergence of market societies.[75] Specifically, Hayek argues that religion made possible the transition from small-scale, hunter-gatherer societies characterized by direct personal relations and the pursuit of common goals in a group, to a market society characterized by impersonal exchange and the pursuit of diverse individual goals.[76] The former were characterized by "instinctual" forms of behavior: high levels of mutual trust, solidarity, altruism, and mutual assistance within the group. Such behavior was a condition of individual survival in the world of primitive societies.

As the human population and material wealth increased, a new form of society emerged in which the instinctual behavior appropriate to small-scale groups was no longer suitable. A world of long-distance trade and increasingly impersonal systems of social cooperation required individuals to control their instincts of altruism and aggression toward outsiders, and to adapt to the rules required by the extended social order: rules concerning property, honesty, contract, trade, competition, and privacy. These rules represented a new form of morality that regulated behavior in ways appropriate to a more complex, developed society; these rules constrained and governed the behavior of self-interested individuals in a world with many more opportunities for the exploitation of others.[77]

Although these rules would often be experienced as irksome, constraining instinctual behavior and conflicting with egotistical impulses, and although their rationale was not obvious, because the social benefits that accrued from them would only be understood with hindsight, they nonetheless survived. What enabled the new rules of the extended order to survive and proliferate was religion, which provided a rationale for moral rules that could restrain human instincts, discourage antisocial behavior, and produce social benefits. Religious beliefs were powerful enough to sustain beneficial customs even when the social benefits could not be easily perceived by those practicing them.[78] Hayek remarks, "As an order of human interaction became more extended, and still more threatening to instinctual claims, it might for a time become quite dependent on the continuing influence of some such religious beliefs—false reasons influencing men to do what was required to maintain the structure enabling them to nourish their enlarging numbers."[79] Religion ensures that rules of conduct that conflict with instinct and reason are transmitted from generation to generation, where they otherwise might be abandoned as irrational or irksome. These rules did not develop through rational discussion and construction because reason is too weak to foresee the benefits and effects of particular moral ideas in complex social systems. They emerged through a process of natural selection, in which traditions and moralities that shape conduct in socially beneficial directions survived because they advanced social stability and human well-being. According to Hayek, "We can hardly be said to have selected them [social rules]; rather, these constraints selected us: they enabled us to survive."[80] Thus, the values that protect property and the family survive because they make a certain stability in human society possible.

Religion for Hayek develops through a similar competitive process of natural selection. Religion was historically a carrier for the values that enabled human society to grow, but there is no intrinsic connection between religion and positive social institutions. Religion can—and does—just as easily support destructive and antisocial institutions, but the religions that do this will not last long. Religions that survive are those that foster socially beneficial values; religions that do not are fated to disappear: "Among the founders of religions over the last two thousand years, many opposed property and the family. *But the only religions that have survived are those which support property and the family.* Thus the outlook for communism, which is both anti-property and anti-family (and anti-religion), is not promising.... In communist and socialist countries we are watching how the natural selection of religious beliefs disposes of the maladapted."[81] For Hayek, then, the religions that undermine the central social institutions of market society are not only destructive to society, but are also self-destructive. Given free reign, the religions that make a positive social contribution will thrive, but antisocial traditions will not survive long. In the short term, "bad" forms of religion may be propped up by political support, or to support the interests of a ruling elite.[82] But over the long term, the decisive fact—far more important than the support or opposition of a particular regime—will be the question of whether the rules of conduct promoted by a particular form of religion contribute to the stability, welfare, and expansion of the community. One implication of this, which Hayek does not explicitly develop, is that religious freedom is good for religion and good for society because it creates the conditions in which religions that are badly adapted to society (and therefore not fulfilling their ultimate function as religion, from the neoliberal standpoint) are eliminated through a process of natural selection.

Whereas Mises provides a rationale for keeping religion out of political and economic life, Hayek provides a rationale for keeping the state out of religion. Mises is concerned for religion to be *religion* in the modern sense of the term: private, subjective, otherworldly, and respectful of the ability of market cooperation and competition to secure human material well-being. He is nevertheless happy for religious groups to be socially involved if they leave religion at the door, respecting and working through the conventions of secular spheres and endorsing their values.

Hayek puts greater emphasis on the role that religion can play in legitimizing and sustaining the moral values on which a stable market society depends. However, his strictures on respecting the boundary between the spiritual and the temporal, and his understanding of religion as essentially a source of general principles and values, rule out any substantive critical challenge to the organizing principles of market society. Hence, it could be argued that Hayek's vision of secularism is ultimately similar to Mises's and that the difference between the two is ultimately one of emphasis. For both thinkers the meaning of religion is given by its relation to the institutions of market society: "good" religion is that which is compatible with this form of social organization; "bad" religion is disruptive of it. However, as we shall argue in the remainder of this section, this would be a hasty conclusion.

Neoliberalism is a project that transcends the economic sphere and shapes distinctive understandings of politics, the economy, and science that inform dominant versions of secularism. Hayek's emphasis on religion as a source of legitimacy for the neoliberal order is not just the product of an economic standpoint, but of a distinctive position on the limits and possibility of scientific knowledge. Hayek's approach is the product of an "epistemology of limited knowledge" that stands in sharp contrast with Mises's modernist scientific outlook.[83]

Mises argued that religion should remain private and confined to the innerworldly sphere of the individual because it was incapable of providing the rational foundation for the organization of the social order. The claims of religion, he contended, could not be rationally demonstrated, unlike those of liberalism, which rest on verifiable social scientific theories. For Hayek, Mises's view was the expression of what he variously described as "utilitarian rationalism," "constructivist rationalism," and eventually "erroneous rationalism," namely, "a conception which assumes that all social institutions are, and ought to be, the product of deliberate design."[84] Hayek rejected this view on the grounds that the modern extended order is the product of an extraordinarily high number of variables that no single political institution could grasp in their totality. This view has two main implications.

First, Hayek considers political ideologies such as socialism and institutions such as central banks—both of which claim to be able to achieve a better social, economic, or financial order through the centralization of knowledge—to be an expression of the modern "pretence of knowledge."[85] This is the idea that human beings may effectively achieve true knowledge about the complex social order and therefore be able to devise institutions and procedures aimed at improving and bettering its functioning.[86] This "fatal conceit"[87] will inevitably translate into the "arbitrary power" of some people over others and eventually manifest into a "tyranny"—such as that experienced in communist countries—that will reduce people to a condition of "serfdom."[88] The second implication follows directly from the first. In order to eschew this "serfdom," we should rely on the neoliberal market—and, specifically, on its mechanism of competition—as a system of social coordination. For Hayek, markets are decentralized institutions that have an innate capacity to organize and coordinate the fragmented pieces of knowledge possessed by individuals and institutions. They have a spontaneous ability to produce order, the efficient allocation of goods and service, growth, and ultimately progress, while not impinging upon our freedom.[89]

Hayek's "deep skepticism about the possibilities of objectively true knowledge"[90] signals an important "postmodern" rejection of modern epistemologies that "held out the promise that the unknown could be made known" and that "time and space truly could be brought under human control through Reason."[91] It is important to stress that we use the label "postmodern" in an extremely narrow sense here: not to include Hayek in the already large and fuzzy group of "postmodernists," but to emphasize how his "epistemology of limited knowledge" differs from scientific modernist outlooks à la Mises. The implication of this difference can be seen in Hayek's distinctive "religious" understanding of the neoliberal market.

Whereas for Mises the market is the expression of a liberal human-made rational order and religion is an untestable and unverifiable system of beliefs that should be confined to the private domain, for Hayek the market is a product of human action but not of human design. Its capacity to deliver growth is not always scientifically "verifiable or testable."[92] For Hayek, however, this nonverifiability is not a problem because he considers that the very advancement of progress and civilization are also products of "beliefs which are not true . . . in the same sense as are scientific statements and which are certainly not the result of rational argumentation."[93] These beliefs, or "symbolic truths," as Hayek refers to them when he quotes the book of Genesis, have forcefully encouraged "their adherents to 'be fruitful and multiply and replenish the earth and subdue it' (Genesis 1:28)."[94] Indeed, he concludes, "nonfactual beliefs" have crucially contributed to the establishment of "the extended order that we now enjoy" to the effect that "now the loss of these beliefs, whether true or false, creates great difficulties."[95]

This argument brings us back to the Hayekian distinction between "good" and "bad" religions, which now appears in a new guise. Whereas "bad" religions are those that do not support or actually reject the extended order of neoliberalism—including ideological belief-systems, such as communism—"good" religions are not simply those that *support* this order but are the very conditions of possibility of the neoliberal order, which would simply not exist without an underlying logic of belief. This means that the neoliberal extended order is itself a nonverifiable and nontestable system of beliefs. This lack of a foundation is the result of the inherent sheer complexity of the market. Because it is made of scattered fragments of knowledge, it is impossible for governments and other political institutions to transcend its inherent unknowability.

Hence, in Hayek's account, the market becomes a mystical and almost sacred space where the *impossibility of knowledge* becomes the very condition for the *possibility of progress*. Indeed, Hayek maintains, to participate in the neoliberal market is to undertake "a voyage of exploration into the unknown, an attempt to discover new ways of doing things better than they have been done before."[96] For Hayek, the mysteries of the unknown of the neoliberal market are governed by a logic of faith that holds the promise of future salvation, namely, the possibility of an extended order characterized by material progress and wealth. This logic of faith at the heart of Hayek's thought has been perceptively observed by Néstor Míguez, Joerg Rieger, and Jung Mo Sung, who ask:

> If it is true that we cannot sufficiently understand the factors and dynamics of the market so that we can intervene in it, how can we know that the market always produces beneficial effects or that it is essentially a "force for good"? Is knowing that the market always produces beneficial effects not a pretension of knowledge of the market? Since one cannot prove this providential character of the market, we have here a "leap of faith" in the affirmation of the essentially beneficent quality of free market.[97]

The argument advanced in this section importantly complicates the idea that the process of societal differentiation has separated religion from other societal spheres and provided a set of differentiated standpoints and rationalities from which religion is shaped, transformed, and disciplined. Hayek's argument does indeed offer a neoliberal secular standpoint from which to evaluate and discipline religion. Yet Hayek's neoliberal standpoint is not separate from religion because, however secular, it also draws on the registers and sensibilities that modernity has corralled as "religious." For Hayek it is *rational* to believe in the market because of our epistemological incapacity to grasp the complexity of the social order in its totality (rational argument), even if the capacity of the market to act as a force for good cannot be demonstrated, and even if the market delivers shocks, crises, and failures, as these may be the means for the market to achieve order and deliver future prosperity (leap of faith). To think otherwise would be a "pretence of knowledge" (rational argument).

Hence, whereas Hayek's justification for trusting the market is the expression of an eminently scientific rationality—our epistemological incapacity to fully grasp the complexity of the social world and its sheer intricacy—his secular approach also demands that we have "faith" in the market as a benevolent entity, the only one truly able to deliver economic growth and advance the pathway of civilization. Hayek's neoliberalism thus articulates a distinctive vision of secularism as a regime of power and knowledge that, in colonizing the religious domain by imposing its shapes and functions, turns the market order into a transcendent, sacred, and totalizing domain. Hayek's view is ultimately the instantiation of a colonialism internal to the western episteme: a self-colonialism in which neoliberalism transcends the economic domain to become the overarching condition of possibility and framework of meaning for the secular order.

Conclusion

We began an investigation of the neoliberal rationalities at the heart of secularism. Our approach departed from state-centric accounts. Actually existing secularist projects in modern nation-states have undoubtedly been projects of "political" secularism. As such they have been concerned with state-building and with the expression of a modernist scientific outlook that sees in secularism a rational foundation for the organization of the social order. However, when the national imaginary is increasingly under siege by the transnational forces of global capital and when neoliberal discourses and practices appear to relentlessly conquer new social and political domains, the power to define religion and secularity is also shifting away from traditionally conceived political standpoints. Neoliberal rationalities within and beyond the nation-state are rewriting existing understandings of the political, of science, of the economy, and, crucially for our argument, of what it means to be secular and religious.

In order to grasp the contours of these neoliberal rationalities, we have sought to extract from the writings of two of the most prominent theorists of neoliberalism, Mises and Hayek, an understanding of how religion is constructed in the foundational corpus of neoliberalism and how the latter contributes to shaping a distinctive understanding of secularism. The analysis juxtaposed Mises's "modernist" account to Hayek's "postmodernist" one. Mises's construction of religion as otherworldly, nonrational, normatively private, personal, and opposed to the this-worldly, public, pragmatic, and scientific rationality of neoliberalism resonates with traditional renderings of secularism. Hayek, on the other hand, while sharing some of Mises's ideas, ultimately departs from his modernist outlook.

Moving from an epistemology of limited knowledge, Hayek questions the modernist pretension of achieving true knowledge and devising overarching policies that may be able to improve social and economic outcomes. For Hayek, neoliberalism is not the scientific foundation of a rational order, but the recognition that the extended order that we enjoy is certainly the product of human action, but not of human design, because we—as individuals but also as members of states, along with national and international organizations—only possess scattered fragments of a complex reality. To embrace neoliberalism is to believe that the market is the most sophisticated yet effective mechanism for coordinating these scattered agencies and knowledges. It is to believe this because the market has an innate and spontaneous capacity to produce order.

Hence, for Hayek, the beliefs associated with religions are often "useful" because they have encouraged those practices that have contributed to the emergence of the modern extended market order. For Hayek, the neoliberal market itself is the expression of an act of belief, of a leap of faith in its capacity to deliver prosperity and growth. The distinctive secularism that emerges from Hayek's perspective is not simply one, as in Mises's account, where religion is constructed from the standpoint of neoliberal secularism; it is one in which a fideistic religious sensibility is reabsorbed as an integral part of neoliberal secularism. Hayek remarks: "You might call every belief in moral principles, which are not rationally justified [such as the norms that govern the neoliberal market], a religious belief. In the wide sense, yes, one has to be religious."[98] With Hayek, neoliberalism becomes a religion.[99]

Depictions of neoliberalism as a religion, a system of belief, a "kind of faith," as a "theology disguised as social science," as "theological free-market ideology," and as an expression of "market fundamentalism" have recently multiplied, particularly in the aftermath of the 2008 financial crisis.[100] To date, however, the analyses that have pointed at the religious nature of neoliberalism have mostly done so to denounce the "irrationality" of neoliberalism as an economic system whose hegemony is unhampered by its failures and incapacity to generate wealth for the most and not just for the few. Our aim here has been to suggest that the "religious" dimension of neoliberalism goes deeper than an irrational or dogmatic attachment to neoliberal ideology that is evident among some of its proponents. The reason, we argued, is that neoliberal secularism is the instantiation of the internal reduplication of the logic of coloniality: a *self-colonialism* in which neoliberal secularism transcends the economic domain and colonizes all other spheres of human existence to the point of incorporating its religious antagonist and becoming itself a religion.

For a vivid illustration of this dynamic, one needs to look no further than the recent COVID-19 pandemic and how its governance has been framed as a trade-off between saving the market and saving lives. The attempts to resist the adoption of lockdown measures by the likes of Donald Trump, who repeatedly stated that the "cure" (the lockdown) would be "worse than the disease" and that an economic recession would kill more than the virus,[101] and Boris Johnson, who advocated "herd immunity," namely, "allowing the disease . . . to move through the population, without taking as many draconian measures" because the "coronavirus should not be allowed to segregate the market," are not just the infamous utterances of irresponsible populist leaders.[102] They are part of a broader neoliberal "regime of truth."[103] In this regime it can be claimed that spending "billion[s] to prolong the lives of a few hundred thousand mostly elderly people is an irresponsible use of taxpayers' money" because the elderly are "for the most part in retirement, not indispensable to the country's productive effort" and ultimately, "from an entirely disinterested economic perspective, the COVID-19 pandemic might even prove mildly beneficial in the long term by disproportionately culling elderly dependents" who should sacrifice themselves to save the economy.[104] In the neoliberal secular order, it is the market that is sacred, not life: life can and must be sacrificed to preserve the existence and smooth functioning of the market.

Jamie Peck, Nik Theodore, and Neil Brenner have pointed out that "neoliberalism invariably exists in an essentially parasitical relationship with those extant social formations with which it has an antagonistic relationship, such as state socialism, social democracy, or neoconservative authoritarianism."[105] The analysis carried out in this chapter suggests that the parasitism of neoliberalism has also become a defining and still largely unrecognized feature of dominant manifestations of secularism governed by neoliberal rationalities. Neoliberal secularism has colonized its religious antagonist to the point of becoming itself "an essentially religious phenomenon."[106] Our argument complicates the existing map of secularisms by suggesting that beyond national differences and beyond societal differentiation, the triumphant logic of neoliberalism has ushered in a new historical phase in which the economization of all social domains also entails a project that deconstructs, merges, and rewrites secularism and religion as foundational categories of modernity.

Finally, our argument is also an invitation to consider the coloniality of neoliberal secularism beyond strictly geographical characterizations in which this regime of power and knowledge travels from the western "center" to the non-western "periphery." The coloniality of neoliberal secularism is also *internal* to the western episteme. It is a *self-colonialism* that blurs the distinction between economic and noneconomic, sacred and profane, religious and secular. It is this amorphous neoliberal space that future research on secularism and religion needs to confront to grasp, and possibly resist, the neoliberal manifestations, transformations, and transmutations of secularism.

NOTES

1. Karl Marx, "Towards a Critique of Hegel's Philosophy of Right: Introduction," in *Karl Marx: Selected Writings*, ed. David McLellan (Oxford: Oxford University Press, 2000[1844]), 71–82; Max Weber, *The Protestant Ethic and the Spirit of Capitalism*, trans. Talcott Parsons (New York: Courier Dover Publications, 2003[1905]).

2. Jürgen Habermas, "Notes on a Post-Secular Society," Signandsight.com, June 18, 2007, http://www.signandsight.com/features/1714.html; Habermas,

Between Naturalism and Religion: Philosophical Essays (Cambridge: Polity Press, 2008); Jürgen Habermas et al., *An Awareness of What Is Missing: Faith and Reason in a Post-Secular Age* (Cambridge: Polity Press, 2011).

3. Giorgio Agamben, *Profanations*, trans. Jeff Fort (New York: Zone Books, 2007), 80–85; Joseph D. Stiglitz, "Moving beyond Market Fundamentalism to a More Balanced Economy," *Annals of Public and Cooperative Economics* 80, no.3 (2009): 345–60; Pope Francis, *Evangelii gaudium* (2013), http://www.vatican.va/evangelii-gaudium/en/files/assets/basic-html/page1.html; Fred Block and Margaret R. Somers, *The Power of Market Fundamentalism: Karl Polanyi's Critique* (Cambridge, MA: Harvard University Press, 2014); Luca Mavelli, *Neoliberal Citizenship: Sacred Markets, Sacrificial Lives* (Oxford: Oxford University Press, 2022); Mavelli, "Neoliberalism as Religion: Sacralization of the Market and Post-Truth Politics," *International Political Sociology* 14, no. 1 (2020): 57–76.

4. Joel Robbins, "The Globalization of Pentecostal and Charismatic Christianity," *Annual Review of Anthropology* 33 (2004): 117–43; José Casanova, "Global Catholicism and the Politics of Civil Society," *Sociological Inquiry* 66, no. 3 (1996): 356–73.

5. Kate Bowler, *Blessed: A History of the American Prosperity Gospel* (Cary, NC: Oxford University Press, 2013); William Connolly, "The Evangelical-Capitalist Resonance Machine," *Political Theory* 33, no. 6 (2005): 869–86; John Milbank, "Stale Expressions: The Management-Shaped Church," *Studies in Christian Ethics* 21, no. 1 (2008): 117–28; Robert Weller, "Living at the Edge: Religion, Capitalism, and the End of the Nation-State in Taiwan," *Public Culture* 12, no. 2 (2000): 477–98.

6. Bethany Moreton, *To Serve God and Wal-Mart* (Cambridge, MA: Harvard University Press, 2009).

7. Mona Atia, *Building a House in Heaven: Pious Neoliberalism and Islamic Charity in Egypt* (Minneapolis: University of Minnesota Press, 2013).

8. Jeremy Carrette and Richard King, *Selling Spirituality: The Silent Takeover of Religion* (London: Routledge, 2005).

9. David A. Harvey, "A Brief History of Neoliberalism (New York: Oxford University Press, 2007), 16, 165–69. For a critique, see Pierre Dardot and Christian Laval, *The New Way of the World: On Neoliberal Society* (London: Verso, 2013).

10. Michel Foucault, *The Birth of Biopolitics: Lectures at the Collège de France, 1978–1979*, trans. Graham Burchell (Basingstoke: Palgrave Macmillan, 2008), 16.

11. Wendy Brown, *Undoing the Demos: Neoliberalism's Stealth Revolution* (New York: Zone Books, 2015), 31; Foucault, *The Birth of Biopolitics*, 242; Dardot and Laval, *The New Way of the World*, 17.

12. Gisela Carrasco Miró, "Encountering the Colonial: Religion in Feminism and the Coloniality of Secularism," *Feminist Theory* 21, no.1 (2020): 96.

13. Linda Martín Alcoff, "Mignolo's Epistemology of Coloniality," *The New Centennial Review* 7, no. 3 (2007): 79–101. On the "coloniality of power," see Aníbal Quijano, "Coloniality of Power, Eurocentrism, and Latin America,"

Nepantla: Views from the South 1, no. 3 (2000): 533–80; see also Walter D. Mignolo, "Introduction: Coloniality of Power and De-Colonial Thinking," *Cultural Studies* 21, no. 2–3 (2007): 155–67.

14. Aníbal Quijano, "Colonialidad del Poder, Cultura y Conocimiento en America Latina," *Anuario Mariateguiano* 9, no. 9 (1997): 17; cited in Walter Mignolo, *Local Histories/Global Designs: Coloniality, Subaltern Knowledges, and Border Thinking* (Princeton, NJ: Princeton University Press, 2000). For an analysis of the colonial/religion nexus, particularly in relation to missionizing, see Lynch (chapter 5) in this volume.

15. Étienne Balibar, *We, the People of Europe? Reflections on Transnational Citizenship* (Princeton, NJ: Princeton University Press, 2004), x. Our chapter thus focuses on the economic rationalities of neoliberalism and their relevance for the internal "reduplication" of the logic of coloniality. For a discussion of political liberalism and its relationship with coloniality and modernity, see Slabodsky (chapter 1), Fadil (chapter 2), and Sayyid (chapter 3) in this volume.

16. Walter Benjamin, "Capitalism as Religion," in *Walter Benjamin: Selected Writings*, Vol. 1 *1913–1926*, ed. Marcus Bullock and Michael W. Jennings (Cambridge, MA: Harvard University Press, 2004[1921]), 288–91.

17. Agamben, *Profanations*, 81.

18. Ibid.

19. Ibid., 82.

20. See Mignolo, *Local Histories/Global Designs*.

21. Talal Asad, *Formations of the Secular: Christianity, Islam, Modernity* (Stanford, CA: Stanford University Press, 2003); Elizabeth Shakman Hurd, *The Politics of Secularism in International Relations* (Princeton, NJ: Princeton University Press, 2009); Erin Wilson, *After Secularism: Rethinking Religion in Global Politics* (Basingstoke: Palgrave Macmillan, 2012).

22. Talal Asad, *Genealogies of Religion: Discipline and Reasons of Power in Christianity and Islam* (Baltimore: John Hopkins University Press, 1993); Peter Beyer, *Religions in Global Society* (Abingdon: Routledge, 2006); Timothy Fitzgerald, *The Ideology of Religious Studies* (Oxford: Oxford University Press, 2000); Saba Mahmood, "Secularism, Hermeneutics, and Empire: The Politics of Islamic Reformation," *Public Culture* 18, no. 2 (2006): 323–47; Tomoko Masuzawa, *The Invention of World Religions: Or, How European Universalism Was Preserved in the Language of Pluralism* (Chicago: University of Chicago Press, 2005); Brent Nongbri, *Before Religion: A History of a Modern Concept* (New Haven, CT: Yale University Press, 2013).

23. Nilüfer Göle, "Manifestations of the Secular-Religious Divide: State, Self and the Public Sphere," in *Comparative Secularisms in a Global Age*, ed. Linell E. Cady and Elizabeth Shakman Hurd (Basingstoke: Palgrave Macmillan, 2010), 44.

24. Linell E. Cady, "Reading Secularism through a Theological Lens," in Cady and Hurd, eds., *Comparative Secularisms in a Global Age*, 247–64; Göle,

"Manifestations of the Secular-Religious Divide"; Peter van der Veer, "Smash Temples, Burn Books: Comparing Secularist Projects in India and China," in *Rethinking Secularism*, ed. Craig Calhoun, Mark Juergensmeyer, and Jonathan Van Antwerpen (Oxford: Oxford University Press, 2011), 270–81.

25. Göle, "Manifestations of the Secular-Religious Divide," 134–46.

26. Abdullahi Ahmed An-Na'im, "Islam and Secularism," in Cady and Hurd, eds., *Comparative Secularisms in a Global Age*, 3–24; Cady, "Reading Secularism through a Theological Lens."

27. Part 2 of Linell E. Cady and Elizabeth Shakman Hurd, eds., *Comparative Secularisms in a Global Age*; see chapters by Bhargava, Stepan, Katzenstein, Madsen, and van der Veer, in Calhoun, Juergensmeyer, and VanAntwerpen, eds., *Rethinking Secularism*.

28. Cady and Hurd, "Comparative Secularisms and the Politics of Modernity: An Introduction," in Cady and Hurd, eds., *Comparative Secularisms in a Global Age*, 7; Michael Warner, Jonathan VanAntwerpen, and Craig J. Calhoun, eds., *Varieties of Secularism in a Secular Age* (Cambridge, MA: Harvard University Press, 2013).

29. David Lyon, "Book Review of *Varieties of Secularism in a Secular Age*," *Canadian Journal of Sociology* 35, no. 3 (2010): 474.

30. Asad, *Formations of the Secular*, 5.

31. Ronaldo Munck, "Neoliberalism as Politics, and the Politics of Neoliberalism," in *Neoliberalism: A Critical Reader*, ed. Alfredo Saad-Filho and Deborah Johnston (London: Pluto Press, 2005), 60–69.

32. Brown, *Undoing the Demos*, 27.

33. Rainer Bauböck, "What Is Wrong with Selling Citizenship? It Corrupts Democracy!," in *Should Citizenship Be for Sale?*, ed. Ayelet Shachar and Rainer Bauböck (EUI Working Papers, 2014/01), 19.

34. Mavelli, *Neoliberal Citizenship*; see also Luca Mavelli, "Citizenship for Sale and the Neoliberal Political Economy of Belonging," *International Studies Quarterly* 62, no. 3 (2018): 482–93.

35. Michael Taggart, "The Nature and Function of the State," in *The Oxford Handbook of Legal Studies*, ed. Peter Cane and Mark Tushnet (Oxford: Oxford University Press, 2003), 101.

36. John Glenn, *Globalization: North–South Perspectives* (London: Routledge, 2007), 128; see also Philip G. Cerny, "Structuring the Political Arena: Public Goods, States and Governance in a Globalizing World," in *Global Political Economy: Contemporary Theories*, ed. Ronen Palan (New York: Routledge, 2000), 21–35.

37. Max Weber, "Religious Rejections of the World and Their Directions," in *From Max Weber: Essays in Sociology*, ed. Hans H. Gerth, and C. Wright Mills (Oxford: Oxford University Press, 1991[1915]) 323–62; Weber, "Science as a Vocation" (1915), in Gerth and Mills, eds., *From Max Weber*, 129–57.

38. Weber, "Religious Rejections of the World and Their Directions," 331.

39. Peter Beyer, "Conceptions of Religion: On Distinguishing Scientific, Theological, and 'Official' Meanings," *Social Compass* 50, no. 2 (2003): 141–60.

40. Jonathan Z. Smith, *Imagining Religion: From Babylon to Jonestown* (Chicago: University of Chicago Press, 1982), xi.

41. Beyer, "Conceptions of Religion."

42. Beyer, *Religions in Global Society*, 36.

43. Ibid., 29–49.

44. See, for example, John Locke, *A Letter Concerning Toleration* (Indianapolis: Hackett, 1983[1689]); Elizabeth Shakman Hurd, "International Politics after Secularism," *Review of International Studies* 38, no. 5 (2012): 943–61; Elizabeth Shakman Hurd, *Beyond Religious Freedom: The New Global Politics of Religion* (Princeton, NJ: Princeton University Press, 2017); Atalia Omer, "When 'Good Religion' Is Good," *Journal of Religious and Political Practice* 4, no. 1 (2018): 122–36.

45. For example, Jürgen Habermas, "Religious Tolerance—the Pacemaker for Cultural Rights," *Philosophy* 79, no. 307 (2004): 5–18.

46. Michael Walzer, "Citizenship," in *Political Innovation and Conceptual Change*, ed. Terence Ball, James Farr, and Russell L. Hanson (Cambridge: Cambridge University Press, 1989), 211–19.

47. Jean-Jacques Rousseau, *The Social Contract* and *The First and Second Discourses*, ed. Susan Dunn (New Haven, CT: Yale University Press, 2002[1762]), 245–53; Robert Bellah, "Civil Religion in America," *Daedalus* 96, no. 1 (1967): 1–21.

48. For example, Richard Dawkins, *The God Delusion* (London: Transworld, 2006); Sam Harris, *The End of Faith: Religion, Terror and the Future of Reason* (London: Simon & Schuster, 2005).

49. Philip Mirowski and Dieter Plehwe, eds., *The Road from Mont Pèlerin: The Making of the Neoliberal Thought Collective* (Cambridge, MA: Harvard University Press, 2009); Jamie Peck, "Remaking Laissez-Faire," *Progress in Human Geography* 31, no. 1 (2008): 3–43.

50. Adam Gaffney, *To Heal Humankind: The Right to Health in History* (London: Routledge, 2017), 124.

51. Nicholas Gane, "The Emergence of Neoliberalism: Thinking through and beyond Michel Foucault's Lectures on Biopolitics," *Theory, Culture & Society* 31, no. 4 (2014): 3–27.

52. Ludwig von Mises, *Human Action: A Treatise on Economics*, 4th ed. (San Francisco: Fox and Wilkes, 1996[1949]), 315.

53. Ibid., 146.

54. Ibid., 144.

55. Ibid., 152–53, 693.

56. Ibid., 148.

57. Ibid., 153–55

58. Ibid., 147.

59. Ludwig von Mises, *Liberalism: The Classical Tradition*, ed. Bettina Bien Grieves (Indianapolis: Liberty Fund, 2005), 33.

60. Mises, *Human Action*, 155.

61. Ibid., 156.

62. Ibid., 155.

63. Ibid., 724–30.

64. Ibid., 729.

65. Ibid., 147–48.

66. Ibid., 157.

67. Ibid., 155.

68. Mises, *Liberalism*, 33.

69. Mises, *Human Action*, 154, 178–84.

70. Charles Taylor, "A Catholic Modernity?," in *A Catholic Modernity? Charles Taylor's Marianist Award Lecture*, ed. James L. Heft (Oxford: Oxford University Press, 1999), 13–38.

71. Mises, *Liberalism*.

72. Friedrich Hayek, *Individualism and Economic Order* (Chicago: University of Chicago Press, 1948), 2.

73. Friedrich Hayek, *The Constitution of Liberty*, ed. Ronald Hamowy (Chicago: University of Chicago Press, 2011[1960]), 528.

74. Friedrich Hayek, *The Fatal Conceit: The Errors of Socialism*, ed. W. W. Bartley III (London: Routledge, 1988), 137.

75. Ibid., 135–40.

76. Ibid., 11–20.

77. Ibid., 11–28, 48–64.

78. Ibid., 135–42.

79. Ibid., 138.

80. Ibid., 14.

81. Ibid., 137 (emphasis original).

82. Ibid., 138.

83. Jeremy Walker and Melinda Cooper, "Genealogies of Resilience: From Systems Ecology to the Political Economy of Crisis Adaptation," *Security Dialogue* 42, no. 2 (2011): 149.

84. Friedrich August Hayek, *Friedrich A. von Hayek Interviewed by Earlene Craver, Axel Leijonhufvud, Leo Rosten, Jack High, James Buchanan, Robert Bork, Thomas Hazlett, Armen Alchian, and Robert Chitester*, Oral History Program University of California, Los Angeles, 1978, UCLA Library, https://static.library.ucla.edu/oralhistory/text/masters/21198-zz0008zd21-4-master.html?_ga=2.1250 41802.1475096235.1701957426-1135896703.1701957426; Hayek, *Law, Legislation and Liberty: A New Statement of the Liberal Principles of Justice and Political Economy* (London: Routledge, 1998), 5; Hayek, *The Road to Serfdom* (Abingdon:

Routledge, 2005[1944]), 210. Hayek remarks: "Mises remained to the end a utilitarian rationalist. I came to the conclusion that both utilitarianism as a philosophy and the idea of it—that we were guided mostly by rational calculations—just would not be true. That [has] led me to my latest development, on the insight that we largely had learned certain practices which were efficient without really understanding why we did it; so that it was wrong to interpret the economic system on the basis of rational action. It was probably much truer that we had learned certain rules of conduct which were traditional in our society. As for why we did, there was a problem of selective evolution rather than rational construction"; Hayek interviewed by Jack High, cited in Alan Ebenstein, *Hayek's Journey: The Mind of Friedrich Hayek* (New York: Palgrave, 2016), 54.

85. Friedrich A. Hayek, "The Pretence of Knowledge," *American Economic Review* 79, no. 6 (1989): 3–7.

86. Ibid.

87. Hayek, *The Fatal Conceit*.

88. Hayek, *The Road to Serfdom*, 205.

89. Friedrich A. Hayek, "The Theory of Complex Phenomena," in *Studies in Philosophy, Politics and Economics* (London: Routledge and Kegan Paul, 1967), 22–42; see also Walker and Cooper, "Genealogies of Resilience."

90. Theodore A. Burczak, "The Postmodern Moments of F. A. Hayek's Economics," *Economics & Philosophy* 10, no. 1 (1994): 32.

91. Jack Amariglio, "Economics as a Postmodern Discourse," in *Economics as Discourse*, ed. Warren Samuels (Boston: Kluwer Academic, 1990), 18; cited in Burczak, "The Postmodern Moments," 33.

92. Hayek, "The Pretence of Knowledge," 137.

93. Ibid.

94. Ibid.

95. Ibid.

96. Friedrich Hayek, *Individualism and Economic Order* (Chicago: University of Chicago Press, 1948), 101; cited in Burczak, "The Postmodern Moments," 49.

97. Néstor Míguez, Joerg Rieger, and Jung Mo Sung, *Beyond the Spirit of Empire: Theology and Politics in a New Key* (London: SCM Press, 2009), 82.

98. Robert Leeson, *Hayek: A Collaborative Biography: Part VII* (New York: Palgrave, 2017), 56.

99. See also Mavelli, *Neoliberal Citizenship*; and Mavelli, "Neoliberalism as Religion."

100. David Graeber and Thomas Piketty, "Soak the Rich," *The Baffler*, no. 25, July 25, 2014, https://thebaffler.com/odds-and-ends/soak-the-rich; Ivan Petrella, *Beyond Liberation Theology: A Polemic* (London: SCM Press, 2008), 127. Jamie Peck, Nik Theodore, and Neil Brenner, "Postneoliberalism and Its Malcontents," *Antipode* 41, no. s1 (2010): 99; Stiglitz, "Moving beyond Market Fundamentalism," 346; see also Fred Block and Margaret R. Somers, *The Power*

of Market Fundamentalism: Karl Polanyi's Critique (Cambridge, MA: Harvard University Press, 2014).

101. Maggie Haberman and David E. Sanger, "Trump Says Coronavirus Cure Cannot 'Be Worse Than the Problem Itself,'" *New York Times*, March 23, 2020, https://www.nytimes.com/2020/03/23/us/politics/trump-coronavirus-restrictions.html.

102. Charlie Cooper and Ashleigh Furlong, "Going Viral: Boris Johnson Grapples to Control Coronavirus Message," *Politico*, March, 16, 2020, https://www.politico.eu/article/going-viral-british-prime-minister-boris-johnson-grapples-to-control-coronavirus-covid19-message/.

103. Michel Foucault, *Power/Knowledge: Selected Interviews and Other Writings, 1972–1977* (New York: Pantheon Books, 1980), 131.

104. See Toby Young, "Has the Government Overreacted to the Coronavirus Crisis?," *The Critic*, March 17, 2020, https://thecritic.co.uk/has-the-government-over-reacted-to-the-coronavirus-crisis/. Giovanni Toti, president of Italy's northern Liguria region, cited in Frances D'Emilio, "Salvini: 'In Graying Italy, the Old Defy Biases Laid Bare by Pandemic," AP News, January 2, 2021, https://apnews.com/article/international-news-pandemics-italy-coronavirus-pandemic-rome-fefe4c3814aafd09da55cf7ac02f932f; Jeremy Warner, "Does the Fed Know Something the Rest of Us Do Not with Its Panicked Interest Rate Cut?," *The Telegraph*, March 3, 2020, https://www.telegraph.co.uk/business/2020/03/03/does-fed-know-something-rest-us-do-not-panicked-interest-rate/. Texas lieutenant governor Dan Patrick, cited in Lois Beckett, "Older People Would Rather Die Than Let Covid-19 Harm US Economy—Texas Official," *The Guardian*, March 24, 2020, https://www.theguardian.com/world/2020/mar/24/older-people-would-rather-die-than-let-covid-19-lockdown-harm-us-economy-texas-official-dan-patrick.

105. Peck, Theodore, and Brenner, "Postneoliberalism and Its Malcontents," 104.

106. Benjamin, "Capitalism as Religion," 288.

PART II

Challenging Colonial Paradigms

Nationalisms and Humanitarianism at the Edges of Modernity

CHAPTER 5

Modernist Epistemological Webs

The Complex Legacies of Missionizing and Humanitarianism for Decolonizing Religion in Africa

CECELIA LYNCH

Abstract

This chapter marks an important intervention in emerging discussions about "decolonizing religion," particularly in African contexts and with an emphasis on humanitarian praxis. The manifold interlocking violences of colonization and missionizing have done significant harm to African religions, leaving a complex and varied landscape. Despite selective forms of engagement with "traditional" and "Indigenous" religions, both religious and secular forms of postcolonial humanitarianism perpetuate colonial and missionizing violences across epistemic and ontological registers—with profound material and sociopolitical consequences for the populations they claim to serve. Foregrounding examples of burial customs, efforts to eradicate female circumcision, and colonial suppression and/or co-optation of native languages and healing practices, this chapter charts a range of impositions, accommodations, and resistances that complicate any easy claims about the forms that "decolonizing religion" might take across the African continent.

In this chapter, I question any fixed results for the project of "decolonizing religion" in contexts across much of the African continent, even while I emphasize the need to explore ontological and epistemological possibilities raised by such a project.[1] In using these terms, I am referring to the possibilities of understanding ways of being and knowing that differ from those shaped by what we might call the "modernist project," that is, centering the human as the focus of agency and value in global relations, emphasizing the belief in and necessity of linear "progress" toward specific developmentalist ends, and reinforcing confidence in particular modes of scientific inquiry and measurement toward those ends. These aspects of the modernist project can be contrasted to those of other "onto-epistemologies" or "cosmologies"—ones that connect ways of being and knowing to situate humans as one form of value and agency in a broader universe marked by "worldviews and spiritualities" that presuppose human/nonhuman and cross-temporal forms of relationality, and that value ecological well-being.[2] My analysis is shaped by my work on humanitarianism and religion, and my observations about historical and ongoing forms of suppression of African religions, on the one hand, and extraction and commodification of their features, on the other. European colonization and Middle Eastern missionizing in Africa are dual sides of an interventionist coin; their lasting effects are coloniality and the spread of Weberian "world religions," such as Christianity and Islam.[3] Religion itself, in postcolonial societies, preceded colonialism (even taking into account the modern origins of "religion" as a category).[4] As a result, decolonizing religion in postcolonial sites entails, as Atalia Omer and Joshua Lupo write in the introduction to this volume, "the reclaiming of land *along with* cultural practices, epistemologies, and ways of knowing that decenter the western European and Christian-centric universalizing, yet parochial, epistemes." Teasing out some of the issues in contemporary religious/humanitarian interactions vis-à-vis Africa demonstrates the complexity of that task.

My reflection here probes constructions of "traditional" or "Indigenous" religion in ways that call into question the developmentalist logics of "colonial religion." It also raises questions about the definition, content, and possibilities of "decolonized" religion. I do so by examining connections between colonial and missionary legacies and humanitarian trends in relations between the Global North and Africa. Focusing on the enduring yet dynamic character of African religious traditions that preceded colonialism, I examine ways in which contemporary postcolonial humanitarianism, including both its religious and "secular" components, continues to ignore and delegitimize practices, memories, and commitments to indigeneity, while simultaneously attempting to learn about and appropriate aspects of them. The legacy of cosmological and onto-epistemological violence done by European colonialism and European and Middle Eastern missionizing to African religious traditions is extensive, but it did not and could not exterminate them.[5] At the same time, African religious traditions do not and have never remained static, "cultural" forms. Taken together, they have produced a range of accommodations that may be difficult to categorize, complicating the analysis of decoloniality. This is true even with the reconfiguration of modernity as relationality proposed by Santiago Slabodsky (chapter 1 in this volume).

After an initial discussion of the early modern development of the colonial/religion nexus (emphasizing its slotting of indigeneity into relatively strong premodern/modern categories in Africa), I discuss several historical and contemporary issues that indicate the complexity of enacting decolonial praxis in contexts of clashes between "colonial" and "African" religions. These include tensions over rites of passage and healing. I address their connections to themes of modernity, "secularism," and geospatial hierarchies examined by other contributions to this volume, but more specifically I connect these issues to processes and practices of global humanitarianism and its missionary antecedents. The fact that African religions are dynamic and not ahistorical, interacting with these issues and humanitarian trends, further complicates the definition and content of "decolonial religion." In the end, the cautionary note I put forth in this chapter is in a dialectical relationship with the possibilities outlined by those at the forefront of attempts to decolonize religion.

A Note on Positionality

In investigating the possibilities of decolonizing religion in Africa, the scholarship and ideas of African scholars must of course be prioritized. As a white female scholar[6] with a Catholic upbringing in the United States, I do not purport to articulate what the content of decolonial religion in Africa (or anywhere) should be. This positionality means that my knowledge and access to forms of spirituality and religion on the continent are etic, that is, that of an outsider. Through working with my colleagues on the *Critical Investigations into Humanitarianism in Africa* (*CIHA*) blog over the past fifteen years, I have been privileged to discuss aspects of the layered legacies of religious encounters on the African continent. Still, my own perspective is of necessity partial, even though no single perspective, including those of African nationals, can be all-encompassing given the vastness of experience as well as the complexity and richness of religious expression across the continent. Outsider (in this case, western) perspectives can be useful in making new observations for analysis, particularly if they interrogate unequal western and African relations of power, but they should not dominate the narratives and be seen as conclusive. In my case, there are potentially interesting points of access (I say "potentially" to indicate the tentativeness of this claim), primarily from growing up with a strong sense of (transplanted Irish) Catholic religiosity, including praying for the intercession of a panoply of saints with different characteristics for different causes. Thus, the idea that spirituality extends into the everyday was never foreign to me. Curiosity about the nature of missionary Catholicism in my formative years (Mass included at least annual appearances by missionary priests), family devotion to the Marian tradition and a range of saints with different spiritual endowments, and diasporically colored connections to Irish folklore and Celtic spirituality, also likely contribute to my ongoing desire to explore "Indigenous" religious cosmologies. In addition to my work and collaborations with colleagues on the *CIHA* blog, my positionality also includes being a scholar of humanitarianism and religion who has conducted research in Africa, the Middle East, and Europe for the past fifteen years.[7] My intention, therefore, is to raise questions stemming from these points of interest and potential access.

"Religion" as a Modern, Contested Category: Implications for Decoloniality

The concept of "religion" is of course a heavily contested one. Numerous critical interlocutors see it as a parochial, ethnocentric, and Eurocentric category, tracing its historical origins to early modern Europe and its genealogy to Christian traditions of (1) differentiation yet symbiosis with western secularism, (2) sets of practices and beliefs infused by Christian understandings of temporality, politics, scriptural hermeneutics, and history, and (3) inapplicability to societies where the good/evil/politics/

society/hierarchy/family/public/private tend to be overtly fused in everyday practice.

I appreciate the critique of religion as a category and agree with much of it, especially the idea that the rise of something we now call "secularism" has many variants, is historically specific within different parts of the world, and is not politically neutral. But in my view the difference between "pre modern" and "modern" practices and norms regarding the personal/political, public/private, religion/culture was never as socially bounded as critics of modernity have tended to assume.[8] These critics include scholars of modernity, religion, and secularism, from Talal Asad and Saba Mahmood to Charles Taylor.[9] The conventional story about modernity is that, in Europe, individual reason and corresponding conceptions of rights progressively replaced communal thinking and corresponding communal duties. In this story, the categories of public and private (along with political and personal) increasingly distinguish areas that should be publicly "governed" from those that should be beyond any authority but the individual's own. Discursive recognition of the individual and private spheres of action have certainly increased with modernity, but other aspects of the premodern/modern dichotomy are more difficult to substantiate. For example, a major corollary for the premodern story is that people did not follow their own inclinations, that is, did not act out of individual interests or motivations, but instead behaved in ways that inevitably followed religiously derived communal norms. Strong categories of public and private in the premodern period made little sense in this story because divine authority reached into every area of life, from the subconscious to interpersonal family relations to governance by lords, kings, and the pope.[10]

Left unexamined in these narrative constructs, however, is how and why vociferous debates took place in the premodern era about the interpretation of religious mandates, for example, as demonstrated by the monastic reform movements spanning many centuries; or the women who refused to adhere to religious dictates, many of whom were then castigated as "witches"; and how and why forms of spirituality, even within Europe, incorporated and embodied a range of spiritualities (examples include Celtic, Umbrian, Arctic). In short, the conventional narrative slides over questions regarding how and why multiple cosmological and political orientations jostled and coexisted, sometimes becoming constitutive of each other.[11] The modern era has not put an end to such coexistence and jostling, as merely scratching the surface of

Indigenous thought can demonstrate. Moreover, contra Taylor,[12] for many people even within Europe and North America, the expectation or mandate that one should believe in a certain way according to the precepts and authority of a certain tradition (including secular/religious hybrids, as in the Nordic countries) far outweighs any conscious "choice" that scholars may think people have in the matter. And even for those who affirm such a choice, either in the name of secularism or in the name of a religious tradition, other pressures at the intersection of public and private realms of life remain.

Thinking through this issue—the conventional temporal bifurcation of "premodernity" and "modernity"—is important for thinking about decolonial possibilities, both in Africa and elsewhere in the world. In particular, lessening this temporal binary opens the way to forms of being that both support and contrast with "modern" understandings (e.g., of property and ideas about the importance of individual reason). For example, early modern precepts of *terra nullius* and the fifteenth-century papal "doctrine of discovery" that were employed by both missionaries and colonizers around the globe show linkages that perpetuated not only sovereign territorial competition, but also "liberal" notions linking "rational use" to rights to property (i.e., property rightly belongs to those who use it for "rational" productive purposes).[13] At the same time, investigating the complex historical layers involved in religious and secular humanitarianism in the present exposes the tenuous legitimacy of these notions. Reifying the modernist tale, therefore, risks stiffening definitions of religion that already mask its dynamism within and across historical periods. In other words, viewing religious/political developments as dynamic and difficult to confine to "eras" opens the way to recognizing the elements of "indigeneity" and "traditional religion" that (though also dynamic) have always been there.

What Was/Is "Colonial Religion"?

The simple answer to this question is that the content of "colonial" religion was crafted and disseminated by those who colonized the African continent. As a result, Christian missionaries have the strongest claim to colonial religion. Christianity is generally tied to successive waves of European colonization across most of the continent, despite its ancient roots in and around Egypt and Ethiopia. Still, missionaries varied in their commitment to European versions of Christianity (Methodism, Presbyterianism, Catholicism, Anglicanism, Lutheranism, Baptism, etc.), and their openness to inclusionary or even syncretist understandings of their faith.

Islam, in contrast, arrived across North Africa and the Sahel in the ninth century. Waves of Muslim traders crossed North Africa and the Sahel (medieval African kingdoms fusing forms of Islam and African religion), and the Ottoman Empire took over much of present-day North Africa. These religious forms then became part of northern African and Sahelian power struggles, resulting in modes of internal coloniality that differed considerably from Christian-European configurations.[14] The spread of Islam to other regions has been more recent—for example, the British brought South Asian Muslim and Hindu laborers to eastern and southern Africa in the nineteenth and early twentieth centuries to construct much of its imperial infrastructure. Nevertheless, though Islam has an extensive historical and geographic reach across much of the continent that is not exclusively tied to conquest, it is still considered a "foreign" religion by some African groups.[15]

More recently, newer Islamic movements have intentionally proselytized and evangelized on the continent. "Reformist" Salafis and variants from Saudi Arabia and elsewhere in Southwest Asia/North Africa, for example, have been attempting to reverse the influence of the Sufi brotherhoods of West Africa and the Sahel. Some of the latter (e.g., the Mouride brotherhood) originated in tandem with French colonialism, with a complex relationship of resistance and accommodation to colonial authorities in the midst of their own consolidation of their religious objectives.[16] Similarly, the contemporary proselytizing and evangelizing by Evangelical and Pentecostal Christians (foreign and African) overlays an already complex matrix of religious humanitarian outreach. Many of the Christian organizations in this matrix eschew proselytizing, but some do not.[17] Christian-African hybrids and Muslim-African syncretic traditions are also common in much of the continent.[18] These contexts, therefore, suggest that there is no "pure" form of decolonial religion, and that even determining its boundaries is not a simple task.

The discussion thus far suggests that the place of "Indigenous" or "traditional" religions in Africa is one of ongoing conceptualization and excavation. The term "traditional" religion has perhaps caught on more in

Africa than elsewhere to distinguish it especially from mainline Catholic and Protestant Christianity and also Islam. This is seemingly in part because of the relatively recent colonization and decolonization of the continent as compared to Latin America or South Asia. Christian theologians, especially, often use the acronym "ATR" (African Traditional Religion) to denote religious traditions existing before Christianity.[19] Some, however, reject the "traditional" adjective for its connotations of something static that lacks coevality, and prefer "African religion" instead. Finally, the terms "indigeneity" and "Indigenous religion" are used less commonly across the continent, but the UN and the African Development Bank recognize the San, Maasai, and Amazigh (among others) as Indigenous.[20]

Because I am interested in connections between mission/colonial trajectories and the humanitarian present in this contribution, I focused in this section on (1) the historical legacy of Christian missionizing and Islamic expansion, the latter primarily through trade, across the African continent, but with ongoing missionizing by sects of both religious traditions; and (2) the resistances and partial accommodations to that missionizing and expansion, resulting in numerous reinterpretations of both of these major traditions and of more geographically contained, "Indigenous" ones. However, I do not mean to suggest that any of these religious traditions is merely a product of colonialism. The less simple answer to the question, "What was/is colonial religion?" therefore, must acknowledge that many African Christians and Muslims are less interested in excavating missionary pasts than in claiming and interpreting their religious traditions for their concerns in the present. In other words, they do not necessarily see their present commitments as shaped by the colonial past. As a result, even though I am interested in how colonial and missionary legacies have reinforced epistemological and cosmological hierarchies, influencing the contexts in which Christian and Islamic NGOs, aided and funded by international agencies, assert difference and superiority vis-à-vis "traditional" practices, I am also keen to emphasize the difficulty of creating rigid boundaries around either "indigeneity" or "the colonial." African religious practitioners are engaged in a range of practices and commitments that embrace, reconfigure, and/or reject Islamic and Christian forms of authority. Moreover, each of these perspectives is dynamic, again making the content of decolonial religion difficult to determine.

Cosmological and Onto-Epistemological Contestations

Colonial and missionary authorities intentionally worked to discipline, suppress, and refashion African religions in the interests of conquest and conversion. Regulatory strategies had both material and cosmological targets, seeking to discipline African peoples into forms of Christianity that would also make them "proper" colonial subjects. Rites of passage (from this world to another; from childhood to adulthood) became significant sites of contestation between missionaries, colonial authorities, and advocates of African religion. Ongoing legacies include interreligious tensions over burial rites; they also include the contemporary humanitarian focus on eradicating female circumcision. In addition, colonial extraction and commodification of African resources extended to herbs and other plants used in "traditional" forms of healing, which are an important component of spiritual traditions. These issues highlight legacies of ongoing cosmological disturbance that influence contemporary humanitarianism and raise questions about aspects of the onto-epistemological damage that any decolonial attempt must confront.

Colonial strategies of conquest and repression blatantly violated African religious sensibilities and communal practices. Ngũgĩ wa Thiong'o's *Dreams in a Time of War* (2010) and *Something Torn and New* (2009) discuss the killing and dismembering of African resistance leaders by the British colonial authorities in ways that intentionally desecrated African religious burial grounds and burial rites.[21] For example, "Waiyaki wa Hinga . . . one of the most important figures in Agikuyu anticolonial resistance lore," was captured and buried alive by the British. But they "removed Waiyaki from his region," and "buried him alive at Kibwezi, head facing the bowels of earth—in opposition to the Gikuyu burial rites' requirement that the body face Mount Kenya, the dwelling place of the Supreme Deity. Similarly, in Xhosaland . . . the British captured King Hintsa of the Shosa resistance and decapitated him, taking his head to the British Museum."[22] Ngũgĩ shows how such dismembering represented intentional strategies on the part of colonial authorities, not only to subdue through epistemological and physical violence, but also to preclude re-membering. These examples indicate the cruelties involved in colonial violations of African religious practices, which prevented African peoples from carrying out respectful and ethical action according to African onto-epistemologies. Cosmological and onto-epistemological features of burial rites are also, of course, important in numerous other religious traditions, including Christianity and Islam.

Today, burial rites remain a source of active contestation, according to my interviews, discussions with colleagues and friends, and recent scholarship.[23] The cruelties of the colonial era are less in evidence, but these contestations reflect the dynamic pressures of European Christian evangelization. One Catholic priest of European origin in the Anglophone region of Cameroon told me that he engaged in dialogue with traditional authorities for community peacebuilding purposes, but concluded there was "no way of mingling the two different burial rites." He acknowledged that people who were both Catholic and traditional were "very confused at times" about what was allowed and what was not allowed in the Church. He permitted some cross-fertilization of African religion and Christianity in his own parish, but he drew the line at burials and even forbade the use of herbs as part of burial ceremonies. Colleagues from the continent have also shared experiences of tensions within families about whether to follow African or Christian burial traditions.[24]

What appears to be at stake in contemporary Christian–African contestations of burials concerns beliefs and corresponding practices that regulate modes of connection between immanent and spiritual worlds, including but not limited to the Christian promise of redemption and transcending death versus African religious responsibility to ancestors as an ongoing part of life.[25] Disputes over burials concern ways of being and acting, forms of knowledge (of self, others, of embodiment versus spirit) and cosmologies that connect temporal responsibilities to the self, other, and universe.

Tensions over burials, then, occur between practitioners of different religious traditions who interpret what forms of ethical action are required by cosmological and onto-epistemological commitments.[26] Contestation over other important rites of passage, however, especially those marking the transition from childhood to adulthood, are gendered, and reinforced by financial power and "donor proselytism" in contemporary humanitarian practice.[27] Specifically, female circumcision became a significant site of Christian condemnation and suppression in the late nineteenth and early twentieth centuries.

The missionary campaigns to eradicate female circumcision in the late nineteenth and early twentieth centuries, among other rituals with onto-epistemological significance, became especially fraught, provoking (along with other issues) the creation of "African Initiated Churches" (AICs; also called African Instituted or African Indigenous Churches). Missionaries condemned circumcision rituals, especially for girls, as religiously dangerous, physically harmful, and atavistic.

My concern here is with the first part of this condemnation: the missionaries' stance was part of a more general condemnation of rites of passage that attacked significant temporal markers of African communal and religious life. Scholarship on the debates about circumcision—see especially the work of Stanlie M. James and Claire C. Robertson[28]—have examined both the religious/cultural and the physical/ritualistic aspects of circumcision through an intersectional and transnational lens, showing the numerous biases in the assumptions of western and white feminist writings on circumcision, including those evident in missionary histories. Here, I note that female circumcision became an early example of the kinds of tensions noted by Omer and Lupo in the introduction, that is, over "reclaiming . . . cultural practices, epistemologies, and ways of knowing that decenter the western European and Christian-centric . . . epistemes."

For the past twenty years or so, moreover, the campaign against female circumcision has become secularized, receiving a new lease on life through the work of numerous NGOs and the UN. Since 1997, multiple UN agencies have condemned "female genital mutilation" (FGM; the preferred term used by the UN and NGOs to distinguish it from male circumcision),[29] and many governments on the continent have followed suit.[30] NGOs, in designing anti-FGM/FGC (female genital circumcision) programs, frame them as a central part of "saving women and girls" from a combination of African patriarchal society and/or African cultural violence. But, as Adomako Ampofo and Signe Arnfred have argued about the general trendiness of women's and girls' issues, transnational NGO and faith-based organization (FBO) campaigns tend to fund programs that promote simplistic narratives of women and girls' empowerment.[31]

Moreover, Islamic NGOs and human rights groups have joined Christians, secular NGOs, and the UN in condemning practices of FGM as "cultural" in order to distance themselves from these practices. This is because a common misconception, in their view, is that FGM is accepted and even encouraged in Islam. In opposition to this idea, Islamic Relief stated in 2019, "Islam must never be used to justify FGM."[32] Another

Muslim group representative in eastern Kenya noted: "People are holding onto traditional, cultural rights more than their religion. . . . What we are trying to do—we are coming up with a program that will pick up all the traditional practices and say this is not Islam; [or] this is Islam but this is not the way Islam says we should do it."[33] I am not claiming that circumcision itself is "religious," but I note that these examples provide yet another indication of modernist attempts to "fix" not only religious boundaries, but also religious hierarchies.

In countering the narrative connecting FGM to Islam, Muslim groups both reinforce their own religious and humanitarian *bona fides* and increase their standing as legitimate, significant, and "modern" religious voices on the African continent. And by reinforcing their own religious standing and referring to such practices as "cultural," they, along with Christian and secular groups, distinguish themselves from African religious communities, for whom rites of passage are key. But isolating and pathologizing specific aspects of these rites also provokes backlash. For example, when I visited a Maasai community in southern Kenya, the two young men who met me at the entrance to the village had barely introduced themselves when they warned me that they would not discuss FGC. I said that I had not planned to ask them about FGC, to which they responded that Christian groups were always coming to lecture them about it.[34]

This experience is similar to that encountered by Islamic Relief in collaboration with four Christian and secular NGOs (Tearfund, World Vision, Christian Aid, and ABAAD), who used their programs as case studies for a report done through the Joint Learning Initiative on Faith & Local Communities (JLI). Funded by the British government, this part of their work concerned finding ways to work with faith communities against "harmful traditional practices," prominently including but not confined to FGM/FGC. However, the project's discursive framing ran into difficulties from the very beginning. The very first "key finding" in the report noted "the 'harm' in 'harmful traditional practices'": "The five case study organisations use the term little or not at all at community level—mainly because it creates resistance and hinders the process of engaging people in local communities to challenge injustice and violence to people, in particular women and girls."[35]

Thus, religious (Islamic and Christian) and secular NGOs have historically created onto-epistemological barriers against African religious traditions by either suppressing or condemning practices associated with communal celebrations of critical life passages. They have also at times encountered resistance to their attempts to transcend such barriers (attempts that are simultaneously reinforced by donor agencies) in their current work. Their framing complicates the work of African feminists and activists, leading to additional questions about what might constitute decolonized religion and/or decolonized humanitarianism.

The NGO Mpanzi, for example, works to prevent FGC through an empathetic understanding of the meaning of the rite of passage and discussion about alternate forms of celebrating it. This organization, founded by Kenyan Jackie Ogega, provides a different model for engaging "traditional" societies and religious norms, relying strongly on community-based onto-epistemologies and on lessons drawn from Ogega's own experience with FGC. Ogega notes that "the cutting is only one component of the rituals undertaken as a rite of passage that form the cultural way of life for the Gusii. The entire rite of passage embodies, in fact, one of the most culturally valued ways of being."[36] What is at stake, therefore, are cosmologies that emphasize how to be human and how to engage in the reproduction of communal values around these ways.[37]

African feminists have frequently criticized FGM/FMC, but they have also criticized anti-FGM campaigns. Fuambai Ahmadu, for example, points out that framing FGM as harmful can also cause harm.[38] Feminist critics assert that, in isolating FGM as the primary evil faced by African women, African women are exoticized and made exclusively into victims of African patriarchal traditions, instead of agents who participate in circumcision (or other) rituals for religious or community reasons, and African "culture" as a result becomes (for those who promote anti-FGM campaigns) an example of violence toward women instead of a place of communal engagement. Moreover, Ahmadu disputes the myth that circumcised women cannot enjoy their sexuality, noting the implications of the discourse of "mutilation."[39] Jackie Ogega of Mpanzi argues that it is critical "to counter . . . [the] pathologizing of the rite of passage as a barbaric, illiterate, abnormal practice."[40] Such pathologizing, however, was at the root of former missionary campaigns against rites of passage rituals, and remains (albeit in partially different form) an important component of many contemporary NGO programs.

Knowledge Suppression and Knowledge Commodification

Primary conduits of Indigenous knowledge include language and nature, perhaps especially vegetation. Missionaries forcibly suppressed African languages in many instances, and Ngũgĩ wa Thiong'o (among many others) movingly describes how British mission schools in Kenya punished students for speaking their own languages.[41] In other cases, however, missionaries deployed African languages to reorder African spiritualities, including their ontological and cosmological assumptions, to accord with European Christian interpretations.

Because language is constitutive of onto-epistemologies (and more specifically of memory), Ngũgĩ has asserted the necessity of preserving African (and other Indigenous) languages as a primary means of decolonizing the mind.[42] But how those languages are maintained is also critical, and Ngũgĩ upholds both oral traditions and written forms of Indigenous language use. Others, however, show how the missionaries' translations of the Bible into African languages, which were intended to aid in conversion, also worked to suppress African religions. African feminist theologian Dora Mbuwayesango, for example, shows how Anglican, Methodist, and Catholic missionaries' translations of the Bible into Shona represented "in effect the religious usurpation of the Shona."[43] Such translations "fixed" specific Shona terms to understand God and human mediators of God's message to other humans, doing so in ways that closed down the more expansive Shona understandings of God (including Spirit as neither male nor female) and how God communicates with humans, and supplanting Shona monotheism with European biblical interpretations. Similarly, South African Nokuzola Mndende criticizes Christians' practice of gendering God: "If I were using my language, I would use 'U-Qamata' (God) 'U' (is), a term which is gender-neutral."[44] To do otherwise, she argues, is a "distortion" that "confuses African Christians who believe in their roots."[45]

Colonial and missionary authorities, then, have employed varying strategies vis-à-vis African languages, but almost always with the intention of suppressing African epistemologies and cosmologies. Reactions to these strategies varied, but one of the primary forms of resistance was the creation of the breakaway African Christian churches mentioned previously (AICs, referring to African Initiated Churches, African Indigenous Churches, or African Instituted Churches). AICs (primarily located in eastern, central, and southern Africa) maintain both linguistic and cosmological ties to African religions. Their independence from both Protestant and Catholic denominational control means that they pose a self-described "challenge to the ecumenical [Christian] movement."[46] In a foreword to a World Council of Churches (WCC) document on AICs—I note that the WCC includes several AIC representatives—Walter Hollenweger describes the intimate connection among forms of religious discourse, theology, and cosmology when describing differences with mainline church denominations: "The means of communication [in AICs] are not statements but stories, not theological arguments but testimonies, not definitions but participatory dance, not concepts but banquets, not systematic arguments but songs, not hermeneutical analysis but healing."[47]

Hollenweger misses the fact that there is indeed a connection between hermeneutical analysis and testimonies, healing, and stories; still, he also indicates an important openness to African onto-epistemologies: "Western theologians could have learned long ago that these categories have theological dignity."[48] Nevertheless, AICs have been largely sidelined by religious and secular humanitarians on the continent.

Before synthesizing the implications of such moves for the possibilities of decoloniality (both from the perspective of AICs and on the part of mainline European and North American church representatives), I want to discuss one additional example, concerning the threat of commodification of African knowledge about healing. Humanitarians and related actors engage in yet another, at first glance contradictory, move vis-à-vis aspects of African religion. On the one hand, its members selectively emphasize some practices (e.g., FGC/FGM) that have been labeled "harmful traditional practices," in the process exoticizing African "culture" and religion while representing their own onto-epistemology as superior. Yet, on the other hand, actors from the colonizers to those in the humanitarian international also extract and attempt to co-opt aspects of African traditions for other objectives. These purposes may include an effort to respect or even learn from "local knowledge" or "local practices,"[49] but they may also include the attempt to deploy African knowledge for pharmaceutical extraction and gains in market share.

During a December 2017 *CIHA* conference, participants (including a plurality of Senegalese scholars) toured the archives at Cheikh Anta Diop University. We saw rows and rows of carefully labeled herbs from across the African continent, collected over decades by French colonial authorities. Each herb was glued to a paper with a description of its African and French names, and a notation about its use.[50] Learning about herbs and their uses in healing is laudable, but insofar as this process becomes part of colonial (or neocolonial) extraction, it is not. Moreover, extractive forms of medical knowledge production occur today. Charles Masango, for example, notes that "most drug industries exploit medicinal properties in plants to treat illness"; as a result, western pharmaceutical companies stand to make significant profits from the knowledge of healers.[51]

The relationship between "traditional" and "conventional" forms of healing remains fraught in many parts of the world. Still, a number of medical research communities, from universities to the World Health Organization (WHO), have recognized the influence and importance of healers in the global provision of health. The WHO has worked with PROMETRA (Promotion of Traditional Medicine, headquartered in Senegal but active in many countries on the continent) to find ways to boost immunity for people with HIV/AIDS and other diseases, resulting in several collaborative projects. PROMETRA has been a willing participant in UN health forums and has become increasingly active in recent years in framing traditional medicine in ways that resonate in academic and other professional forums. For example, its website currently states that PROMETRA "works to improve the health and well-being of global communities through the use of quality traditional medicine and indigenous science and building bridges between modern and traditional systems of health care."[52] The WHO's Africa office regularly celebrates African Traditional Medicine Day on August 31 of each year; the WHO has also published a series of reports that emphasize both advancing and developing policy frameworks for traditional medicine.[53] Collaboration is constructive, but the problem of knowledge extraction and threat of commodification remains. The August 2021 message of the WHO regional director for Africa, Dr. Matshidiso Moeti, demonstrates the contradictory stance of international organizations vis-à-vis African knowledge systems in the context of addressing the COVID-19 pandemic. Moeti notes, for example, that "as part of the COVID-19 response, promising traditional medicine therapies are emerging." But the message also encourages their marketization: "Major pharmaceutical companies are also looking to Africa for new active ingredients. With the right partnerships and investment, tried-and-tested African traditional medicines could find a broad global market."[54]

Thus, contemporary collaborations between healers and humanitarians can easily slide into extractive modes of knowledge production, raising the question of to what degree African modes of healing can be separated from their cosmological and onto-epistemological (and geographically situated) purposes?

PROMETRA's website, for example, emphasizes spirituality, and promotes an organized trip to Benin as a "Way of Remembering Pilgrimage into African Spirituality."[55] The pilgrimage is intended to connect participants to ancestors and "put the universal spirituality at the Heart of Humanity." Spirituality is almost always emphasized by healers themselves. PROMETRA's international president, Dr. Erick Gbodossou, introduced our *CIHA* group to healers from central Senegal who made it clear that healing was a spiritual and religious vocation. This understanding is also in line with healers I met in eastern Kenya and Cameroon. In Kenya, I visited the town of Kilifi during a "promotion of traditional medicine day." Healers had gathered from surrounding villages to dance and drum their way through the town, ending up at the town square for more dance and music, because movement is an integral component of the healing process for body and mind. The healers then spread out their herbs and medicines to discuss their methods of healing with potential patients. In Cameroon, I met with a well-known healer who showed me various plants and their uses, but also told me that he was a priest and a healer, and that these aspects of his vocation were constitutive of each other.[56]

Healer-priests and priestesses train from generation to generation, passing down experiential and spiritual knowledge. At the same time, PROMETRA provides additional training to professionalize, to a degree, the traditional healing vocation.[57] As in language preservation, however, there is still debate regarding whether to codify healing methods to preserve them in written form for posterity. The PROMETRA website states, "When a healer dies, a library burns."[58] Traditional practitioners are all too aware of the material and religious risks involved in revealing and codifying knowledge. Masango explains: "Traditional medicines embrace herbal and nonherbal elements. While traditional healers may reveal the former, the latter may not be revealed as it involves spiritual features."[59]

These examples, then, beg questions similar to those the debates regarding rites of passage do about what constitutes decolonized religion and decolonized humanitarianism. Can African herbs be extracted from the broader healing practices of which they are a part, reflecting cosmologies and onto-epistemologies that differ starkly from those embedded in globalized extraction and marketing strategies? In what ways do such strategies "work"? For what purposes (medical, economic)? And for whose benefit—African healers/communities or the WHO and/or pharmaceutical companies? Are there permissible levels of extraction in attempts to further decolonized religion and decolonized humanitarianism? Such questions bring to the fore important contrasts in conceptions of interconnectedness by, on the one hand, neoliberal mechanisms of power and subjectivity—as addressed by Luca Mavelli and Edmund Frettingham (chapter 4) in this volume, among others—and by African religious cosmologies, on the other.

Responses and Conclusions

How questions such as the ones above are addressed has important implications for the possibility of decolonial religion. There are a range of responses from the African continent, including those discussed in the preceding sections of this chapter. I add two more kinds of responses here. First, the Centre for Constructive Theology at the University of KwaZulu-Natal (UKZN) has initiated a dialogue with representatives of AICs to discuss theological and onto-epistemological issues and the potential for collaboration. One result of this initiative was a series of lectures in September 2021 on the occasion of the 150th anniversary of the birth of J. L. Dube, a cofounder of the African National Congress (ANC), who was Christian and a member of an Indigenous community. UKZN scholars noted the tensions in this dual identity for Dube, who during his life advocated for decolonization, repossession of land, and education in order to promote "self-reliance." One speaker, Taruona Kudzai, stressed the need to decolonize ontologies, epistemologies, and medicine today, but argued that the current ANC Party had lost the political will to do so, thereby also losing touch with its roots.[60] These and other aspects of the dialogue indicate that decolonial projects also confront political tensions, and remind us once again that decolonization is an onto-epistemological, cosmological, and religious task. In other words, decolonial projects beg questions of what kinds of beings are valued and granted agency and what modes of knowledge are conceptualized and accessed to engage in politics. In turn, political projects can be interrogated regarding whether or not they engage in holistic understandings of well-being for both human and nonhuman agents.

The Afrikania movement, headquartered in Ghana, with some presence in Côte d'Ivoire and Togo, represents a second, very different kind of decolonial project. Founded by a former Catholic priest, Afrikania is based on the recovery of African religion (treated as a singular form) and the establishment of a series of beliefs and rituals to go along with it. Afrikania seeks to establish what it considers to be genuine African religion above and against colonial religious impositions. Components of this effort include creating replacement rituals for Christian sacraments and Muslim rites to commemorate birth, adulthood, marriage, and death. Communities all over the continent continue to perform these rites, but Afrikania interestingly seeks to systematize them.[61]

Afrikania is a fascinating if limited (at least thus far) response to colonial religion as it is understood in this volume, and to colonial and contemporary humanitarianism. It also represents its own type of modernist appropriation of resistance, one that includes branding of religion in the service of promotion (and proselytism). It is also modernist in its work of ahistorical categorization of what is African, what is colonial, what is "authentic," and therefore superior for Africans. Marleen de Witte writes that Afrikania provides a fascinating response to "the question of how to be an African and a modern religion at the same time,"[62] a statement that replicates assumptions that "African" and "modern" religions are incompatible. Still, Afrikania's founding in the early 1980s was anything but ahistorical, representing a partial reaction to the Ghanaian nationalism of "what has come to be known as the 'Second Coming' of [the regime of] Flight Lieutenant Jerry John Rawlings."[63] Thus, Afrikania, which over time has drawn from both Ghanaian nationalism and pan-Africanism, purports to update and modernize African religion as an integral component of contemporary African liberation from colonial religious authority.

Nevertheless, the number of Afrikania's followers appears to be quite small in comparison to the number of those who continue to juggle African/Christian or African/Muslim commitments. Afrikania, therefore, represents a minority response to the dilemma of how to decolonize religion. Is it more or less decolonial than the dialogue at UKZN, or the work of PROMETRA with the WHO? Of course, the decolonial, like other categories of analysis (and aspiration), is dynamic. But each of these movements and organizations raises dilemmas for reclamation projects that are constitutive of both material and intangible goods (i.e., land, onto-epistemologies, and cosmologies). Each suggests that decolonial projects must work through multiple layers and registers produced by historical encounters with people from Europe and the Middle East, as with Christianity and Islam, and by multiple, ongoing forms of postcolonial economic, military, and religious intervention. They also suggest that it is difficult, at best, to determine at which layer of excavation (or addition) decoloniality can arguably begin.

I have indicated in this contribution how European colonialism and European and Middle Eastern missionizing have left complicated legacies across the African continent for both religion and humanitarianism. Today, dominant religions include a range of Christianities and Islams, some reflecting African communal religious practices, others departing from them and/or condemning them. Still others represent seemingly contradictory modes of onto-epistemological and cosmological accommodation and condemnation. Humanitarian legacies include schools and health clinics, but establishing each has also created hierarchies of knowledge and of religious expression. I do not purport to answer the question of what constitutes decolonized religion, but I have attempted to show some of the ways in which contemporary humanitarianism makes the onto-epistemological excavation required for decolonial projects more difficult. Examples include the ongoing roles of "missionary religion" and the complex of humanitarian actors in disciplining rites of passage, and the material and onto-epistemological threats to African systems of healing by pharmaceutical companies, international organizations, and, potentially, NGOs. These examples show the durability of (in Slabodsky's words in chapter 1) the "relationship between the altruism of forced inclusion and the virulence of forced exclusion as partners in the construction of hier-archies of populations." Nevertheless, in such multifaceted contexts, attempts such as that by the Afrikania movement to throw off "foreign" religious influence also become constitutive of modernist epistemological webs. I cannot define what decolonial religion looks like in and for Africa or Africans, but I conclude by asserting the necessity of openness to African onto-epistemologies, cosmologies, and forms of spirituality if we are to be able to delineate and debate decolonial possibilities.

NOTES

1. I also note as a partial disclaimer that I agree with those who problematize the idea that "Africa" is a cohesive unit while also decrying attempts to create artificial barriers, for example, between "north" and "sub-Saharan" Africa. In other words, treating "Africa" as a given entity is problematic but necessary because of its historical and imaginary role in international politics. Of course, the same is true for "the west" or "the Global North," so I try (only partially successfully) to minimize my use of these terms. V. Y. Mudimbe has famously pointed out that the idea of Africa is a construction of Europeans, and "the very name of the continent is a problem"; Mudimbe, *The Idea of Africa* (Bloomington: Indiana University Press, 1994), xi.

2. Maggie Fitzgerald speaks of "onto-epistemology" to describe such ideas. See Fitzgerald, *Care and the Pluriverse, Rethinking Global Ethics* (Bristol: Bristol University Press, 2022); see also Cecelia Lynch, "Centering Global Humanitarianism in Africa," *Global Africa* 1, no. 1 (2022): 80–92.

3. Christianity existed in the Horn of Africa before successive waves of European colonization; colonization also brought Hinduism to East Africa and southern Africa. I distinguish between the historical process of colonization, which took place over several centuries in the early modern through modern periods, and "coloniality," which refers to the dynamics and mechanisms of power relations that resulted (and continue in the postcolonial period). Similarly, I distinguish between "missionizing," which refers to the processes of proselytism that were led by missionaries, primarily Christians, sometimes in advance of and sometimes following waves of colonization. Nevertheless, in much of Africa both Christianity and Islam are considered to be "missionary" religions, but the contexts and relations of power differ greatly among societies and religious traditions.

4. Regarding the modern origins of "religion" as a category, I refer to the groundbreaking work of several scholars, including Talal Asad, *Genealogies of Religion: Discipline and Reasons of Power in Christianity and Islam* (Baltimore: Johns Hopkins University Press, 1993); José Casanova, "The Secular, Secularizations, Secularisms," in *Rethinking Secularism*, ed. Craig Calhoun, Mark Juergensmeyer, and Jonathan VanAntwerpen (Oxford: Oxford University Press, 2011), 54–74; and Charles Taylor, *A Secular Age* (Cambridge, MA: Harvard University Press, 2007). Each places the origins of "religion" as a category in the early modern era, but the purpose of each in doing so differs. In each case, however, the origin of religion becomes Eurocentric, and I want both to acknowledge the development of the religious/secular binary in this era and to recognize the importance of premodern and modern systems of practice, ritual, and belief that link worlds of experience with worlds of spirits in African cosmologies.

5. The concept of "onto-epistemology" (and also ethico-onto-epistemology) has been increasingly taken up by scholars interested in the symbiosis between

ontology and epistemology, on the one hand, and ethics and the politics of knowledge construction, on the other, and by those interested in the implications of all of these interrelated concepts. See, for example, Karen Barad, who coined the term "ethico-onto-epistemology," in Barad, *Meeting the Universe Halfway: Quantum Physics and the Entanglement of Matter and Meaning* (Durham, NC: Duke University Press, 2007). See also Fitzgerald, *Care and the Pluriverse*; and Lynch, "Centering Global Humanitarianism in Africa." Onto-epistemology is very close in nature to cosmology, but the latter term also refers to understandings about the origins, development, and relationship (or interrelationship) among human and nonhuman beings in the universe. Religious traditions, then, incorporate cosmologies in different ways: a given religious tradition may strongly reflect a specific cosmology and onto-epistemology, or there may be contestation (as is currently the case in Christianity between western and non-western perspectives). As a result, cosmologies can also, like religious traditions, be syncretic in their worldly manifestations.

6. The politics of capitalization of "Black" versus "white" is tricky, as demonstrated by a brief search of news media editorial desk debates and decisions from March 2020 to the present. I have preferred in this piece to keep "white" lowercase to de-emphasize its usual status. Of course, by then drawing attention to the choice in this footnote (as requested by editors) I have perhaps undone any attempt at de-emphasis. We live in a complicated world.

7. In addition to collaborations through the *Critical Investigations into Humanitarianism in Africa (CIHA)* blog (cihablog.com), these include a project on women and religion in Cameroon funded by the Contending Modernities research initiative at the University of Notre Dame.

8. Cecelia Lynch, *Wrestling with God: Ethical Precarity in Christianity and International Relations* (Cambridge: Cambridge University Press, 2020).

9. Asad, *Genealogies of Religion*; Taylor, *A Secular Age*; Saba Mahmood, *Religious Difference in a Secular Age: A Minority Report* (Princeton, NJ: Princeton University Press, 2015); Atalia Omer, "Modernists Despite Themselves: The Phenomenology of the Secular and the Limits of Critique as an Instrument of Change," *Journal of the American Academy of Religion* 83, no. 1 (2015): 27–71. Although their purposes and focuses differ, Asad and Mahmood, on the one hand, and Taylor, on the other, analyze genealogies of early modernity to the present. Omer provides a trenchant critique of the "secularism studies" of the former.

10. In a more explicitly theological vein, proponents of the radical orthodoxy movement, such as John Milbank, *Theology and Social Theory: Beyond Secular Reason* (Malden, MA: Blackwell, 2006), and William Cavanaugh, *Theopolitical Imagination: Christian Practices of Space and Time* (London: T&T Clark, 2002), have even made the case that modernity itself is a theological heresy in need of premodern correction. That Asad and Milbank refer to each other's work in their respective scholarship is thus perhaps no coincidence.

11. I read Slabodsky's arguments in this volume to stop the "hermetically sealed" comparisons between temporal eras and geographic spaces as similar to the one I am making here.

12. Taylor, *A Secular Age*.

13. I have used similar examples to muddy the waters between premodern and modern in my own genealogical work on Christianity and international relations (see Lynch, *Wrestling with God*), and in a more recent piece calling for global humanitarianism to be recentered in Africa (see Lynch, "Centering Global Humanitarianism in Africa"). So have others, including Slabodsky in this volume.

14. Ousmane Oumar Kane, *Beyond Timbuktu: An Intellectual History of Muslim West Africa* (Cambridge, MA: Harvard University Press, 2016); Osman B. Bari, *A Comprehensive History of Muslims & Religion in Ghana*, Vol. 1 (Accra: Dezine Focus, Printing & Publications, 2009); Souley Mane, *L'islam en Pays Bamum, de Ibrahim Njoya a Ibrahim Mbombo Njoya (1895–2016)* (Paris: L'Harmattan, 2017); Elizabeth Isichei, *A History of Christianity in Africa* (Grand Rapids, MI: William B. Eerdmans, 1995).

15. For example, the Afrikania Mission, founded in Ghana in 1982 by a former Catholic priest renamed Osofo Okomfo Damuah, sees itself as pan-African traditional religion "come alive." Afrikania Mission leaders frequently call for observa-tions similar to those accorded both Christianity and Islam (for example, the call for a public holiday in Ghana), and they have created a "handbook" of teachings, which they compare (and contrast) with the Bible and Qur'an. See Ama Nunoo, "Afrikania Mission, the Neo-Traditional Movement That Champions Africanism," Face2Face Africa, June 8, 2020, https://face2faceafrica.com/article/afrikania-mission-the-neo-traditional-movement-that-champions-africanism.

16. See, for example, Khadim Mbacké, *Sufism and Religious Brotherhoods in Senegal*, trans. Eric Ross, ed. John Hunwick (Princeton, NJ: Marcus Wiener, 2005); Rüdiger Seesemann and Benjamin F. Soares, "'Being as Good Muslims as Frenchmen': On Islam and Colonial Modernity in West Africa," *Journal of Religion in Africa* 39 (2009): 91–120.

17. Cecelia Lynch and Tanya B. Schwarz, "Humanitarianism's Proselytism Problem," *International Studies Quarterly* 60, no. 4 (2016): 636–46.

18. Some of these hybrids are explicit, as in the African Initiated Churches (AIC), which I discuss below, but others are covert, as reflected by one of my interlocutors, who said that people go to the healer and don't tell the priest, and go to the priest but don't tell the healer (Mamfe, Cameroon, January 2007).

19. Mercy Amba Oduyoye, *Introducing African Women's Theology* (Sheffield: Sheffield Academic Press, 2001); Emanuel Martey, *African Theology: Inculturation and Liberation* (Maryknoll, NY: Orbis Books, 1996).

20. African Development Bank, "Development and Indigenous People's in Africa," *Safeguards and Sustainability Series* 2, no. 2 (Abidjan: African Development Bank Group, 2016).

21. Ngũgĩ wa Thiong'o, *Decolonising the Mind: The Politics of Language in African Literature* (London: James Currey; Nairobi: EAEP; Portsmouth, NH: Heniemann, 1986); Ngũgĩ wa Thiong'o, *Dreams in a Time of War* (New York: Pantheon Books, 2010).

22. Ngũgĩ wa Thiong'o, *Something Torn and New: An African Renaissance* (New York: Basic Civitas Books, 2009): 3–4.

23. My own interviews (which ranged across western, central, eastern, and southern parts of Africa) did not focus on burial rites, but it was an issue I found quite interesting when it did arise in formal and informal encounters. Some overviews of related debates include Innocent Ogbona Nweke, "Juxtaposition of Burial Rites in African Traditional Religion: Igbo Land as a Case Study," *Journal of African Studies and Sustainable Development* 3, no. 1 (2020): 40–59; Rebekah Lee and Megan Vaughn, "Death and Dying in the History of Africa Since 1800," *Journal of African History* 49, no. 3 (2008): 341–59.

24. Personal interview in the northwest region of Cameroon, January 2007; personal communication after a panel presentation, International Studies Association annual meeting, Atlanta, 2016.

25. Both African and western sources make similar points. See, for example, Kofi Asare Opoku, *West African Traditional Religion* (Accra: FEP International Private Limited, 1978); T. N. O. Quarcoopome, *West African Traditional Religion* (Ibadan: African Universities Press, 1987); John S. Pobee and Gabriel Ositelu II, *African Initiatives in Christianity: A Challenge to the Ecumenical Movement* (Geneva: WCC Publications, 1988); and the Lutheran World Federation, *Ancestors, Spirits and Healing in Africa and Asia: A Challenge to the Church* (Geneva: LWF Studies, 2005).

26. In other work, I call this process of interpretation "popular casuistry." See Lynch, *Wrestling with God*.

27. Lynch and Schwarz, "Humanitarianism's Proselytism Problem."

28. See Stanlie M. James and Claire C. Robertson, eds., *Genital Cutting and Transnational Sisterhood: Disputing U.S. Polemics* (Champaign: University of Illinois Press, 2002). This book represented cutting-edge work more than two decades ago, but it is telling that the public sphere debate about FGC/FGM has changed so little.

29. The terminology, of course, matters a great deal. "Circumcision" connotes a (general) form of practice that males and females both undergo; "mutilation" highlights bodily violation and injury.

30. See, for example, WHO, *Eliminating Female Genital Mutilation: An Interagency Statement* (WHO, 2008), http://www.un.org/womenwatch/daw/csw/csw52/statements_missions/Interagency_Statement_on_Eliminating_FGM.pdf.

31. Akosua Adomako Ampofo and Signe Arnfred, "Introduction: Feminist Politics of Knowledge," in *African Feminist Research and Activism: Tensions, Challenges, and Possibilities*, ed. Akomako Ampofo and Signe Arnfred (Uppsala: Nordic Africa, 2009), 5–27.

32. Islamic Relief, "Islam Must Never Be Used to Justify FGM," February 6, 2019, https://islamic-relief.org/news/islam-must-never-be-used-to-justify-fgm/.

33. Personal interview, June 29, 2007.

34. Nevertheless, they did not condemn Christian groups as a whole, and expressed appreciation for the World Vision funding that had enabled them to attend secondary school (Maasai Mara visit, July 2007).

35. Elisabet Le Roux and Brenda Bartelink, "No More 'Harmful Traditional Practices': Working Effectively with Faith Leaders," London, Tearfund, UK Government, October 2017. In the interests of full disclosure, I also had email conversations with one of the authors regarding my discomfort with the project, especially the term "harmful traditional practices." I want to thank Brenda Bartelink for her generous reflections on my and others' criticisms, and her rethinking some of the conclusions to take account of them.

36. Jackie Ogega, "A Talk by Jackie Ogega on Ending Female Genital Cutting," University of California, Irvine, February 6, 2014.

37. It is important to acknowledge that numerous African women's organizations have worked to eradicate these practices, often designing and promoting alternative rites of passage that do not involve genital cutting. A Swiss NGO representative's organization also worked in this way. Personal interview, Geneva, June 2007.

38. Brenda Bartelink, "No More 'Harmful Traditional Practices!' Gender Activism and Faith Leaders in International Development," *The Critical Investigations into Humanitarianism in Africa (CIHA) Blog*, June 14, 2018, https://www.cihablog.com/no-harmful-traditional-practices-gender-activism-faith-leaders-international-development/.

39. Fuambai S. Ahmadu and Richard A. Schweder, "Disputing the Myth of the Sexual Dysfunction of Circumcised Women: An Interview with Fuambai S. Ahmadu by Richard A. Shweder," *Royal Anthropological Institute*, November 26, 2009. See also James and Robertson, eds., *Genital Cutting and Transnational Sisterhood*.

40. At the same time, it is important to note that Ogega is highly critical of the gendered implications of these practices.

41. Ngũgĩ wa Thiong'o, *Dreams in a Time of War*.

42. Ngũgĩ wa Thiong'o, *Decolonising the Mind*; Ngũgĩ wa Thiong'o, *Something Torn and New*.

43. Dora R. Mbuwayesango, "How Local Divine Powers Were Suppressed: A Case of Mwari of the Shona," in *Other Ways of Reading: African Women and the Bible*, ed. Musa W. Dube (Geneva: WCC Publications, 2001), 63–77.

44. Nokuzola Mndende, "Ancestors and Healing in African Religion: A South African Context," in *Ancestors, Spirits and Healing in Africa and Asia: A Challenge to the Church*, ed. Ingo Wulfhorst (Geneva: LWF Studies, 2005), 13–24.

45. Ibid.

46. John S. Pobee and Gabriel Ositelu II, *African Initiatives in Christianity: A Challenge to the Ecumenical Movement* (Geneva: WCC Publications, 1998).

47. Ibid, ix.

48. Ibid.

49. Séverine Autesserre, *Peaceland: Conflict Resolution and the Everyday Politics of International Intervention* (Cambridge: Cambridge University Press, 2014).

50. The University Herbarium link can be found at https://www.cabdirect.org/cabdirect/abstract/20006782409.

51. Charles Akwe Masango, "Indigenous Knowledge Codification of African Traditional Medicine: Inhibited by Status Quo Based on Secrecy?" *Information Development* 36, no. 3 (2020): 327–38.

52. Promotion of Traditional Medicine, PROMETRA, "Way of Remembering Pilgrimage into African Spirituality," 2021.

53. These include Regional Committee for Africa, 63 (2013), "Enhancing the Role of Traditional Medicine in Health Systems: A Strategy for the African Region (Document AFR/RC63/6), WHO Regional Office for Africa, https://apps.who.int/iris/handle/10665/94185; Regional Committee for Africa, 70 (AFR/RC70/INF.DOC/2, 2020), "Progress Report on the Implementation of the Regional Strategy on Enhancing the Role of Traditional Medicine in Health Systems 2013–2023, information document," WHO, https://apps.who.int/iris/discover?query=Progress+report+on+the+implementation+of+the+regional+strategy+on+enhancing+the+role+of+traditional+medicine+in+health+systems+2013%E2%80%932023.

54. Matshidiso Moeti, "Message of WHO Regional Director of Africa," WHO, August 25, 2021, https://www.afro.who.int/regional-director/speeches-messages/african-traditional-medicine-day-2021.

55. PROMETRA, "Programs and Causes," https://prometra.org/programs-causes.

56. Personal interviews and participant-observations: Yaounde, Cameroon, November 2017; Fatick, Senegal, December 2017; Kilifi, Kenya, August 2008.

57. Erick Vidjin' Agnih Gbodossou, "Traditional Healers' Self-Proficiency Training," Dakar, Edition Metraf, 2005.

58. PROMETRA, "Education," https://prometra.org/education.

59. Masango, "Indigenous Knowledge Codification of African Traditional Medicine"; Ossy M. J. Kasilo and Emmanuel K. A. Sackey, "Intellectual Property Approaches to the Protection of Traditional Knowledge in the African Region," *African Health Monitor* 14 (2010): 89–102.

60. Albert Billy Bangirana, introduction to Taruona Kudzai, "African Traditional Medicine and COVID-19 Vaccine," *CIHA Blog*, September 15, 2021, http://www.cihablog.com/african-traditional-medicine-covid-19-vaccine/.

61. Interview, Accra, Ghana, 2012.

62. Marleen de Witte, "Spirit Media: Charismatics, Traditionalists, and Mediation Practices in Ghana" (PhD diss., Utrecht University, 2008), 218.

63. Samuel Gyanfosy, "A Traditional Religion Reformed: Vincent Kwabena Damuah and the Afrikania Movement, 1982–2000," in *Christianity and the African Imagination: Essays in Honour of Adrian Hastings*, ed. David James Maxwell and Ingrid Lawrie (Leiden: Brill, 2002), 271.

CHAPTER 6

Linking Identity and Solidarity

A Reflection from the Periphery

SLAVICA JAKELIĆ

Abstract

At a time of ascendant and increasingly polarized populist politics, how might we understand and negotiate the ethical tensions between increasingly particularist forms of political identity and the need for a viable politics of solidarity? This chapter complicates the bifurcated western logic that views particularist forms of national identity as inherently in tension or opposition to universalizing forms of solidarity often expressed in explicitly religious terms. Drawing on postcolonial and decolonial insights and the ambivalent status of the Balkans as neither wholly European nor wholly Other, the chapter considers the work of Fr. Tvrtko Barun, S.J., the director of the Jesuit Refugee Service for South-East Europe, to problematize the western identity/solidarity dichotomies but also to highlight the ethical and theoretical constraints of the monolithic understanding of "Europe" emerging in decolonial thought. Centering Fr. Barun's response to the "migrant crisis" in the Balkans reveals the co-constitutive nature of Christian and national identities, eliminating the logic of opposition by showing how the universalizing impulses of Barun's solidarity are enacted from within specific, situated national identities, experiences, and imaginaries.

Is it necessary to transcend the ascribed or particular forms of group identity—to eschew the affects, passions, and sentiments one attaches to them—in order to be in solidarity with others with whom one does not share history or culture, and in the name of more universal ethical commitments?

This question is especially pertinent in the time of "redemptive" populist politics,[1] whose successes are less a sign of pathologies of democracy and more an indication of neglect of a vital social question—that of democratic formation of particular group attachments in pluralistic societies.[2] It is hardly an accident that the achievements of both progressive and right-wing populist parties greatly rely on the unitary notion of the "we" to which individual supporters attach their passions and commitments. And although the latter, as Chantal Mouffe and Ernesto Laclau have argued,[3] can revitalize democratic life by increasing agonistic engagements, it can also affirm collective identities in ways that constrict both democratic contestation and deliberation, particularly when populists organize their idea of belonging by politically exploiting xenophobic tendencies in the general population.[4] Populisms thus raise the stakes in any attempt to reconcile several democratic concerns: with that which binds individual citizens into a political community; with the responsibility that citizens have toward those outside their own particular group; and with pluralism as a platform for citizens' deliberation and disagreement about the ideals of national identity and the common good—a framework for a "healthy conflict," to recall Jason Springs's astute usage of this phrase.[5]

In this chapter, I explore these challenges of populist politics, most specifically the way they compel us to probe the languages and practices that would allow for individuals to belong to national and religious communities in ways that are both particular and capacious. I do so by focusing on the relationship between *the ethics of identity* and *the ethics of solidarity*, with the former referring to particular forms of group attachments and the latter denoting the imperatives of responsibility to those outside such allegiances. Overwhelmingly, western social thinkers posit the ethics of identity and the ethics of solidarity as distinct from, and often opposed to, one another[6]; they associate particular attachments with the traditional and universal commitments with the modern forms of social life. These views,

I argue here, ought to be problematized: they result from, to use Julien Go's term, the "analytic bifurcation" of western social thought.[7]

I examine the analytic bifurcation underwriting western considerations of identitiarian and solidary commitments by engaging the insights of postcolonial and decolonial thinkers in the context of the refugee and migrant "crisis" in the Balkans.[8] I begin by uncovering the anti-identitarian thrust of the identity/solidarity distinctions in the usual approaches to both nationalisms and religions: on the one hand, the differentiation between "ethnic" and "civic" nationalisms (particular, affective, collectivistic versus universal, rational, individualistic national commitments), and, on the other hand, the juxtaposition of "identitarian" religions and the universalist, "belief-centered" expressions of religions (i.e., group-oriented religious exclusion and violence versus theologies of inclusion and tolerance).

While these binary conceptualizations of nationalism and religions have long been subject to scrutiny and critiques, they are revived in the recent attempts to explain away the surge of populist religio-nationalist identities. My critique of such bifurcated thinking about national and religious belonging follows some of Meghan Tinsley's decolonial considerations of the civic/ethnic nationalism binary; it also probes Boaventura de Sousa Santos's insights about the "abyssal line." According to him, the abyssal line defines western forms of thinking and living that seek to establish the irreducible differences between the colonizers and the colonized—with the world of the former designated as the dichotomy between regulation and emancipation, and of the latter by appropriation and violence (or, otherwise, nonexistence).[9] The Balkans, I contend here, are a geopolitical, historical, and cultural site that challenges the abyssal line but also requires us to interrogate the confines of decolonial engagements with this central dimension of colonial thought and practice. Focusing on what Santos calls the "sociology of absences," I uncover the discursive formation of religious and national narratives of belonging as intertwined with the narratives of solidarity with refugees and migrants. More specifically, instead of focusing on nationalism in relation to nation-states[10] (i.e., instead of critiquing the centrality of nation-states in the colonial matrix of power[11]), and instead of considering the Christian universal humanist propositions as the source of solidarity with refugees in the Balkans (i.e., instead of thinking about Christian humanism in ways that are problematic on decolonial grounds),[12] I consider both Christian and national identities as entwined ways of being and living locally by looking at the case of Fr. Barun, the director of the

Jesuit Refugee Service for South-East Europe (JRS). Barun is central for the argument here because he was at the forefront of work with migrants and refugees in the Balkans, and because his discourse on solidarity arises at the intersection between the particular histories of suffering in this region and the particularized (rather than totalizing) ethics of Christian humanism. For this Jesuit, to be sure, solidarity is a universal proposition, but it is a disposition inhabited and enacted within visceral identity attachments rather than distinct from them, that is, it is situated in the range of lived experiences of exile from one's home.

With this reading, I seek to unsettle the analytic bifurcation in western considerations of the ethics of identity and the ethics of solidarity by uncovering their deep relationality. The latter, I also propose, represents one alternative to "abyssal thinking" that emerges on the periphery of both "sides of the line," the "metropolitan society" and "the other."[13] Put another way, I look at the Balkans as a periphery and a bridge that has long existed between the colonizer and the colonized, is not reducible to either,[14] and which points to the "silenced, and marginalized knowledges" and practices[15] that have been "suppressed, discredited, disqualified ... by being outside epistemological and social monocultures."[16] These are knowledges and practices that neither merely resist nor mimic western modernity; rather, they reframe and reconfigure it through relational subjectivities.

This chapter, then, is not another attempt at theorizing the ambiguous, hybrid forms of identity, but their retrieval as coeval. In probing the potential of the liminal and distinctive status of the Balkans in relation to and within Europe, *and* in relation to the South; in suggesting that the discursive formation of identity-solidarity links carries, to echo Arturo Escobar, the "non-dualist worlds" organized around "a deeply relational understanding of life,"[17] I argue that the Balkans challenge the totalizing effects of the modernist view of history and the totalizing decolonial perspectives on "Europe" of which the Balkans are a part yet are also "the other."[18]

This last point helps alert us to the possibility that the decolonial rejection of the "abyssal line" could also help sustain it. The latter is not a risk merely because critiques often reaffirm the very categories and modes of thought that they subject to critique. Rather, I want to propose that the reassertion of abyssal thinking is possible if decolonial considerations confine our analytic lenses within the colonizer/colonized view of the past and the present, that is, if they do not allow us to see places shaped by complex, multiple peripheralities. The Balkans are one such place. To assess their liminal historical legacies and experiences is not to reassert their significance as an "area study" or to suggest another intra-European perspective on the possible ways to understand and tackle the populist challenges in our moment.[19] It is rather to think of the Balkans as a challenge to a hermetic understanding of "Europe" and, more importantly, to take their historical legacies as instructive for how we might envision forceful, particular, and pluriversal challenges to the exclusionism and violence established by various forms of populist identitarianism and by "identitarian essentialisms."[20] I am appealing here to an expansive vision of pluriversality, in which decoloniality, as Walter Mignolo stresses, is one option and truth with parentheses,[21] focused not only on the critique of dualism but also on the perseverance of "non-dualist worlds . . . that reflect a deeply relational understanding of life."[22] This expansive vision of pluriversality would allow a relational, non-Eurocentric critique of and alternative to Eurocentrism that can arrive from Europeans, once Europe is not only provincialized but also decentered.[23]

IDENTITY AND SOLIDARITY BIFURCATED

Disciplinary preoccupations along with ethical and political challenges affect and sometimes dictate the ways in which scholars approach the notion of solidarity.[24] The shifts in the meanings of this notion and ideal,[25] and disciplinary and normative complexities in the approaches to it notwithstanding, western conceptualizations of solidarity most often emerge from the juxtaposition of particular group attachments and the imperatives of responsibility to those outside such loyalties.

One paradigmatic example of this framing of solidarity is Émile Durkheim's discussion of mechanic and organic solidarity: the former indicating the bonds we have with others because of fate, similarity, and ascription (what I term in this chapter the "ethics of identity"), and the latter pointing to the association of individuals by virtue of difference, functional necessity, and rational attachments (what I designate as the "ethics of solidarity"). Since Durkheim first posited this binary, social thinkers presented significant theoretical and empirical challenges to the western modernist bias built into his view that mechanic solidarity characterizes traditional societies and organic solidarity structures the life of modern societies.[26] Nonetheless, his is a vision that still configures many sociological analyses of the ethics of particular attachments and universal ethical commitments.[27] Moreover, as we shall see shortly, the idea that modernity carries an unavoidable, and, for many, coveted, shift from affective, ascribed, and particular to reasonable, chosen, and universal attachments is central to the considerations of nationalisms and religions.

At first sight, the discussions of the ethics of identity and the ethics of solidarity in moral and political philosophy appear to be more complicated than those in the social sciences. Jürgen Habermas reserves the notion of solidarity for the particular community of attachments and responsibilities to one another held because of the shared interests, while he sees the universal ideals of justice as the other side of such particular attitudes toward solidarity.[28] For Alasdair MacIntyre, too, solidarity stands for the communal and particular rather than universal (impersonal and rational) moral obligations. But whereas Habermas elevates the universal ideals as the guiding principles of solidary relations in modern societies, as especially evident in his affirmation of the values of "constitutional patriotism," MacIntyre declares that solidarity emerging from the strength of communities is the only kind of solidarity that can be truly moral.[29]

Another influential western philosopher links the notion of solidarity principally to particular experiences and attachments: for Richard Rorty, the power of solidarity depends on the historical and national specificity of the "we." Solidarity is *"made,"* he declares, rather than found, *"produced in the course of history rather than recognized as an ahistorical fact."*[30] Nonetheless, Rorty asserts that the ideal of solidarity is the ability—the willingness and the agency—to enlarge our sense of belonging with and responsibility to others beyond the particular "we." He recognizes that the (Kantian) ideal of obligation to other human beings "as such" serves as "a means of reminding ourselves to keep trying to expand our sense of 'us' as far as we can."[31] In assuming precisely such a universalistic meaning of solidarity, Keith Banting and Will Kymlicka gauge similar terrain that Rorty explored in terms of solidarity's particularity, that is, its practice. In pluralistic societies, Banting and Kymlicka thus warn, solidarity is not "self-enacting": because it is unlike identity, solidarity may "be left untapped" or "politically blocked," and thus ought to be continuously championed.[32]

The ethics of solidarity—the one reflecting a sense of responsibility to others beyond the bonds of particular attachments—therefore appears in very different incarnations and under different names in sociology, theology, ethics, and moral and political philosophy. Yet, underneath these terminological differences, specific disciplinary preoccupations and individual normative positions, lies one concern: the *relationship* between the particular and universal grounds of one's ethical commitments to others. On my reading, regardless of disciplinary flavor or normative orientations, western social and philosophical theorizing of these questions most often entails two dimensions. The first is the separation of the ethics of identity from the ethics of solidarity, that is, the detachment of the domain of belonging that is ascribed and affective from the space of intentionality that is agential and deliberative. The second feature of western thinking about the ethics of identity and the ethics of solidarity is a gesture toward the ethics of rational, willed commitments as a fact of, or a norm needed for, modern pluralistic societies (i.e., a historical development that needs to be affirmed, probed, or, as is the case with MacIntyre, problematized and critiqued).

The ideas of the American historian David Hollinger display these features explicitly. He contends that if identity and community express an ascribed sense of belonging in ways that are quasi-mystical and conducive for violence,[33] solidarity represents agency—one's choice of commitment to others and expectation of commitment from others in how they constitute and reconstitute the "we." Solidarity, Hollinger maintains, transcends the membership in a group into which one is born; it is an "experience of willed affiliation, " of "conscious commitment," and it entails a level of deliberation and choice.[34] Most importantly, Hollinger argues that solidarity is most needed and most difficult to achieve when we have a choice to cross the lines of difference to develop a commitment to the larger constituted "we." Such a "we" "applies paradigmatically to moral obligations within communities in the face of oppression"; it is indispensable in those moments when there is a need for reimagining the sources of moral obligations to one another.[35]

Ours is a moment that calls for this kind of reimagining: the unprecedented levels of migration challenge the boundaries and the borders between particular (national, religious, ethnic, linguistic) identities and more expansive (global, human) solidarities. Such challenges result in "the politics of threatened majorities"—a democratic imagination that is, as Ivan Krastev writes, often reduced to a demographic one,[36] and as such provides the backdrop for the antipluralistic impulses of most populist politics. The imperative to reimagine the boundaries of our ethical obligations in effect raises a twofold question: Should we tackle the described challenges by reiterating the opposition between the ethics of identity and the ethics of solidarity? Or, is it possible to *retrieve* and *affirm* other types of ethical, cultural, and political imaginaries through which identity and solidarity inform and embolden one another—the imaginaries quelled, marginalized, silenced, untapped? Western social thinkers, I propose, share the assertion of difference and opposition between the ethics of identity and the ethics of solidarity. This same understanding organizes the still influential theories of nationalisms and religions, specifically the concepts of ethnic versus civic nationalisms, and of identitarian versus belief-centered religious commitments. Despite the important critiques of such binary constructs, they are revived today, yet again, to frame both the scholarly and the political responses to populists' nativist religio-national projects.

Identity versus Solidarity as Ethnic versus Civic Nationalisms

The opposition between the ethics of identity and the ethics of solidarity is easily traceable in one of the most influential articulations of ethnic and civic nationalisms, that of Hans Kohn.[37] He contrasts the ethnic nationalism—blood, tribalism, peoplehood, emotional attachment to history, "monuments and graveyards" (i.e., the identitarian logic of ethical commitments)—with the civic nationalisms—"a rational and universal conception of liberty,"[38] individual political agency, and "creative self-fashioning"[39] (i.e., a political community whose members are in solidarity with one another through assent to the shared civic ideals and deliberation about their civic bonds).

A range of social theorists and social scientists critiqued and disputed Kohn's view of the universality of civic national ideals and bonds of citizenship as desirable for liberal modernity, suggesting that such bonds possess no ties to, or dependence on, particular and identitarian attachments. From Anthony Smith, Rogers Brubaker, and Craig Calhoun, to Bernard Yack, Geneviève Zubrzycki, Rasma Karklins, or Yael Tamir, just to mention some of his critics, scholars argued that the sharp separation or opposition between ethnic and civic nationalism—between identitarian and more universal civic bonds of citizenship—is both historically and analytically problematic, and normatively biased against identitarianism as unchanging and antimodern.⁴⁰ The critics in question underscore that there are no pure civic nationalisms, just as there are no pure ethnic nationalisms; that civic nationalism, just as ethnic, can be the source of exclusion, domination, and is always particular in character. Moreover, contrary to Kohn's approach, critics suggest that it is the relationship, not the disconnect between the civic and ethnic, that merits attention.⁴¹

Despite these critiques, Kohn's binary easily lent itself to the widespread usage in the analysis and interpretations of the 1990s wars in the Balkans, and most specifically wars in Bosnia and Croatia. In this instance, Kohn's opposition between ethnic and civic nationalism was additionally appealing because it paralleled another contrast Kohn drew—that between eastern and western values and versions of modernity. With rare exceptions, scholars and practitioners, foreign and from the region, presented the ethnic/civic binary as the perfect explanatory tool for the ways in which the "ethnic" nationalisms in the newly formed nation-states were in fact the remnants of the Balkan centuries-old tribalisms and of the primordialist group identities that were the threats to the virtues of liberal democracy.⁴² In those narratives, the Balkans have always been the European "other."

In the face of populist challenges, scholars and policymakers alike returned to Kohn's ethnic/civic nationalism dichotomy as if all the critiques of its ahistoricity and modernist bias never occurred or carried no merit. If Kohn used the ethnic/civic distinction to lionize the "liberal achievement" against "an illiberal challenge to it"⁴³—if, furthermore, the notion of ethnic nationalisms explained the phenomena of the Balkan postcommunist societies as "intrinsically alien to Western civic and supposedly civilized nationalism,"⁴⁴ then western scholars and policymakers today employ the notion of civic nationalism to combat the success of the populist nativist and exclusionary nationalist platforms in their midst. We can trace the normative logic of the ethnic/civic binary—the ideas about the irreconcilability between the ethics of identity and the ethics of solidarity, and about the former as a threat to pluralism—in the affirmations of "liberal" or "civic" forms of nationalism, in the quick retreats into "patriotism" and "constitutional patriotism" as a tool against nativist nationalisms, or in the celebrations of the American "civil religion."⁴⁵ All these notions stand for universal principles of civic attachments in contrast to the threats of culture wars but especially as a tool against populist nationalisms and identitarianisms. Ethnic nationalism is the watchword for scholars of religion and politics who identify this phenomenon as the same as "white nationalism," and who locate civic nationalism as its opposition and the perpetual promise of liberal democracy.[46] Even Jill Lepore's nuanced historical work on "new Americanism" keeps intact the idea of particular attachments as exclusionary and dangerous, and of solidary bonds based on universal principles of citizenship as open, inclusive, and tolerant.[47]

Identity versus Solidarity as Identitarian versus Belief-Centered Religions

Scholarly approaches to identitarian religions—those configurations of religious traditions tied to, or embedded in, some form of specific group identity—most often entail the view of such religions as intolerant and an obstacle to coexistence with, or acceptance of, those with whom one does not share particular culture, history, language, nationality, and religion. Social scientists and scholars of religion alike especially critique the links between religions and nationalism, which they often perceive as a signifier of the victory of secularization and politicization of religious traditions or, as the critics of secularism argue, the ineluctable consequence of the powers of the secular and of modernity that these powers help establish and justify.[48] And, while these critical perspectives involve the analyses of a range of religious traditions—from Christianity to Hinduism and Islam—it is in the studies of Christianity and nationalisms that we can discern most clearly the assumptions about the opposition between particular religious attachments (i.e., Christianity configured along the identitarian logic of belonging) and religion as a source of universal ethical obligations (i.e., solidarity with others articulated around the theological premises of Christian faith and the values of universalist humanism).[49]

The Balkans are the case study in such scholarly and policy arguments. Just as scholars and practitioners deployed the ethnic/civic binary to explain the roots of the wars in Bosnia and Croatia, the dichotomy between identitarian and belief-centered religiosity provided the framework for the critiques of the role of religious tribalisms. Historians, social scientists, scholars of religion, Christian theologians—they all lamented the cultural, collectivistic configurations of Christianity.[50] Miroslav Volf, a distinguished Yale theologian and Croatian by birth, saw religions in the former Yugoslavia as a problem because they served as a cultural resource rather than an active faith. The late Croatian sociologist of religion and a devout Catholic Željko Mardešić argued that the only way out of the "vicious circle" in which Catholicism and other religions "fall into the worldly traps" was the affirmation of faith that was not historically grounded but founded in "the personhood of every human being."[51]

Peace studies scholars, among them Marc Gopin, R. Scott Appleby, and Gerard Powers, called for more complex approaches to the role of religion in the Bosnian and Croatian conflicts. Using some of their insights, and especially building on the discussions of religious studies scholars in the genealogical approaches to "religion," my earlier work explored the range of identitarian Christianities from the European periphery—the Balkans and Eastern Europe in particular—in the *longue durée* perspective. With this lens, I probed a theory of religion that was modernist in character and theologically skewed against religious identitarianism in ways that prevented an exploration and understanding of the peacebuilding potential of collectivistic Christianities. This theory of religion, similarly to the ethnic/civic nationalism binary, builds on the distinctions between ascription and choice, particularism and universality, embedded and culturally unencumbered forms of experience.[52]

With the emergence of religio-national agendas in the populist politics of many western democratic societies, the above-described dichotomies returned in full force to ground the statements of Christian theologians, religious studies scholars, and social scientists concerned about the ties between Christianities and populism. To reject the nativist, antipluralist, and isolationist "new nationalism" that had been articulated in the conservative journal *First Things*, American Christian theologians and public intellectuals—including Cornel West, Miroslav Volf, Stanley Hauerwas, Anthea Butler, and Eddie Glaude Jr.—asserted the universality of Christian faith. Unlike states and nations, they declared, the church has no borders, and only if it "welcomes the stranger, embraces the orphan, and binds wounds of all who are our neighbor" is it the church living the integrity of Christian faith.[53]

The universal tenets of Christian faith asserted here are undoubtedly powerful as a condemnation of the publicly awakened "white nationalism" and its links to Christianity. But what the affirmation of abstract Christian universal humanism also did was to leave out all embedded, particular instantiations of Christianity, not least those arising in the historical experience of the Black church, which powerfully responded to and rejected Christianity's complicity in slavery and racism. What is more, the exclusive and ahistorical focus on Christian humanism also omitted the long and violent history of that humanism's role in colonial projects and racial oppression around the globe. It is this hegemonic Christian humanism that postcolonial and decolonial thinkers so forcefully reject; it is this unencumbered Christian humanism that is probed by the students and advocates of humanism who are conscious of the humanisms' propensity to exclude and dehumanize.[54]

The recent analyses of identitarian Christianities and populist nationalisms and "civilizationism" in Europe succumb to the same particular/universal, identitarian/faith dichotomy. Nadia Marzouki, Olivier Roy, and Rogers Brubaker write about identitarian religions and identitarian Christianities as secularized, politicized forms of Christianity that signify eroded faith and doctrine[55] and the separation of Christianity from theology and spirituality. Just as this was the case with civic nationalism, these recent discussions of Christianity and populism entail an assumption that universally oriented commitments are more tolerant and inclusive of others by virtue of that universality, while those that are identitarian in character are not reconcilable with the ethics of solidarity by virtue of their particularism. Can we, however, sustain affirmations of Christian universalisms as the unqualified theo-political response to today's populist religious nationalisms if we probe, with all the intellectual, moral, and political seriousness required, the role of Christian humanism in colonial projects, or Mignolo's arguments that "universality is always imperial and war driven"?[56]

Overcoming Analytic Bifurcation: Linking the Ethics of Identity and the Ethics of Solidarity as an Alternative to Abyssal Thinking

The identity/solidarity divide I have highlighted thus far organizes two sets of binary concepts that arise in the scholarly and policy responses to populist religio-national exclusionism: "ethnic" versus "civic" nationalism and "identitarian" versus "belief"-driven religious commitments. In these discussions, particular national and religious attachments stand as the domain of exclusion, intolerance, and violence, while the universal ethical commitments that push one beyond particularisms arise as inclusive, tolerant, and thus desirable as a source of bonds in and between contemporary, pluralistic societies.[57] Should we settle for this unreflexive reiteration of universal commitments as a remedy for the predicaments of our moment, or should we strive to trace and interrogate the complex ties between ethnic and civic national commitments, between identitarian and belief-centered types of religious attachments—to open our analytic tools beyond the normative horizons, exclusionary tenets, and often violent historical legacies of different iterations of universalist ethics and the politics shaped by them?

For the latter to happen, the binary understanding of the ethics of identity and the ethics of solidarity ought to be disrupted. Postcolonial and decolonial perspectives provide productive trajectories for that endeavor. When binary thinking about particular and universal ethical obligations is explored with postcolonial and decolonial lenses, they do not arise as an exception but as yet another aspect of "analytic bifurcation" that, according to Julian Go, characterizes much of the western social thought. The latter analytically separates social relations that "might not have been separate at all," thus overlooking their "'truer' history."[58]

On my reading, the conceptual and normative distinctions between identity and solidarity do not result from what some scholars see as "*European* Universalism," but from the universalization of the singularly *western* European experience of progress that posits "a presumably universal template of development and theoretical categories" and "in turn reduce[s] cultural difference to temporal difference and presuppose[s] the superiority of Western experience."[59] As a result, the conceptualization of the ethics of identity and the ethics of solidarity as opposed to each other most often carries a teleological claim that there is and that there ought to be a movement, and a shift, away from ascription and toward rationality and the universality of subjectivities and intersubjectivities.[60] While this essay represents an inquiry into the "relational over substantialist understandings of the social world,"[61] it also reflects that dimension of decolonial projects that, following Boaventura de Sousa Santos, seeks to move us beyond "abyssal thinking." For Santos, this colonial thinking gives reality and value only to the rational (regulative and emancipating) metropolitan societies of the west (which also refers to the universal principles of ethics and social bonds resulting from western modernity), while it denies the colonized world, or the South, any legitimacy except the one of violence (seeing the latter as also arising from the configurations of identity that emerge from local knowledges and experience, including particular attachments).[62]

Meghan Tinsley draws on Santos's idea of the abyssal line and on Frantz Fanon's zones of being and nonbeing to assert that civic nationalism thus construed obscures racialized patterns of exclusion of the Other and therefore cannot be presented as a global ideal. On these grounds, Tinsley presents a powerful decolonial critique of Kohn's binary and a critique of civic nationalism as predicated on ethnic nationalism. Tinsley contends that, after the essentialist movements of anticolonial solidarity, such as pan-Africanism and pan-Arabism, the Global South is presenting us today with the new forms of solidarity emerging in the movements for Indigenous rights or for Black lives. These strive to transcend "the binary of the Self and Other" and as such, Tinsley is convinced, can be a forceful rebuttal to global populist politics.

I concur with much of Tinsley's decolonial critique of civic nationalism. But rather than assuming with her that the Balkans are different from the South because the exploitative European intrusion into the region "historically has been *far less politically invasive, economically extractive, and culturally devastating* than the Othering of the global South by the North,"[63] rather than following Santos's understanding that the abyssal global lines of separation between the metropolitan societies and colonial territories are fixed,[64] and that the Balkans might be considered a mere variation of western modernity,[65] I point to the Balkans as a border that belongs to neither side of the abyssal line. Its historical and sociological experiences of neither the colonizer nor the colonized, its liminality as multiple peripherality, I maintain, challenges the totalizing effects of the modernist view of history and the totalizing perspectives on "Europe" that arise in some decolonial trajectories.

Particular Attachments and Bonds of Solidarity: The "Dual" Periphery as a Bridge

The free nations tend to sink into "spheres of influence" and investment centers, and then often succumb into disfranchised colonies. All this has been rationalized by universal sneering at small nations, at "Balkanization" and helpless Haitis, until the majority of the world's people have become ashamed of themselves.
    —W. E. B. Du Bois, Color and Democracy

Linking Identity and Solidarity   183

The word "Balkanization," writes the Bulgarian American historian Maria Todorova, had come to denote not only "the parcelization of large and viable political units but also had become a synonym for a reversion to the tribal, the backward, the primitive, the barbarian," that space that is the "other" of Europe, with the inhabitants who "do not care to conform to the standards of behavior devised as normative by and for the civilized world," that is, western Europe in particular.[66] The "othering" of the Balkans in the western European imaginaries came with another perception: the Balkans as a boundary space. The latter perspective had become prominent among all those who recognize the Balkans as a category of their own identity, a self-designation, if only to resist it.[67] Living in the Balkans and being from there means being neither in Europe nor outside of it, perhaps especially today when several Balkan countries are EU members, yet their status, and the status of the citizens from the Balkans (or southeast Europe), has never become equal to the status of the western European members.[68]

The western perception of the Balkans as frozen in time, then, merits attention not because it still is "one of the most powerful pejorative designations in history, international relations, political science, and . . . general intellectual discourse."[69] This western (European) perception of the Balkans is particularly of interest here for two other reasons: it complicates the division of the world into the colonizer and the colonized separated by the abyssal line, and it brings into question any essentialist notion of Europe. On the one hand, the drive to "Europeanize" or "modernize" the Balkans, to make "it less what it was," signified, according to Todorova, the western European view of the Balkans as not only "an incomplete other" but also "an incomplete self." On the other hand, there was in the Balkans a powerful resistance to such attempts and, more importantly, the resistance through the affirmation of the distinctive Balkan identity—of not merely an agency for resistance to the attempts of Europeanization but of "autonomy."[70] That drive, I argue here, was also formative for the configurations of identity, community, and thus of a different kind of modernity.

Todorova's historical work on the discursive construction of the Balkans was one of the most significant interventions in the long discussions about the relevance of postcolonial studies in critical Balkanist studies.[71] Some scholars argued that the studies of the Balkans (and the notions that often accompanied it, those of "Eastern Europe" and "southeast Europe") should be considered as a subspecies of the studies of Orientalism,[72] but Todorova disagreed. She critiqued Edward Said's notion of Orientalism as pertinent for the study of the Balkans because she saw the Balkans as possessing "historical," "geographic,"[73] and "unimaginative concreteness"[74] as "opposed to the intangible nature of the Orient."[75] With two legacies, one of Byzantium and the other of Ottoman rule—to which one should also add the distinctive experience of communist modernity—Todorova revealed the Balkans as the region that was not part of colonial projects, with societies whose histories were not determined by some empire's civilizing missions, or the abyss between metropole and dependencies. The Balkans might have been "semicolonial, quasi-colonial," Todorova writes, but they were "clearly not purely colonial."

In this discussion, I take Todorova's approach to the Balkans as a circumscribed geopolitical and cultural location, and as a region with its own historical legacies, yet nonetheless a region that is part of Europe. By situating the Balkans in the liminal space, and by highlighting its "in-betweenness" and "transitionary character,"[76] Todorova does not only complicate the totalizing view of Europe; she also stresses the importance of historical specificities of the study of a region. In so doing, she uncovers the analytic potential of the Balkans as the periphery[77] shaped by both western and eastern Christianity, both Christianity and Islam, both western and Ottoman empires.[78] As so powerfully suggested in the Nobel laureate Ivo Andrić's novel *Na Drini ćuprija* several decades ago,[79] the Balkans thus emerge as a periphery that is also a bridge, a bridge that allows for the relationality between identity and solidarity, of particularity and openness. The latter shapes the work of Fr. Barun, and it is that to which we turn next.

PARTICULAR AND CAPACIOUS:
THE CASE OF FR. TVRTKO BARUN AND THE JESUIT RELIEF SERVICE IN SOUTH-EAST EUROPE

Kad me netko pita o njima, ja bih najradije da se svi zagrlimo i zajedno plačemo.

(When someone asks me about them, what I want us all to do is hug each other, and cry.)

—Šuhret Fazlić, the mayor of Bihać, Bosnia
and Herzegovina, speaking of migrants in his city[80]

The waves of migrants seeking refuge in the EU—1,321,560 asylum claims in 2015[81]—are just an element in the migratory upheavals occurring on a global scale: according to the UN High Commissioner for Refugees (UNHCR), the recent migrations of forcibly displaced people, from refugees to economic and political migrants, are the highest since World War II.[82] As the numbers of the first-time asylum applicants greatly decreased for most member countries of the EU since early 2017,[83] this development did not change much for the Balkan region, which continues to experience waves of migrants from a range of countries. These include people from Afghanistan, Syria, and Iraq, in particular, all of whom are seeking passage to western Europe.

One Balkan country whose geopolitical and cultural status highlights the challenges of being a bridge toward, but also a border of, western Europe is Croatia. In Europe and in the Balkans by virtue of its history and its culture, Croatia is the most recent addition to the EU and became part of its Schengen area only in 2023. The country's infrastructure for hosting and integrating migrants into Croatian society is young and not fully institutionalized—it has been in place only since 2006. At the same time, this is a society with an unfortunate advantage when it comes to questions surrounding immigration and refugees, because of its own recent firsthand knowledge and experience of forced migrations. During the wars in Bosnia and Herzegovina, Croatia, and Kosovo in the 1990s, Croatia's citizens were refugees all over western Europe, all while the country hosted 750,000 refugees from various countries of former Yugoslavia (two-thirds from Bosnia and Herzegovina).

Between September 2015 and March 2016, 658,068 refugees and migrants passed through this country of 4 million people. During that most intense period of the European migrant crisis, the country's government did its best to secure help and temporary camps for refugees and migrants. Positioning itself explicitly against the likes of Orbán, with Croatia's minister of foreign affairs, Vesna Pusić, publicly declaring that "Croatia would not be building walls" but treat migrants with respect for their dignity and rights, Croatia's policy of openness was one of the reasons why some EU countries did not see it as ready for the Schengen border system.[84] The period during which Croatia enacted both the humanitarian and human rights principles toward the migrants, however, was followed with the new government, keen on protecting "Croatian interests" and European borders.[85] Over the last several years, Croatian and international media have been filled with reports about violence against migrants and their mistreatment at the hands of Croatian police and border forces.[86] The Bosnian city of Bihać, which is on the border with Croatia, became just one of the Balkan cities that acutely felt the change in the Croatian and EU immigration policy, suddenly facing thousands of refugees, economic migrants, and asylum seekers in their midst, in a country impoverished by recent war and a deep political crisis of its institutions, with almost no resources to provide assistance to all those for whom the Balkans are a gateway to the west.

It is in the context of this humanitarian crisis and the closure of the EU to receiving more immigrants that the work of the Jesuit Refugee Service and its offices in southeast Europe—with centers in Prizren, Belgrade, and Zagreb—became especially significant. The organization has a global structure—it is active in fifty countries all over the world, and in fifteen European countries—and quickly became one of the few organizations in the region that could and did assist all types of migrants. For his work and the work of his organization in the Balkans, the director of this NGO, Jesuit Tvrtko Barun, won the 2017 European Citizen's Prize. Barun's presence in the Croatian media has been constant, before and after he received this award. In all of his public statements—from the organization's official documents to his interviews for TV and newspapers—his message was one of nonnegotiable ethical obligation that European Christians have toward the migrants: "As Christians, if we truly live our Christianity, . . . we should never be concerned about dividing the Good news" because it is "directed not only to all Christians but to all people of good will."[87] Barun and his organizations, as he puts it, ground their work on "the values of the Gospel of hope, human dignity, and justice, [and] respect for other cultures and values. . . . Our actions and work," this Jesuit not embarrassed to echo St. Francis declared, "are an attempt to 'preach' the acceptance of others who are different. Remember the Gospel of Matthew, verse 25: 'I was a stranger and you took me in.'"[88]

While Barun and his organization have been advocating ethical responsibility toward the migrants out of their Christian commitment, his appeals to people's conscience linked Christian humanism to humanist values more generally—to a sense of shared humanity.[89] Condemning the words of another Croatian priest who stated that Croatia shouldn't be helping the migrants, "'not to even give them water or food,'" Barun said,

> We can have different political ideas, different opinions, but to say something like this, regardless of who the other is—a Muslim, an atheist, a Buddhist, or something else—it's clear that this has nothing to do with Christianity. Good works and the works of charity are the foundation of Catholic social teaching and there is no space for negotiation in this regard. In fact, when we speak about such basic things it does not matter if we were Christian or not—what matters is that we are human beings.[90]

From the same position, Barun criticized European populist parties and politicians building walls to keep out migrants.[91] In a statement that echoed some of the appeal of the German chancellor Angela Merkel to return to the roots of Christian faith in opening the door to the migrants,[92] Barun proclaimed that "Christian Europe cannot be proud of its role in the migrant crisis. It lacked solidarity."[93] The problem in Europe, he concluded, "[is] not the migrants; it is the Christians."[94]

For Barun, then, Christian humanism and humanist values in general shape his vision and practice of solidarity. He links it to empathy, which to him is inseparable from getting to know the migrants personally. "You know," he explains in his interviews, "we react one way when we deal with ideologies or beliefs, and another way when we deal with the real people."[95] Just like the Polish pope, John Paul II, Barun understands solidarity not as a battle against someone in order to affirm someone else, but first and foremost as an encounter with others.[96] "Every experience of meeting someone who is different," Barun stated, "changes us," "opens new horizons, new worlds," as long as "we are open to being enriched with that difference."[97] Perhaps more than anything else, solidarity is to Barun, in accord with the Catholic social thought, about action.[98] Solidarity with migrants, he is very clear in his interviews, needs to move beyond humanitarianism: it needs to be about developing reasonable, rational practices for the migrants' integration into a new society, to enable those seeking asylum to fully live in their new homes—not in ghettos for foreigners, he emphasizes, but in true neighborhoods, with everyone else.

In practically every interview he gives, Barun debunks the fears of difference in the European midst. He is less interested in the statistics that stress that Muslims make up only 6 percent of the total European population, and more in a nuanced understanding and elaboration about "identity and culture" as always in motion, changing. It is the latter notion that allows him to argue against fears of more immigrants and demographic politics concerned with what more immigrants will do "to the Croatian identity."[99] "What matters the most," he maintains, is not what Europe was, but what "kind of Europe we see and want to create with all these people who want to live here, with us, to see how to integrate them so that they can make a contribution to building our societies. Respecting the laws and Constitution of some country, that is what matters, the rest of it—what clothes you will wear, what food you will eat, ... what beliefs you will have, what life-style you want to nurture,"[100] all that is not important.

By situating his work in universal humanist values, Christian and non-Christian, by insisting on the reasonableness and action in solidarity with all migrants, Barun seems to affirm the separation of particular identity—national, religious, cultural, historical—and humanist values that transcend all forms of particular attachments. This is certainly one way to interpret his words that "[my] relationship with God, of me as a Christian, is a more important value than my pride about being Croatian."[101] Yet, to see his statement only as a dismissal of religious identitarianism—as a proclamation that his religious identity is grounded only in transcendence and signifies leaving behind other particular attachments—is to leave out the second important dimension of his message, which is the affirmation of pride about his national identity and the responsibility that emerges from it. For Barun, one's sense of national attachment is not a problem in itself (it is important to recall here his articulation of the changing meanings of Croatian identity and culture). Rather, he sees such attachments as a problem only when and if they preclude the embodiment of the transcendent horizon of Christian faith, which happens and matters in this world only in relation to others, Christians and non-Christians, and only if it helps expand our view of different others so that we are in solidarity with them as equal in their humanity and dignity.

This reading of Barun—as affirming the coexistence of particular attachments with theological beliefs and their universal horizons, wherein the former is being informed by the latter—gains an additional layer of relationality when he speaks of particular historical experiences of suffering as embedding, rather than precluding, a sense of solidarity with different others. In several of his interviews, Barun appeals to Croatian Catholics to open their homes and their country because of their own recent experience of war and displacement. For him, the "sad experience of our Domovinski rat" (here he uses the notion "the war for our homeland," not a generic notion of conflict), means that "our own" refugee experience should help "us understand the refugees" coming "to our country."[102] The particularity of history and the visceral memories of it do not signify here an obstacle to solidarity but a shared experience with the migrants and thus an important foundation of solidarity with them. In Barun's rendering, the particularity of identity attachments to one's country indicate the capacity to know and understand what it means to be without it. It is that concrete historical experience of homelessness, Barun is suggesting, that should embolden ones' solidarity with others with whom we share not only humanity but also the immediate knowledge of suffering.

Barun is hardly alone in asserting that the experiences of *living* on the Balkan borders can lead toward the linking of the ethics of identity and the ethics of solidarity—what decolonial thinkers might recognize as a relational way of being characteristic of border thinking and doing. In her interviews with people who, along the western Balkans route, help refugees and asylum seekers, Chiara Milan finds that the solidarity that these individuals have with the migrants is anything but the upshot of some universal humanist values. Rather, the sense of solidarity arises from the range of sources, and among them is the awareness of particular histories— the perception of "having undergone a similar experience of displacement and/or uprooting in the past." Echoing much of Barun's own discourse about the work with refugees, one activist in Macedonia states that she, just like the others who are helping the migrants, can "still remember clearly what it means to seek refuge from a war: I am a Bosniak, we had a refugee crisis . . . I felt how war affects people. Also the Albanians [living in Macedonia] remember the refugee crisis in Kosovo, and the refugees used the same path the Macedonians used during the Great War when the Greeks expelled them."[103]

Just as was the case with Barun, the discursive aspects of such an understanding of particular identity and national belonging is not tied to or trapped within the frameworks of the nation-state; it is instead part of a narrative of belonging whose meanings are configured by the experienced trauma of exile from one's home, shifting the boundaries of belonging toward a close encounter and solidarity with others who also know what it means to lose one's home.

Conclusion as an Opening:
Toward a More Relational Ethics of Identity and Solidarity

Recognizing the languages and practices that can link a sense of belonging, religious and national, with the humanist drive toward solidarity with all human beings is today more important than ever. This act, I have argued, counters the identity/solidarity bifurcation shaping much of western theological and social thought dismissive of and normatively skewed against identitarian subjectivities. The bifurcation in question, as decolonial thinkers also helped us see, entails the western "abyssal thinking" that ultimately deems all particularities except one's own as "nonexistent," that is, something to overcome in the name of universalisms "fictionally" conceptualized in the North and western world.[104]

I furthermore proposed that both the bifurcation in question and the decolonial rejection of its grounding remain silent on the existence of betwixt/between subjectivities, such as those we can trace in the Balkans, which is the periphery of both the colonizer (western Europe) and the colonized (the South). Yet only by undertaking the sociology of silences in the places that various theories and types of politics marginalize is it possible to recognize and examine the links between identitarian and solidary subjectivities. As we saw, when solidarity is read through the lenses of particular belonging that evoke the specific historical experience of exile, it is possible to inhabit ties and responsibilities to others while affirming humanisms that build on rather than transcend one's attachment to a particular group—religious and national. In identifying the complex and productive relationship between the narratives of particular identities and the more universally framed ethics of responsibility and solidarity—in seeing the insights of border living in regions like the Balkans, which are, and have historically been, defined by multiple peripheralities—we might accomplish three things: first, identify frameworks of social cohesion and give concreteness to various forms of moral commitment; second, trace existing discourses that can powerfully challenge the exclusionary nationalist and nativist narratives; and third, in so doing, make an important step toward developing a less bifurcated, truly pluriversal world where coexistence arises "in cooperation among compatible universes based on truth in parentheses and in antagonism and conflict with universes of meaning based on truth without parentheses."[105]

If Barun's actions, and the work of organizations like his, might not resolve the questions of borders that "cross everyone, including those who never cross borders,"[106] they can certainly make those borders more porous and more humane. What is more, they can provide discourses for a different way to address the challenges, and perhaps for many temptations, of various types of exclusionary identities, including those disguised in forms of uncritical universal humanist ethics. I pointed to Barun as an example of a way of being that is not dictated by the norms of knowledge and political practices of the European "center," but that emerges on the European borders that, to so many, have long been a home, not an obstacle to cross.

NOTES

1. Margaret Canovan. "Populism for Political Theorists?," *Journal of Political Ideologies* 9, no. 3 (2004): 241–52.

2. Three decades ago, Craig Calhoun noted that the "problems of collective identity formation are commonly ignored by democratic theory" even though they are "endemic to modern political life"; Calhoun, *Nations Matter: Culture, History, and the Cosmopolitan Dream* (London: Routledge, 2007), 80. Similarly, some scholars of populism correctly note that populisms provoke debate about social problems that traditional political parties marginalize or ignore; see interview with Benjamin De Cleen, "Populism, Nationalism, and Transnationalism," openDemocracy, October 25, 2016, https://www.opendemocracy.net/en/can-europe-make-it/you-can-use-populism-to-send-migrants-back. For some recent discussion of this problem in political theory, see Keith Banting and Will Kymlicka, eds., *The Strains of Commitment: The Political Sources of Solidarity in Diverse Societies* (Oxford: Oxford University Press, 2019).

3. Chantal Mouffe, *Deliberative Democracy or Agonistic Pluralism* (Vienna: Institut für Höhere Studien, 2000); Chantal Mouffe, *On the Political* (London: Routledge, 2005); Ernesto Laclau, *On Populist Reason* (London: Verso, 2005).

4. See Josip Kumpes, "Religioznost i Stavovi Prema Imigrantima u Hrvatskoj," *Migracije i Etničke Teme* 34, no. 3 (2018): 275–320; for the European "new radical right" that affirms the idea of "a fortress Europe" to exploit "the fears and anxieties of citizens who feel threatened by socio-economic changes and resent a rise in the number of immigrants, asylum seekers and refugees," see Montserrat Guibernau, *Belonging: Solidarity and Division in Modern Societies* (Cambridge: Polity Press, 2013), 89.

5. For the discussion of "healthy conflict" in American society, see Jason Springs, *Healthy Conflict in Contemporary American Society: From Enemy to Adversary* (Cambridge: Cambridge University Press, 2018).

6. Twenty years ago, Andrew Vincent argued that political theory needed a new vision that would not draw a sharp contrast between particularity and universality. See Vincent, *Nationalism and Particularity* (Cambridge: Cambridge University Press, 2002).

7. For the idea of "analytic bifurcation" in social theory, see Julian Go, "For a Postcolonial Sociology," *Theory and Society* 42 (2013): 25–55; see also Go, ed., *Postcolonial Sociologies: A Reader* (Bingley: Emerald Group, 2016), 9–16.

8. In her considerations of identity and solidarity using the lenses of feminist critiques, Shannon Dunn also argues for the need to think of these two notions together rather than apart. See Dunn, "Identity Politics, Social Justice, and the Quest for Solidarity," *Soundings: An Interdisciplinary Journal,* 104, no. 4 (2021): 281–98. I am grateful to an anonymous reviewer of my chapter for alerting me to this excellent discussion.

9. Boaventura de Sousa Santos, "Beyond Abyssal Thinking: From Global Lines to Ecologies of Knowledges," *Eurozine*, June 29, 2007, https://www.eurozine.com/beyond-abyssal-thinking/. Santos here explains that modern western thinking designated "the other" as inhabiting the "colonial territories"; in his later work, he opposes the western-centric/Eurocentric abyssal thinking while pointing to the "epistemologies of the South"; see Santos, *The End of the Cognitive Empire: The Coming of Age of Epistemologies of the South* (Durham, NC: Duke University Press, 2018).

10. For the postcolonial and decolonial critiques of nationalism in the context of the Balkans, see Katarina Kušić, Philipp Lottholz, and Polina Manolova, "Introduction: From Dialogue to Practice: Pathways towards Decoloniality in Southeastern Europe," *dVersia* (March 2019): 23. For a critique of nationalist identitarianism as the affirmation of "ethnonationalist capitalism," see Danijela Majstorović, "Postcoloniality as Peripherality in Bosnia and Herzegovina," *dVersia* (March 2019): 133.

11. See, among others, Aníbal Quijano, "Coloniality of Power, Eurocentrism, and Latin America," *Nepantla: Views from South* 1, no. 3 (2000): 533–80, esp. 557–58.

12. On one decolonial reading of Christianity, Christian humanist ideas are not only constitutive of the "totalizing Christian framework," but also generative of

the first articulations of cultural racism, as attested, among others, in the ideas of Bartolomé de las Casas. See Santiago Slabodsky, "Not Every Radical Philosophy Is Decolonial," *Contending Modernities*, June 4, 2020, https://contendingmodernities.nd.edu/decoloniality/not-every-radical-philosophy-is-decolonial/.

13. Santos, "Beyond Abyssal Thinking."

14. For a different take on the decolonial thought pertaining to the Balkans, see Kušić, Lottholz, and Manolova, "Introduction," 24.

15. Santos, *The End of the Cognitive Empire*, 8.

16. "Interview with Boaventura de Sousa Santos," conducted by Roger Dale and Susan Robertson, *Globalisation, Societies and Education* 2, no. 2 (2004): 147–60.

17. Arturo Escobar, "Patterns of COMMONING: Commons in the Pluriverse," https://patternsofcommoning.org/commons-in-the-pluriverse/.

18. In his 1986 piece in *The New York Review of Books*, Timothy Garton Ash ruminated about the "Central European" identity as "Western, rational, humanistic, democratic, skeptical, and tolerant." See Garton Ash, in Pamela Ballinger, "Whatever Happened to Eastern Europe? Revisiting Europe's Eastern Peripheries," *East European Politics and Societies and Cultures* 31, no. 1 (2017): 51.

19. See Slabodsky in this volume (chapter 1).

20. For the importance of envisioning and enacting the alternative forms of identity that affirm pluriversality and epistemological diversity, see Santos, *The End of the Cognitive Empire*, 11.

21. Walter D. Mignolo and Catherine E. Walsh, *On Decoloniality: Concepts, Analytics, Praxis* (Durham, NC: Duke University Press, 2018), 115.

22. Escobar, "Patterns of COMMONING."

23. For Mignolo's careful consideration of the meanings of the non-Eurocentric critique of Eurocentrism, see Mignolo and Walsh, *On Decoloniality*, 151. For Maria Todorova's discussion of the task of Eastern European intellectuals to "deprovincialize Western Europe," see Todorova, "Balkanism and Postcolonialism, or On the Beauty of the Airplane View," in *In Marx's Shadow: Knowledge, Power, and Intellectuals in Eastern Europe and Russia*, ed. Costica Bradatan and Sergie Oushakine (Washington, DC: Lexington Books, 2010), 175–95.

24. In this chapter, I draw on some general propositions put forward in my earlier Slavica Jakelić, "From Law to Solidarity," in *Law, Religion and Love: Seeking Ecumenical Justice for the Other*, ed. Paul Babie and Vanja-Ivan Savić (Oxfordshire: Routledge Press, 2018), 129–48.

25. In Greek and Roman contexts, this notion referred to the "republican civic friendship"; in the Christian theological framing, it came to stand for the ideal of charity; see Hauke Brukhorst, in Simon Derpmann, "Solidarity and Cosmopolitanism," *Ethical Theory and Moral Practice* 3 (2009): 305.

26. See, especially, S. N. Eisenstadt's points about the complex relations between particular and universal in the cultural projects of modernity, in Eisenstadt,

"Multiple Modernities," *Daedalus, Journal of the American Academy of Arts and Sciences, Multiple Modernities* 129, no. 1 (2000): 1–29.

27. The American sociologist Michele Dillon, for example, writes that mechanic solidarity in the American context gives voice "to intersecting identities that do not fit easily within *traditional* structures that emphasize a *single, overarching, and homogenized* identity"; see Dillon, "Multiple Belongings: The Persistence of Community amidst Societal Differentiation," in *At the Limits of the Secular: Reflections on Faith and Public Life*, ed. William A. Barbieri Jr. (Grand Rapids, MI: William B. Eerdmans, 2014), 281 (my emphasis).

28. Jürgen Habermas, "Justice and Solidarity: On the Discussion Concerning Stage 6," *Philosophical Forum* 21 (1998): 47.

29. On Habermas's view of German patriotism "after Auschwitz," and as always carrying the burden of the moral catastrophe of Nazism, see Habermas, as quoted in Jan-Werner Mueller, "Origins of Constitutional Patriotism," *Contemporary Political Theory* 5 (2006): 289. Habermas's critics thus correctly point to the "supplemental particularity" upon which the universal rational principles of his cosmopolitanism rely; see Mueller, "Origins of Constitutional Patriotism." For MacIntyre, one's sense of moral obligation is inseparable from a sense of loyalty to particular communities and their traditions; for one iteration of this argument, see Alasdair MacIntyre, *Is Patriotism a Virtue?*, The Lindley Lecture at the University of Kansas, Department of Philosophy, 1984, 3–20, esp. 10–11. See also the discussion of MacIntyre's ideas in Klaus Peter Rippe, "Diminishing Solidarity," *Ethical Theory and Moral Practice* 3, no. 1 (1998): 365. MacIntyre does acknowledge the philosophical validity of the universal moral claims, but his argument needs to be placed within his larger critique of modernity, especially the legacy of the Enlightenment, where liberal impersonal moral judgments acquired particular prestige, whether in their Kantian, utilitarian, or contractarian flavor; see MacIntyre, *Is Patriotism a Virtue?*, esp. 9; also see MacIntyre, *After Virtue: A Study in Moral Theory* (Notre Dame, IN: University of Notre Dame Press, 2007).

30. See Richard Rorty, *Contingency, Irony, and Solidarity* (Cambridge: Cambridge University Press, 1989), 195 (my emphasis). It is this kind of contextually and historically "bound-up" meaning of solidarity that shaped the sense of obligation and solidarity in the Black America of the early nineteenth century; see Eddie S. Glaude Jr., *Exodus! Religion, Race, and Nation in Early Nineteenth-Century Black America* (Chicago: University of Chicago Press, 2000), 16.

31. Rorty, *Contingency, Irony, and Solidarity*, 196. Insisting on the specificity of solidarity within a particular "we," Rorty writes, "our sense of solidarity is strongest when those with whom solidarity is expressed are thought of as 'one of us,' where 'us' means something smaller and more local than the human race" (ibid., 191).

32. Keith Banting and Will Kymlicka, eds., "Introduction," in *The Strains of Commitment: The Political Sources of Solidarity in Diverse Societies* (Oxford: Oxford University Press, 2019), 7, 27, 33.

33. Here, Hollinger echoes the arguments put forward by Amartya Sen, *Identity and Violence: The Illusion of Destiny* (New York: W. W. Norton, 2006).

34. Solidarity, according to Hollinger, involves "a special claim . . . that individuals have on each other's energies, compassion, and resources"; see David A. Hollinger, "From Identity to Solidarity," *Daedalus* 15, no. 4 (2006): 24.

35. See Jean Harvey, in Simon Derpmann, "Solidarity and Cosmopolitanism," *Ethical Theory and Moral Practice* 12, no. 3 (2009): 305.

36. Ivan Krastev, *After Europe* (Philadelphia: University of Pennsylvania Press, 2017), 50.

37. Kohn was influenced by other thinkers who introduced similar binaries in the discourse and analysis of social theorizing of modernity; for more, see Calhoun, *Nations Matter*; see also John Coakley, "National Identity and the 'Kohn Dichotomy,'" *Nationalities Papers* 46, no. 2 (2018): 252–71.

38. Kohn, as quoted in Bernard Yack, *Nationalism and the Moral Psychology of Community* (Chicago: University of Chicago Press, 2012), 26; from Kohn, *The Idea of Nationalism*, 574.

39. Calhoun, *Nations Matter*, 132.

40. In studies of nationalism, there have been sociologists whose antiidentitarian stance is expressed through skepticism about the analytic usefulness of the notion of "identity," including even calls for the dismissal of the notion as such. See Rogers Brubaker and Frederick Cooper, "Beyond 'Identity,'" *Theory and Society* 29 (2000): 1–47; Siniša Malešević, "Identity: Conceptual, Operational and Historical Critique," in *Making Sense of Collectivity: Ethnicity, Nationalism and Globalization*, ed. Siniša Malešević and Mark Haugaard (London: Pluto Press, 2002), 195–215.

41. See Anthony Smith, *Nations and Nationalism in a Global Era* (Cambridge: Polity Press, 1995); Rogers Brubaker, "The Manichean Myth: Rethinking the Distinction between 'Civic' and 'Ethnic' Nationalism," in *Nation and National Identity: The European Experience in Perspective*, ed. Hanspeter Kriesl, Klaus Armingeon, Hannes Slegrist, and Andreas Wimmer (Chur: Verlad Rüegger), 55–71; and Rasma Karklins, "The Misunderstanding of Ethnicity," *Problems of Postcommunism* 48, no. 3 (2001): 37–44; Calhoun, *Nations Matter*; Geneviève Zubrzycki, "The Classical Opposition between Civic and Ethnic Models of Nationhood: Ideology and Empirical Reality and Social Scientific Analysis," *Polish Sociological Review* 139 (2002): 275–95; Bernard Yack, *Nationalism and the Moral Psychology of Community* (Chicago: University of Chicago Press, 2012); Yael Tamir, "Not so Civic: Is There a Difference between Ethnic and Civic Nationalism?," *Annual Review of Political Science* 22 (2019): 419–34.

42. For the use of ethnic/civic binary (or some variant reflective of their content) in the studies of the wars in Bosnia and Croatia, and also in Serbia, Kosovo, and Slovenia, see, among others, the distinction between "benign" or nonexpansionist nationalisms and the "integral" and aggressive types of nationalism in Ivo Banac,

The National Question in Yugoslavia (Ithaca, NY: Cornell University Press, 1984); Michael Ignatieff, *Blood and Belonging: Journeys into the New Nationalism* (New York: Farrar, Straus and Giroux, 1993); Bogdan Denitch, *Ethnic Nationalism: The Tragic Death of Yugoslavia* (Minneapolis: Minnesota University Press, 1995); Duško Sekulić, "Građanski i Etnički Identitet: Slučaj Hrvatske," *Politička Misao* 40, no. 2 (2003): 140–66; Jelka Zorn, "A Case for Slovene Nationalism: Initial Citizenship Rules and the Erasure," *Nations & Nationalism* 15, no. 2 (2009): 280–98; Anida Sokol, "Between Ethnic and Civic Nationalism: Census and Nation Building in Bosnia and Herzegovina," *medien & zeit* 1 (2016): 12–22; Adrianna Piacentini, "The Weight of Ethnic Collectivism: Youth, Identifications, and Boundaries in Post-conflict Bosnia Herzegovina," *Studies in Ethnicity & Nationalism* 18, no. 3 (2018): 262–80; Laurence Cooley, "To Be a Bosniak or to Be a Citizen? Bosnia and Herzegovina's 2013 Census as an Election," *Nations & Nationalism* 25, no. 3 (2019): 1065–86. For two excellent critiques of this type of analysis and of the west/east and civic/ethnic nationalisms binaries, see Ana Devic, "Ethnonationalism, Politics, and the Intellectuals: The Case of Yugoslavia," *International Journal of Politics, Culture and Society* 11, no. 3 (1998): 375–409; Stephen Shulman, "Challenging the Civic/Ethnic and West/East Dichotomies in the Study of Nationalism," *Comparative Political Studies* 35, no. 5 (2002): 554–86.

43. Kohn posited the civic nationalism of the United States founding documents and of the French Revolution against Germany's anti-Enlightenment turn to "folk"; see Calhoun, *Nations Matter*, 126.

44. Todorova notes the irony in western perceptions of nationalist imaginaries and projects in the Balkans—from seeing the "consciousness of nationality" in the dawn of World War I as "the only basis of European culture and the only bias towards European civilization to be found in the Balkans" to viewing the region through the prism of "the handicap of heterogeneity" in the late 1990s. For the first quotation of the British diplomat who, in the months preceding World War I, wrote the Balkan survey for the Carnegie Endowment, see Maria Todorova, *Imagining the Balkans* (New York: Oxford University Press, 1997), 132; see also Joseph Roucek, *Balkan Politics: International Politics in No Man's Land* (Stanford, CA: Stanford University Press, 1948), as quoted in Todorova, *Imagining the Balkans*, 128.

45. See Emmanuel Macron's speech on patriotism, and his condemnation of nationalism, during the commemoration of the 100th Armistice Day anniversary in Paris; see E. J. Dionne, Norman J. Ornstein, and Thomas E. Mann, *One Nation after Trump: A Guide for the Perplexed, the Disillusioned, the Desperate, and the Not-Yet Deported* (New York: St. Martin's Press, 2017). For Philip Gorski's affirmation of sharp distinctions between "civil religion" and "religious nationalism" wherein the former allows for and the latter constrains democratic pluralism, see Gorski, *American Covenant: A History of Civil Religion from the Puritans to the Present* (Princeton, NJ: Princeton University Press, 2017).

46. Stuart M. Patrick, "The Rise of Ethnonationalism and the Future of Liberal Democracy," Council on Foreign Relations, June 15, 2017, https://www.cfr.org/blog/rise-ethnonationalism-and-future-liberal-democracy; Panel discussion, "Ethnonationalism and Vulnerable Populations," Council on Foreign Relations, November 20, 2017, https://www.cfr.org/event/ethnonationalism-and-vulnerable-populations.

47. Lepore is conscious of both the bonds and the burdens of the American past wherein the promise of inclusion was accompanied by the most radical form of exclusion; see Jill Lepore, *This America: The Case for the Nation* (New York: Liveright, 2019), esp. 30, 41, and 46–47. For my reflections on the problems of Lepore's understanding of patriotism and civic nationalism, see Slavica Jakelić, "Why Nationalism Keeps Surprising Us," *Religion & Its Publics Blog*, December 28, 2020, http://relpubs.as.virginia.edu/why-nationalism-keeps-surprising-us-by-slavica-jakelic/.

48. See Talal Asad, *Formations of the Secular: Christianity, Islam, Modernity* (Stanford, CA: Stanford University Press, 2003); Saba Mahmood, *Politics of Piety: The Islamic Revival and the Feminist Subject* (Princeton, NJ: Princeton University Press, 2005); Elizabeth Shakman Hurd, *The Politics of Secularism in the International Relations* (Princeton, NJ: Princeton University Press, 2008); Markus Dressler, "Public Private Distinctions, the Alevi Questions, and the Headscarf: Turkish Secularism Revisited," in *Comparative Secularisms in a Global Age*, ed. Linell E. Cady and Elizabeth Shakman Hurd (New York: Palgrave Macmillan, 2010), 121–41; also Dressler "Making Religion through Secularist Legal Discourse," in *Secularism and Religion-Making*, ed. Markus Dressler and Arvind-Pal S. Mandair (Oxford: Oxford University Press, 2011), 187–208.

49. Catholic theologian William Cavanaugh critiques Christian identity defined by virtue of one's birth into some specific group as a hindrance for the possibility of true catholicity; see Cavanaugh, "If You Render unto God What Is God's, What Is Left for Caesar?," *Review of Politics* 71 (2009): 607–19.

50. For an early articulation of this idea, see Paul Mojzes, *Yugoslavian Inferno: Ethnoreligious Warfare in the Balkans* (London: Bloomsbury, 1994). On the role of ethno-religious links in the war in Bosnia, see Lenard J. Cohen, "Bosnia's 'Tribal Gods': The Role of Religion in Nationalist Politics," in *Religion and the War in Bosnia*, ed. Paul Mojzes (Atlanta: Scholars Press, 1998), 43–73. For the claims that the identitarian expressions of religions in the former Yugoslav society were a result of religions becoming an ideological substitute for communism, see Vjekoslav Perica, *Balkan Idols: Religion and Nationalism in Yugoslav Societies* (Oxford: Oxford University Press, 2002), 221.

51. The references to Volf and others rely on my discussion of this problematic developed in Slavica Jakelić, "Catholicism and Belonging, in This World," in *Beyond the Borders of Baptism: Catholicity, Allegiances, and Lived Identities*, ed. Michael Budde (Eugene, OR: Cascade, 2016), 104–22.

52. Slavica Jakelić, *Collectivistic Religions: Religion, Choice, and Identity in Late Modernity* (London: Routledge, 2016).

53. See The Editors, "Open Letter: Against the New Nationalism: An Appeal to our Fellow Christians," *Commonweal*, August 19, 2019, https://www.commonwealmagazine.org/open-letter-against-new-nationalism.

54. For Mignolo's decolonial critique of the western European assertion of its humanism as a universal humanism, see Mignolo and Walsh, *On Decoloniality*, esp. 153–76. For Nelson Maldonado-Torres's affirmation of "decolonized humanism," see Maldonado-Torres, "On the Coloniality of Human Rights," *Revista Crítica de Ciênsias Sociais* 114 (2017): 117–36. For Anthony Pinn's critique of universal humanism's implication in racism in the American history and present, see Pinn, *When Colorblindness Is Not the Answer: Humanism and the Challenge of Race* (Durham, NC: Pitchstone Publishing Institute for Humanist Studies, 2017). For my discussion of Talal Asad and Pierre Fassin's critique of Christian-seculo humanism in humanitarianism as circumscribed in their western-centric understanding of humanism, see Slavica Jakelić, "Humanism and Its Critics," in *The Oxford Handbook on Humanism*, ed. Anthony Pinn (Oxford: Oxford University Press, 2021), 265–93.

55. Rogers Brubaker, "Between Nationalism and Civilizationism: The European Populist Moment in Comparative Perspective," *Ethnic and Racial Studies* 40, no. 8 (2017): 1199.

56. See Walter D. Mignolo, "Foreword: On Pluriversality and Multipolarity," in *Constructing the Pluriverse: The Geopolitics of Knowledge*, ed. Bernd Reiter (Durham, NC: Duke University Press, 2018): xii. For the role of Christian universalism in Western European colonial projects and governance, see, among others, Jean Comaroff and John Comaroff, "Christianity and Colonialism in South Africa," *American Ethnologist* 13, no. 1 (1986): 1–22; David Chidester, *Savage Systems: Colonialism and Comparative Religion in South Africa* (Charlottesville: University of Virginia Press, 1996). Some decolonial thinkers argue that the colonial Christian theology of Renaissance humanism continued to operate "under the guise of secular colonial politics" and is still informing the "present global epistemic order"; see An Yountae, "A Decolonial Theory of Religion: Race, Coloniality, and Secularity in the Americas," *Journal of the American Academy of Religion* 88, no. 4 (2020): 947–80.

57. Echoing Sen, Hollinger sees the concept of identity as "quasi-mystical and conducive for violence;" see Amartya Sen, *Identity and Violence: The Illusion of Destiny* (New York: W. W. Norton, 2006).

58. Julian Go, "For a Postcolonial Sociology," *Theory and Society* 42 (2013): 36–37.

59. Ibid., 32 (my emphasis).

60. MacIntyre recognizes this move as a problem, yet in asserting the primacy of the identitarian logic of solidary relations, he also reaffirms the same problem: he ends up cementing the identity/solidarity divide.

61. Go, "For a Postcolonial Sociology," 41.

62. Santos, "Beyond Abyssal Thinking."

63. Meghan Tinsley, "Decolonizing the Civic/Ethnic Binary," *Current Sociology* 67, no. 3 (2019): 355.

64. Santos, "Beyond Abyssal Thinking" (my emphasis).

65. It would be possible to offer this understanding of the Balkans if one were to follow what Santos would deem as "the *marginal* or *subordinate versions* of modern Western thinking which have opposed the hegemonic version" (ibid.) (my emphasis).

66. Todorova, *Imagining the Balkans*, 2.

67. See, especially, Todorova's chapter "Balkans as Self-Designation," in Todorova, *Imagining the Balkans*. For the ways in which scholars saw this resistance to the character of the Balkans, and Balkanness, as something that some in the Balkan region rejected as a way to align with the west, see Milica Bakić-Hayden and Robert Hayden, "Orientalist Variations on the Theme 'Balkans': Symbolic Geography in Recent Yugoslav Cultural Politics," *Slavic Review* 51, no. 1 (1992): 1–15.

68. Among others, the Bulgarians, Romanians, Poles, and Croats, often college-educated, are the ones who were the last to have the license to migrate to Germany, the Netherlands, Ireland, or UK, where they are also the ones to do the lowest-paying jobs.

69. Todorova, *Imagining the Balkans*, 7. For the perpetuation of the notion of the Balkans as unpredictable and immutable in its irrationality among some of the most influential western European political leaders, see Slavica Jakelić, "Boundaries of Freedom, Boundaries of Responsibility: Everyday Religious Life of the Croatian Catholic Women," in *Everyday Life in the Balkans*, ed. David Montgomery (Bloomington: Indiana University Press, 2018), 299–310.

70. Todorova, *Imagining the Balkans*, 17.

71. For one such discussion, see, for example, Costica Bradatan and Serguei Oushakine, eds., *In Marx's Shadow: Knowledge, Power, and Intellectuals in Eastern Europe and Russia* (Washington, DC: Lexington Books, 2010).

72. Among them Milica Bakić-Hayden, "Nesting Orientalisms: The Case of Former Yugoslavia," *Slavic Review* 54, no. 4 (1995): 917–31; and Larry Wolff, *Inventing Eastern Europe: The Map of Civilization on the Mind of the Enlightenment* (Stanford, CA: Stanford University Press, 1994).

73. Todorova, *Imagining the Balkans*, 11.

74. Ibid., 13.

75. Ibid., 11. For Kušić, Lottholz, and Manolova, Todorova's work represents "a cornerstone to what can be referred to as 'critical Balkanist studies,'" which built on Said's work and other postcolonial pivotal interventions, and came to include Milica Bakić-Hayden's and Larry Wolff's writings mentioned in this chapter; see note 10, above. On Todorova's reservations about the usage of postcolonial perspective in the study of this region and its historical legacies, see, especially, Todorova's chapter "Balkanism and Postcolonialism, or On the Beauty of the Airplane View," in Maria

Todorova, *Scaling the Balkans: Essays on Eastern European Entanglements* (Leiden: Brill, 2019), 93–114.

76. Todorova, *Imagining the Balkans*, 18.

77. For an important contribution to the discussion of "periphery" as a valuable tool in the study of the Balkans and Eastern Europe, see Pamela Ballinger, "Whatever Happened to Eastern Europe? Revisiting Europe's Eastern Peripheries," *East European Politics and Societies and Cultures* 31, no. 1 (2017): 51.

78. In this, I only partly depart from Todorova, who emphasizes the Byzantium and the Ottoman legacies as crucial for the historical existence of the Balkans, stressing rather the encounters between those legacies and those of developed in the western European context; see Todorova, *Imagining the Balkans*, 12.

79. I draw here on some of Todorova's reflections on the Balkans. For the bridge as a metaphor for the role of Bosnia in connecting the east and the west, see Andrić's novel *Na Drini ćuprija*. In this interpretation, I differ from those who read Andrić's body of work as affirming a hybridity that reflects a type of Orientalism; for this argument, see, for example, Tomislav Longinović, *Vampire Nation: Violence as Cultural Imaginary* (Durham, NC: Duke University Press, 2011). I take Andrić's writing to affirm particular configurations of identity that reflect the richness of the idea and ideal of the Balkans as a bridge, reducible to neither Occidentalist nor Orientalist imaginaries.

80. Mario Pušić, "Reporteri Jutarnjeg u Najvećem Europskog Gradu Migranata, Nadomak Hrvatske Granice," https://www.jutarnji.hr/vijesti/svijet/reporteri-jutarnjeg-u-najvecem-europskom-gradu-migranata-nadomak-hrvatske-granice-ono-sto-su-kruzeri-dubrovniku-e-to-su-nama-u-bihacu-migranti/9180845/.

81. "Migrant Crisis: Migration to Europe Explained in Seven Charts," BBC News, March 4, 2016, https://www.bbc.com/news/world-europe-34131911.

82. Adrian Edwards, "Forced Displacement at Record 68.5 Million," UNCHR, June 19, 2018, https://www.unhcr.org/en-us/news/stories/2018/6/5b222c494/forced-displacement-record-685-million.html.

83. "Annual Asylum Statistics," Eurostat Statistics Explained, https://ec.europa.eu/eurostat/statistics-explained/index.php?title=Asylum_statistics&oldid=558181.

84. "Croatia Will Not Build Walls for Refugees: Vesna Pusić Expresses Contempt for Hungarian Solution," *Jutarnji list*, August 27, 2015, https://www.jutarnji.hr/vijesti/hrvatska/hrvatska-nece-graditi-zidove-za-izbjeglice-vesna-pusic-iskazala-prezir-prema-madarskom-rjesenju/293875/.

85. The current Croatian prime minister, Andrej Plenković, and his administration approach the question of migrants primarily as a legal matter, a humanitarian issue, or a human rights issue. See "What Will Europe Do about the Great Migrant Crisis? EU Leaders Divided over the Fate of Unfortunate People, Read What the Croatian Prime Minister Said," *Slobodna Dalmacija*, June 24, 2018, https://www

.slobodnadalmacija.hr/novosti/svijet/clanak/id/553008/sto-ce-europa-poduzeti-po-pitanju-velike-migrantske-krize-celnici-drzava-eu-podijeljeni-oko-sudbine-nesretnih-ljudi-procitajte-sto-je-porucio-hrvatski-premijer.

86. The former Croatian president Kolinda Grabar-Kitarović defended the behavior of the police and border forces, stating they used legal tools to protect Croatia's own borders. See Zdravka Grund, "The Ombudswoman Received an Anonymous Letter from a Police Officer, Complaining That Their Bosses Were Ordering Them to Forcibly Expel Migrants," *Telegram*, July 17, 2019, https://www.telegram.hr/politika-kriminal/pucka-pravobraniteljica-primila-anonimno-pismo-policajca-tvrdi-kako-je-istina-da-koriste-nasilje-prema-migrantima/; "Shocking Letter from Mountaineers: 'Migrants Were Just Looking for Water, and Special Forces Were Beating Them and Shooting over Them,'" *RTL.HR*, June 20, 2019, https://www.rtl.hr/vijesti-hr/novosti/hrvatska/3520107/pismo-planinara-koji-je-svjedocio-nasilju-nad-izbjeglicama-na-risnjaku/; Gordan Duhaček, "In a Shocking Interview, Kolinda Admitted That the Croatian Police Were Breaking the Law," July 10, 2019, https://www.index.hr/vijesti/clanak/kolinda-u-sokantnom-intervjuu-priznala-da-hrvatska-policija-krsi-zakone/2099829.aspx.

87. Jasmin Klarić, "Migranti Nisu Problem. Problem su Kršćani." ("It's Not the Migrants Who Are the Problem. The Problem Is the Christians"), *Autograf*, November 18, 2018, https://www.autograf.hr/tvrtko-barun-migranti-nisu-problem-problem-su-krscani.

88. Antun Oršolić, "Father Tvrtko Barun: The Sad Fact That We Had Similar Experiences in the Homeland War Should Help Us Understand Refugees," *Narod*, August 30, 2015, https://narod.hr/hrvatska/pater-tvrtko-barun-zalosna-cinjenica-da-smo-u-domovinskom-ratu-dozivjeli-slicna-iskustva-trebala-bi-nam-pomoci-da-razumijemo-izbjeglice.

89. Thinkers such as Hannah Arendt would see this as a platform for solidarity that partakes "of reason" and is "able to comprehend . . . the multitude of a class or a nation or a people" and "eventually all mankind"; Arendt, *On Revolution* (New York: Penguin Books, 2006), 79.

90. Klarić, "Migranti Nisu Problem. Problem su Kršćani."

91. Ibid.; see also Oršolić, "Father Tvrtko Barun."

92. See, for example, Jan-Werner Mueller, "Angela Merkel's Misunderstood Christian Mission," *Foreign Policy*, March 18, 2016, https://foreignpolicy.com/2016/03/18/angela-merkels-misunderstood-christian-mission-eu/.

93. Tomislav Mamić, "Head of the Jesuit Refugee Service: 'Orban and Barbed Wire Are Our Role Models? Christian Europe Cannot Be Proud of Itself in Refugee Crisis,'" *Jurtanji*, December 25, 2017, https://www.jutarnji.hr/vijesti/hrvatska/voditelj-isusovacke-sluzbe-za-izbjeglice-orban-i-bodljikave-zice-su-nam-uzor-krscanska-europa-ne-moze-se-ponositi-sobom-u-izbjeglickoj-krizi/6873168/.

94. Klarić, "Migranti Nisu Problem. Problem su Kršćani."

95. Ibid.

96. John Paul II, *Sollicitudo rei socialis*, https://www.vatican.va/content/john-paul-ii/en/encyclicals/documents/hf_jp-ii_enc_30121987_sollicitudo-rei-socialis.html. For the understanding of the solidarity with and among workers, see John Paul II, *Laborem excercens*, https://www.vatican.va/content/john-paul-ii/en/encyclicals/documents/hf_jp-ii_enc_14091981_laborem-exercens.html. As Gerald Beyer helpfully notes, Catholic social teaching recognizes three meanings of solidarity: "solidarity as anthropological 'datum,' solidarity as an ethical imperative, and solidarity as a principle concretized in legislative policies and institutions." See Beyer, "The Meaning of Solidarity in Catholic Social Teaching," *Political Theology* 15, no. 1 (2014): 15.

97. Mladen Obrenović, "Barun: Our Small Countries Can Hardly Do Anything on Their Own," Al Jazeera, October 7, 2017, http://balkans.aljazeera.net/vijesti/barun-nase-male-zemlje-tesko-mogu-ista-same-napraviti.

98. See Beyer, "The Meaning of Solidarity in Catholic Social Teaching."

99. Klarić, "Migranti nisu problem. Problem su kršćani." Because of his views and his openness toward and work with the migrants, Barun has been accused of dismissing the responsibility to his "own people" and of being an ally of Soros and Open Society. See Ivona B., "Koga Predstavlja Isusovac Tvrtko Barun i u Čije Ime Govori?" ("Who Does Jesuit Tvrtko Barun Represent and on Whose Behalf Is He Speaking?"), *Kamenjar*, June 21, 2018, https://kamenjar.com/koga-predstavlja-isusovac-tvrtko-barun-i-u-cije-ime-govori/.

100. Klarić, "Migranti Nisu Problem. Problem su Kršćani."

101. Ibid.

102. Oršolić, "Father Tvrtko Barun."

103. Chiara Milan, "Refugees at the Gates of the EU: Civic Initiatives and Grassroots Responses to the Refugee Crisis along the Western Balkans Route," *Journal of Balkan and Near Eastern Studies* 21, no. 1 (2019): 8.

104. On the notion of the human as "the fictional conceptualization" of European Renaissance, see Mignolo and Walsh, *On Decoloniality*, 153.

105. Ibid., 175n18.

106. De Genova as he is quoted in *The Irregularization of Migration in Contemporary Europe: Detention, Deportation, Drowning*, ed. Yolande Jansen, Robin Celikates, and Joost de Bloois (Washington, DC: Rowman & Littlefield International, 2015), 12.

CHAPTER 7

The Fires This Time

GIL ANIDJAR

Abstract

There are many fires today, many emergencies, all burning incandescent, some of them simultaneously; others for longer than we can remember. There are fires that are just beginning, perhaps, but already threatening to engulf us; others yet too numerous, too remote to be counted, or reported. Still, who is it that can scream "fire!"? Who is it that truly decides on the emergency, who is it that declares the state of emergency, the state of exception? Who is it that knows which fire to respond to? Who is it that can call the fire, that can identify and name the fires this time?

"In a theater," Kierkegaard once wrote, "it happened that a fire started offstage. The clown came out to tell the audience. They thought it was a joke and applauded. He told them again, and they became still more hilarious. This is the way, I suppose, that the world will be destroyed—amid the universal hilarity of wits and wags who think it is all a joke."[1]

When it comes to fire, when it comes to emergency, the world is certainly a busy stage. Whether or not it will be destroyed, as Kierkegaard supposed—and accompanied by laughter, to boot—the world in which we live today involves many fires. These are literal and metaphorical, oracular and fictitious, real and imagined, and they are surely burning incandescent. Some of them do so simultaneously, others for longer than we can remember, while more fires, perhaps just beginning, are already threatening to engulf us. Others yet are too numerous, too remote (but for whom?) to be counted, or reported.

Still, who is it that shouts "fire!," who is it that truly (or, famously, falsely) decides on the emergency, on the state of emergency or, allowing for the confusion, the state of exception? *Pace* Kierkegaard, it is after all not the clowns—or so one wonders, given the visibility of comedians as incisive commentators and effective pundits —who know which fire to warn of or respond to (for every fire, there is another fire imposing its claim). But who is it, then, that can call the fire, identify and name the fires this time? James Baldwin's own promissory note notwithstanding, the question has been strangely confined to the juridical and to the political, a question of sovereignty, yet it exceeds both spheres by far.[2] Nor is it reducible to the epistemological, much less to the narrowly theatrical. After all, *anyone* can yell "fire!" and no amount of prior knowledge or established authority is necessary. We ourselves, for instance, we scholars, have the leisure and the presumed capacity to point to the fire and to warn about it. But how do we really know how to identify and call out fire? How do we decide—do we decide?—which fire and which emergency to respond to, which to name and which to interrogate and inquire into? Who is it, then, that can shout "fire!"?

Now, there are strict laws against the frivolous use of the word "fire" in a theater or other crowded venues. This is clearly an effect, once again, of anyone having the capacity to yell "fire!" Anyone—the well meaning and the "woke," the experts and the ignorant, the liars and the deceivers, the deceived and the mistaken too—can do it. And so, finally, the clowns. Let us not presume it is with equal efficacy. Or indeed always possible (sometimes everybody knows about the fire, but no one says a thing). Yet there are circumstances when the word can be uttered, when "fire!" must in fact be uttered, regardless of its anticipated or actual effect (which might be momentous, even massive—or laughter). From this we learn that not all words are created equal (there are strong and weighty words, and there are weak ones). We also learn that words are not merely dependent on the circumstances—the context—in which they are uttered. Some words have an effect regardless of their accuracy, regardless of the power or authority of whoever speaks them. Even clowns. Some words have a force or a power that can produce new circumstances (think of "Fire!" as an order given to an execution squad, or to a terrorist cell). A particular class among felicitous performatives (to be distinguished, no doubt, from "misfires"), some words can and do create new contexts. The word "fire" in a crowded theater or indeed on the world stage is among them. And failure, assuming this is what Kierkegaard's clown actually shows, is always a possibility.

When the circumstances permit (or demand), "fire!" must undoubtedly be uttered, shouted. It is necessary that it be so and it would be criminal, if not necessarily cowardly, to stay silent. When there is no fire, however, when the circumstances do not call for it, that very same utterance becomes criminal in turn. Why criminal rather than nonsensical? Because chaos is likely to ensue (it does not always), people might get hurt. However massively, however minutely, circumstances will have changed, and therefore the play will have been interrupted. Or not. Hero or villain, clown or sovereign, it is important to insist and recognize that anybody has the ability—if not the strength, the authority, or the legitimacy, much less the power—to yell "fire!" and to disrupt, displace, and even create a new play. All things being increasingly unequal, someone today— Steven Pinker, say, or, less reliably, Yuval Noah Harari —might also yell back: "False alarm! Everything is good or getting better!" Or else, "It's a hoax!"

When it comes to fire, an actual voice is not always necessary, for the fire itself might speak. It can do its own "work" with little need for assistance (aside from the proverbial smoke, of course). Besides, there are other ways than giving vocal or aural accompaniment to fire. Sometimes it is enough to signal toward it, with a whisper or a gesture (picking up the fire extinguisher, say, or sounding an alarm, even just running away), any of which might be enough to initiate a response, a panic, the onset of salvation, and a new state of play. Or nothing at all, of course, in spite of the devastation. Intentions may be involved, deception too (and self-deception), and sometimes simply an error, or even genuine belief.

Is a decision made? If there really is a fire, the mere perception of it will often suffice regardless of intention and belief, regardless of decision. If there really was a fire, there might be no need to ask in its aftermath: "Why did you yell 'fire!'?" nor "What made you decide to yell 'fire!'?" Much less: "Why did you run?" "Why at this time?" or "Why so late?" (there are those who will ask nonetheless, investigating the fire or the response to it, rather than its burning causes and effects, secondary benefits included). This is not to say that no alternatives were available, or that no decision was involved, only that the matter is as if already decided. If there is a fire, there is little room for hesitation, no time for deliberation, and therefore nothing to decide. No decision to speak of. It is a fight-or-flight situation, and though it may be called a "choice" or indeed a decision, it is only such to the extent that one is called upon to act (decisively, as we say) in one way or another on the spur of the moment. Which, in this case, means that one must speak and speak up—and run (for help or safety). One might also fail to act and keep quiet, but that too would constitute a response or a reaction. For one cannot but respond to the situation, to the fire, and one must call it by its name, and act accordingly—or fail to do so, with dire consequences.

To speak of decision, or of agency, would not, for all that, be mistaken. And one should indeed insist on giving credit to the courageous individual who acted quickly and forcefully, just as one should swiftly condemn anyone who decided deceptively to abuse their agency, to wrongly exercise their freedom to yell "fire!" when no fire was burning. However, if there is really a fire, there is neither time, nor need, for a decision. No prior experience, no prior experience of agency or of decisiveness, is necessary. No authority or instituted voice. Being in a position to act, standing in that time and place, means that one must act immediately. And it might be the first time. Or the last. It is, in any case, a necessity, not a choice.

Choice and decision might be involved nevertheless. If only because there is the possibility of a delay or of a mistake. Is it really a fire? Or is it only smoke? Is it not a joke? And if it is a fire, how serious or dangerous is it? Does it threaten to spread? Is it certain that it will? Is the fire not intentional perhaps? Is it not meant to be there? Perhaps it is just the way of things, the theater's furnace, and not a raging fire about to engulf the theater? It may even be part of the show, a prop for the next act, a special effect, an off-stage distraction. Perhaps it is nothing.

If the world is a stage, the play is not the thing. Not, that is, if there is a genuine fire. The disruption, and the possibility of fiction (a lie or a mistake, a strategy of deception or distraction, a clown's jest—a play) is impossible to hold at bay, try as the law might.

For all the significance granted to agency and to decision, then, for all the critiques of sovereignty, popular and other, it seems to me that too little attention has been given to those elements that, in case of a fire or of another emergency, exceed the bounds of any agency, of any law or authority, much less sovereignty, those elements that overwhelm an alleged ability to decide and the freedom to choose, even the capacity to speak. Besides, when we name our circumstances, when we call "fire!" on the most pressing emergency, we are not merely seeking a validation of our point of view ("This is just what you think!" "You're saying this because you are who you are! Because of your privileged position or condition!"). We make no subjective claim, no local claim either; nor are we commenting on who we are, professing some identity, exercising our agency, legal or other, much less foregrounding our expertise. We are not necessarily trying to persuade either. We, we who might count ourselves, or be counted, among clowns are issuing a warning and, if anything, bearing witness. Our authority to do so, however small, unjust, or mistaken, however limited, has little to do with our prior record, our legal standing, or even the confidence or the recognition of our peers (assuming it has not been tried too many times, like that boy crying wolf, or fire). And though the crowd—our intended audience—may or may not respond (with laughter, say), granting or withholding thereby the efficacy we sought (rather than the credit to our person and the authority that may inhere in it), the response does not constitute the true measure of our testimony, the confirmation of its accuracy. The force of our utterance and the authority of our testimony stem instead from the fire, from the incendiary circumstances in which we find ourselves. Surely, we might be mistaken, but what we witness, what we see or live, is what grounds and authorizes our conviction and our action, our speech. There *is*—*es gibt*, *il y a*—fire, and so we call it. We call it without delay and with no further mediation. It is the fire that obligates us, to that we respond. And so we scream, "FIRE!"

In the case at hand, in the case of fire, there should be no space and no delay between the actual fire and the word "fire," no interval between the event and the testimony, no distance between the fact and the utterance, no mediation, no arbitration, and no consideration of arbitrariness between the thing and the word. And yet, the very possibility of yelling "fire!" when there is no fire, the very possibility of fiction, or of a word divorced from things and from circumstances—that possibility is necessary and unavoidable. Undeniable. The absence of choice, the impossibility of delay, cannot cancel all lapses and intervals. Regardless of intention and of decision, and for reasons that exceed matters of deception and of delusion, it is impossible to dispense with the word "fire" in its multiple usages, whether erroneous or fictitious, whether real or comical, whether pernicious or courageous.

On the world stage, though, it is not always necessary to yell. Sometimes, everybody can see the fire. And so we (or at least some of us) start to run. And then shout. Only there are many fires. Not all of them equally visible from all vantage points. And there are many, many witnesses. Some of them false witnesses.

Like words, witnesses are not all born equal. Who knows this better than the clown? True, witnesses are effects of the circumstances to which they testify. Yet, by accident, and sometimes by training or even by design, some are better positioned with regard to the event (the fire), the capacity to call out "fire!" and the subsequent behavior of the audience. In the theater, the medium is the voice and the resonant space of the auditorium. On the world stage, the medium is the media, which now includes (and is perhaps overtaken by) social media, the information superhighway on which we now travel, if in smaller (rare) metal boxes. Journalists are witnesses, as are civil servants, the police and the politicians, NGO workers, scholars and researchers, among many other individuals and organizations. Any clown or anyone with a phone. Not to forget ChatGPT. Without media, for now, without journalists and those in a position to observe and report, without witnesses (reliable or not), the word "fire" might remain a dead letter. Depending on the fire, the number of witnesses varies, and the likelihood of resonance—the resonance of "likes"—not to mention subsequent action, fluctuates widely. There are, allow me to repeat, many fires. Most of them destructive. Some of them fictitious (or "fake"). What that means is also that, in the theater, one might call out "fire!" when there is no fire or while referring to another stage, or to some other place outside the theater. There is a fire, but it is not occurring here. It is another fire, which interrupts the play, and another play too, another fire, of which we may or may not have been aware. *Tout autre est tout autre*, Derrida said. Every fire is another fire, a different fire entirely.

I seek no theory of communication, here, no media theory. I am neither prophet nor clown (or so I hope), and I am not really interested in a theory of the event. I merely wish to respond as I am called to do. And like my peers, I very much mean to respond to fire. It seems to me, however, that if we are to understand the nature of the fires that threaten or engulf us, if we are to address and state our emergency (or emergencies) along with our role in it, we scholars might attend to the frame of our considerations: historical, disciplinary, authoritative. The world is a stage (it is many stages) and we start, therefore, *in medias res*. And the fire, if there is one (that is, if there is one at all, and if there is only one) serves as an entry point, but it is not the beginning, nor can it be the only beginning. The fire, even (especially?) fictitious, initiates a disruption, a change in a play that is always already running, a transformation in the existing space of the theater. And like the theater, the fire vies for attention, seeking to compensate for a generalized and permanent attention-deficit disorder, and it might be accompanied by another (or the same) call, "fire!" Yet this fire and its call might not suffice, it cannot suffice to serve as the actual entry point, since there might or might not be a fire, or at least not only this fire, not here, not now.

So who calls out "fire!"? Who decides on the state of the exception?

Sometimes fires just burst. As we have seen, this might suffice. The fire might be enough and not to call it, not to name it or declare a state of emergency would be irresponsible, perhaps impossible. The fire is here and it must be responded to. One—a president of the United States, say—might therefore declare a state of emergency or fail to do so, but the emergency is plain to see, as is the need to respond to it. What if we cannot see the fire? What if the fire is (already) viral? What if we can only see "our" fire? To repeat: It is undoubtedly someone's responsibility to call the fire out. This cannot but mean that someone could always yell "fire!" where there is none. Or at least not yet. Someone might testify to a fire that does not exist, or to one that is taking place elsewhere and bears no perceptible relation to the stage we are at. Someone might declare a state of emergency, a war on terror, on the poor, or else a war on COVID, someone might refrain from it when no fire was (is) burning. Or else it was (it is) a different fire. Witnesses and journalists, jurists and activists, the police and the politicians, scholars and academics, ultimately the public—all had (have) to get on board to ensure that the emergency was (is) acknowledged and dealt with. Sometimes it is a revolution. Sometimes it is many. Sometimes it is laughter. Or else it is nothing. Not an event. Not, legally, a genocide.

Each of the contributions in this volume I respond to here may be described as itself a response or a call, one that warns about and calls out, "Fire!" Each signals toward the world stage, toward a corner or angle thereof, and to its vulnerability to and destruction by fire or violence. Each elaborates on the "ostensible ontological fragility of the social body," as Nadia Fadil (chapter 2) calls it, but Santiago Slabodsky (chapter 1) probably comes closest to telling us that it is the world as a whole that is ablaze. This is the condition he calls, after Aníbal Quijano, "coloniality," and it cannot be confined to an all-too-studied and -reported corner of the earth ("the Global

North as the uncontaminated origin, center, and motor of world history"), nor should it be deemed a recent development, even if we seek to "account for the beginnings and transformation of [a] discourse" that gives it a particular, and novel-looking, form. Coloniality is a centuries-old global condition, which finds its sources in "a program of global domination" and in the mobilization of "common genocidal forces," all of which continue to "structure and order global relations of power (knowledge, race, sexuality, labor)." Coloniality (or perhaps it is genocide) is the fire that must be called and declared, and studied too, and it is that which requires a different response, a different understanding and different forms of knowledge, better methodologies. We scholars must call it and know it, therefore, we must call it as we know it, and if not light a fire ourselves, at least "shed light on a more accurate reading of the current political stage," the world stage. We must report on the fire. We must at least "start a conversation."

Cecelia Lynch (chapter 5) too refers to a global emergency; she declares it and joins others in calling it "religion." The fire this time is in Africa, and it involves the complex relation between the Global North and Africa—colonialism and missionizing, conquest and conversion, religion and humanitarianism—with regard primarily to religious traditions, Lynch says, which these forces "did not and could not exterminate." The fire is therefore not genocide, nor, contrary to a powerful discourse, is it FGM (which Lynch nevertheless addresses with great sensitivity). It is, to repeat, religion, its existence, its forms (Islam, Christianity, "African religion"), its knowledges and its decolonizations. Most directly, and in sympathy with the decolonial turn, Lynch acknowledges and calls for "cosmological and onto-epistemological contestations," for "the necessity of openness to African onto-epistemologies, cosmologies, and forms of spirituality." Burial practices and traditional medicines, "experiential and spiritual knowledge," attempts "to update and modernize African religion as an integral component of contemporary African liberation from colonial religious authority"—these not only confirm what and where the fire is, but also point to ways of extinguishing it.

Slavica Jakelić (chapter 6) brings us closer to the debates that oppose (or confuse) emergency and exception. The fire may be, once again, global insofar as it involves a predicament that Jakelić calls "a vital social question," namely, the possibility of solidarity. It is indeed an urgent social question with regard to belonging and collective action, but it is also a national question.

Does national belonging contradict solidarity? Does religion, and, more specifically, does Christianity? At the border between Europe and the South, between the west and the rest, there are refugees. Refugees at the border—this names the fire, I think, in the clearest manner for Jakelić. And on this she argues that the Balkans emerge as the exception that is the rule. The Balkans "challenge the totalizing effects of the modernist view of history and the totalizing decolonial perspectives on 'Europe' of which the Balkans are a part yet also 'the other.'" We thus learn that neither nationalism nor religion per se are to be seen as causes of the emergency. They did not light the fire, nor are they the fire. Still, we do need a different understanding, a different "theory of religion." Is religion the fire or is it what we need to extinguish it? We must in any case engage in "an exploration and understanding of the peace building potential of collectivistic Christianities." The Jesuit Tvrtko Barun and the Jesuit Relief Service are part of a solution, a way to quench the fire with solidarity and with Christian humanism. The "affirmation of pride" in national identity and theological, that is, Christian, commitment to "historical experiences of suffering" render solidarity possible, sustaining narratives of belonging and practices of solidarity and of coexistence.

There are many fires, and many are those who call them out, many who identify and name the fires. Luca Mavelli and Edmund Frettingham (chapter 4) foreground a number of names (primarily, no doubt, neoliberalism and, judging by their title, secularism) for what seems to be a large number of fires. By invoking proper names (Mises, Hayek), we might venture that Mavelli and Frettingham are also denouncing those who started the fire, the arsonists, as it were (or perhaps these are declaring the absence of fire, just as Margaret Thatcher declared the end, the nonexistence, of society). Upon closer reading, though, matters are more complicated. They certainly cannot be reduced to a formula such as the one Slabodsky proposes ("Convert—for your own good—or I kill you"). Here again, let us note that the fire (or fires) is less genocidal, less obviously destructive, than it is transformative. Moreover, it has, if one may twist the metaphor, a number of moving parts, or, better yet, many spots. Most obviously, the ever-expanding market and market logic constitute the form of and give the name to the fire. Yet such expansion took on a particular dimension, a particular color, with the embrace of neoliberal policies, such as those promoted by Mises and Hayek and their numerous followers (Milton Friedman comes to mind). Whatever the nature of the market, and the many understandings of it we might register, neoliberalism expands it, Mavelli and Frettingham write, well beyond the economic sphere. The logic of neoliberalism must therefore be understood in its spread and in its growth. The market is, no doubt, a raging fire, but its intensification, its escalation is not the effect of some immanent dynamic. Rather (and rather than laissez-faire), neoliberalism actively pushes the market beyond its economic limits. And at this juncture, it seems to acquire (or perhaps require) a new moniker. That moniker is "secularism," and more precisely "the coloniality of secularism." Is secularism—or its coloniality—the ultimate name of the fire? Is there one secularism? The answer is, we are told, no. There are in fact many secularisms, and it is necessary to distinguish between them (we are not told why): "it is necessary to distinguish between political, economic, scientific, and even religious secularisms." It is necessary, in other words, to name the distinct fire spots, to recognize them as separate and unequal "colonial epistemic regimes." But the buck does not yet stop here, since these distinct regimes, which must be identified, called out and further investigated, are themselves derivative, secondary effects of a more originary fire, with which we had, in fact, begun. The different secularisms "have been themselves colonized by neoliberal rationalities." There would thus be one fire after all, and its name is neoliberalism. It is an "economism" whose "proponents believed that the policies, institutions, and rationalities of governance they advocated for in economic affairs were appropriate for all areas of life." What Mises, Hayek, and others promoted was the market as paradigmatic: "the self-regulating free market became the model for human sociality as such, and commercial values such as competitiveness, entrepreneurship, self-interest, and efficiency were celebrated as desirable individual dispositions." Interestingly enough, the market (and the ethical, social, and political dispositions it institutes) does not include a theory of the exception, no procedure to identify or declare, much less manage, a state of emergency (or many), the destruction of a market say, the demise of "niche" customers, whose country (or "economy") has been devastated. Who is it, then, that can shout "fire!"? Who, in "the self-regulating free market"—the current form of the world stage—identifies the real emergency? Who decides on the state of exception?

Be the answer to that question what it may, Mavelli and Frettingham take their own account yet further when they identify the fire as "self-colonizing." It is not the wasteland that grows, in other words, but rather the fire, one that, multiple as it is, jumps from spot to spot and from sphere to sphere and burns stronger as it grows. What the authors ultimately and finally call "neoliberal secularism" is what "transcends the economic domain and colonizes all spheres of human existence," which includes, of course, "religion." Indeed, the colonization, the self-colonization of neoliberal secularism extends "to the point of incorporating its religious antagonist." And at this very point, the fire jumps again and changes nature—and name—"becoming itself a religion." Neoliberalism is a religion, it is a peculiar religion, which is not reducible (but why would it be?) to irrationality or even to belief. Neoliberal secularism is a religion that is "internal to the western episteme," but it has undoubtedly lit a global fire and created a state of emergency. "It is a *self-colonialism* that blurs the distinction between economic and noneconomic, sacred and profane, religious and secular," and it is this "amorphous" fire that must be confronted by those who seek to call out the fire for what it is, for the secularism that it is. Secularism thus names the fire. It constitutes what must finally be called out and named, what must be investigated, what "future research on secularism and religion needs to confront to grasp, and possibly resist, the neoliberal manifestations, transformations, and transmutations of secularism."

What if there's no fire in the first place? No fire on or off the world stage? What if those who yell and shout "fire!" are deceived or mistaken? What if they are too provincial? What if it is even worse, and they are liars, deceivers? What if the fire, what if *this* fire is a fiction, an invention, a fetish? This is what Fadil suggests as she demonstrates the way in which Islam is made into a threat, an imminent fire, the clear and present danger of a firestorm. On the multiple stages of the world theater, in the "several public spaces" that are now found, each operating "according to their own meaning structure but . . . also entangled with one another," some fictions rise up higher to enable the regulation of a world imagined as stable. And just as the world is imagined, so is "Muslim difference"—the fire so many governments and professional (and amateur) fire shouters have rushed to name—which comes to serve as a "fetish" (a term Fadil borrows from Achille Mbembe), the occasion to develop "security policies" and ultimately "attempts at *stabilizing* the idea of a secular order," a world order, a world stage "in confrontation with a Muslim alterity." The fetish is a fiction. Its operations arbitrary and unstable. "It is at once overpowering and unstable. Serious and false." It is akin to "science fiction" and even has "magical-realist components." It is not fire, if there is one, only a fictitious one. It is a desperate mechanism that seeks to defuse another fire, a world understood as being on fire, "the 'chaotic pluralism' that characterizes the social world (i.e., the presence of Muslims as social and political actors and carriers of meaning)." Imagined threats—fictitious fires—are thus being invented, called out, mobilized with devastating consequences, destructive transformations of worlds. The fire is not in the world, nor is the world on fire. Not from this fire, at least. There is rather "a discourse of deception" and "an aura of factuality," an "epistemological and ontological insecurity at the heart of modernity." The site of this insecurity, Fadil tells us, is something called "religion"—a fetish indeed. In other words, there begins more clearly to appear "a continued anxiety over the ontopolitical capacities of the secular state, its ability to recognize and *mark* religion, that is, Islam."

"Religion" did not start the fire. And though there might be something in Islam that triggers the anxieties of the secular state, the fire to which the latter responds, which it keeps calling out and battling, that fire is less self-colonizing than it is self-generated. The "ritual performance of the state," the ongoing fabrication of fetishes that are called out as incendiary—such is the emergency we, we scholars, should name and interrogate.

We write in a time of emergency. We write out of a sense of emergency, and we respond as we must. Someone, anyone, calls out "fire!" And these days, someone else is already poised to deny it. "It's a hoax!" Imagine the scene, in the theater. It has gone well beyond free speech—does ChatGPT have the right to free speech?—and the distinction to which we continue to hold, we historians, we scientists, between fact and fiction (between artifice and intelligence, or between life and choice) has long collapsed. And certainly so when it comes to our ability to discriminate with certainty. There are endless fires, and many of them are fictitious. Others are ablaze and we refuse or simply fail to see them, or to call them by their name. Or else we offer new names, which, laudable as they might be, do not necessarily help with the fire. What fire? And which fire after all? Which name? There is noise (the fire is noise, and noise is a fire). There is a cacophony and there is a mass proliferation of calls, and first of all, of course, of fires. The planet is on fire (the trump card of fire warnings), yet we call out still, as we must, for the smaller, older, or more urgent fires. Who will name the real fire, the true and truly burning fire, when so many deny the fires, when so many sound false alarms? Is Iran not the fire? Or is it the virus and its variants or is it the megalomanic uncontrollability of AI? Is China not on fire or is it Palestine? What about the police, fully militarized? Is it race or gender? Is it not the economy, stupid? Capitalism or colonialism? Illness or war? Is it not, finally, religion that started the fire or is it instead humanity who has lost its way? *All* of humanity equally? Will the real sovereign (please) stand up and finally declare the state of the exception or will it be an ex-president, a non-elect president, the latest TikTok sensation, the next viral celebrity? The next viral variant? The insectocalypse? Or the still growing, still looming nuclear catastrophe? Will it be an old volcano or a new meteorite? The next breakthrough toward antimatter at the Larger Hadron Collider? Is it not too late to fight the fires? So many have ended worlds already. Ideologies (or marketing campaigns) spreading like wildfire or incendiary bombs, plastic, corn syrup, and depleted uranium. But which fires are left? Which yet to call out? And what about the fictitious ones? The made-up fires, so many of which are now too big to fail? Which discipline, which science is authorized, which qualified to tell us what fire to fight? Anthropology? Philosophy? Object Oriented Ontology? Oceanography? The science of evolution or that "crack in creation" Jennifer Doudna fell through and wrote about, along with other (imagine that) gene editors and financial backers? Journal and newspaper editors? The science of the state now known as statistics? Or another mad science entirely, one that, all things being increasingly unequal, will surely bring a change we can believe in?

    I wanted to conclude with yet another fire. I wanted to conclude—but how to conclude?—with the (failed) emergency of a learning tradition that continues to divide knowledges, the arts and the sciences, with none ruling, except STEM or university administrators tentatively lording with the backing of governments and of corporations that, packed with power, increasingly lack authority (the authority of science is, we might recall, not exactly scientific), a tradition of learning and of ruling with neither the mandate nor the ability (not to mention the schooling system) to distinguish between the fires, let alone between the real and the fictitious fires. A learning tradition that does not know priorities—is that a tradition? A tradition of learning? Or is it a devouring fire? Whichever it is, it seems to have transformed itself, disguised itself, into a market (the free marketplace of ideas and the courage of one's opinions, more or less protected by what we insist on calling, as if it could prevent the fire, "freedom of speech"). A market, then, wealthy as it is in exceptions and in emergencies, in free individuals or subjects, but that offers no mechanisms to describe the burning fires, none to identify or rank them otherwise than by sheer addition (of voices, of views, of "likes," of hits and of retweets, and of paywalls too), otherwise than by gargantuan inclusion or else by joining the massive and growing chorus of fire shouters, Instagram posters, and other influencers. What are we burning to learn? Where are we learning to learn? And when did we learn (did we learn?) to discriminate and fight the fires that burn along the monuments that commemorate—and feed—old fires? The archives we stoke, uncover, or destroy? Have we learned to adjudicate on the most pressing noun (or pronoun) that might start a fire, that has already started so very many? Can we say her name and speak a fiery truth to power? Which power? Can we call out the powerful lies that continue to light innumerable fires (or squash the urgent, and truer, votes and voices)? Can we name or shame those that deny the fires? How many fires can we even name? How many fires this time?

NOTES

1. Søren Kierkegaard, *Either/Or, Part 1*, ed. and trans. Howard V. Hong and Edna H. Hong (Princeton, NJ: Princeton University Press, 1987), 30.
2. James Baldwin, *The Fire Next Time* (New York: Vintage, 1963).

CONTRIBUTORS

GIL ANIDJAR teaches in the Department of Religion at Columbia University. He has written a number of books and articles on enmity, Christianity, secularism, the university, Shakespeare, Derrida and, more recently, dance and danger. His latest book, *The Sovereignty of Mothers*, is forthcoming with Columbia University Press.

NADIA FADIL is an associate professor in the Department of Social and Cultural Anthropology at KU Leuven. Fadil's work centers on race, religion, and secularism, with a particular focus on Islam in Europe. Her most recent co-edited publications include *Radicalization in Belgium and the Netherlands: Critical Perspectives on Violence and Security* (2019) and the special issue "Envisioning Hijra: The Ethics of Leaving and Dwelling of European Muslims" of *Contemporary Islam* (2021).

EDMUND FRETTINGHAM is assistant professor of international relations at Leiden University. His primary research interests lie within religion in world politics, with particular focus on Christian politics, the place and role of religion in political life, and approaches to the study of religion in international politics.

SLAVICA JAKELIĆ is the Richard P. Baepler Distinguished Professor in the Humanities at Valparaiso University's honors college. Her scholarly interests and publications center on religion and nationalism, religious and secular humanisms, theories of religion and secularism, theories of modernity, and interreligious conflict and dialogue. Jakelić has worked at, or was a fellow of, a number of interdisciplinary institutes in Europe and the United States. She is a senior fellow of the national project "Religion &

Its Publics," placed at the University of Virginia, where she was a faculty member and co-director at the UVA's Institute for Advanced Studies in Culture for several years. She is also a senior fellow of the international project "Orthodoxy and Human Rights," placed at Fordham University. Jakelić is the author of *Collectivistic Religions: Religion, Choice, and Identity in Late Modernity* (2010), *Pluralizing Humanism* (forthcoming with Routledge), and *Both Freedom and Belonging: Essays on Religion, Nationalism, and Solidarity* (forthcoming with TIM Press, in Croatian). She co-edited three volumes and is currently working on a book titled *Ethical Nationalisms.*

JOSHUA LUPO is the assistant director of the Contending Modernities research initiative. In this role, he serves as the editor and writer for the *Contending Modernities Blog* and the classroom coordinator for the Madrasa Discourses program. He has published articles and reviews in *Sophia, Soundings, Critical Muslim, Reading Religion,* and *Religious Studies Review.* With Contending Modernities co-director Atalia Omer, he is the co-editor of *Religion and Broken Solidarities: Feminism, Race, and Transnationalism* (Notre Dame Press, 2022) and *Religion, Populism, and Modernity: Confronting White Christian Nationalism and Racism* (Notre Dame Press, 2023). His current book project is titled *After Essentialism: A Critical Phenomenology for the Study of Religion.*

CECELIA LYNCH is professor of political science at the University of California, Irvine. Lynch is an expert on international relations, and has researched and published extensively on interrelated themes of religion/secularisms, humanitarianism, ethics, and globalization broadly conceived, including their racialized and gendered character, working from what she calls a "critical interpretivist" approach to all of the above. She co-edits the Critical Investigations into Humanitarianism in Africa (CIHA) Blog at www.cihablog.com. Her most recent book is *Wrestling with God: Ethical Precarity in Christianity and International Relations* (Cambridge University Press, 2020). With Cilas Kemedjio, she is also the editor of *Who Gives to Whom? Reframing Africa in the Humanitarian Imaginary* (Palgrave Macmillan, 2024).

LUCA MAVELLI is a reader in politics and international relations at the University of Kent, UK. His research focuses on neoliberalism, citizenship, migration, secularism, and religion in international politics. He is the author of *Neoliberal Citizenship: Sacred Markets, Sacrificial Lives* (Oxford University Press, 2022) and *Europe's Encounter with Islam: The Secular and the Postsecular* (Routledge, 2012), and the co-editor of *The Refugee Crisis and Religion: Secularism, Security and Hospitality in Question* (Rowman and Littlefield, 2017) and *Towards a Postsecular International Politics: New Forms of Community, Identity, and Power* (Palgrave, 2014). His work has been funded by the UK Economic and Social Research Council, the British Council, and the Leverhulme Trust. His articles have appeared in *Political Geography*, *Citizenship Studies*, *European Journal of International Relations*, *International Studies Quarterly*, *Review of International Studies*, *Security Dialogue*, *Millennium: Journal of International Studies*, *International Politics*, *Critical Studies on Terrorism*, *Journal of Religion in Europe*, and *Resilience: International Policies, Practices and Discourses*.

ATALIA OMER is a professor of religion, conflict, and peace studies at the Kroc Institute for International Peace Studies and at the Keough School of Global Affairs at the University of Notre Dame. She is also the Dermot T. J. Dunphy Visiting Professor of Religion, Violence, and Peace Building at Harvard University and a senior fellow at the Religion, Conflict, and Peace Initiative at Harvard University's Religion and Public Life program. Her research focuses on religion, violence, and peace-building, with a particular focus on Palestine/Israel and on theories and methods in the study of religion. Omer's most recent book is *Decolonizing Religion and Peacebuilding* (Oxford University Press, 2023). Among other publications, Omer is the author of *When Peace Is Not Enough: How the Israeli Peace Camp Thinks about Religion, Nationalism, and Justice* (The University of Chicago Press, 2015), and *Days of Awe: Reimagining Jewishness in Solidarity with Palestinians* (The University of Chicago Press, 2019). She is also a co-editor of *The Oxford Handbook of Religion, Conflict, and Peacebuilding* (2015). Omer is co-director of Contending Modernities, a global research initiative.

S. SAYYID is professor of decolonial thought and social theory and the former head of School of Sociology and Social Policy at the University of Leeds. He reads historical ontologies and writes political theory. His publications have been translated into several languages. He is also the editor of the interdisciplinary journal *ReOrient*. Sayyid's major publications include *Recalling the Caliphate: Decolonization and World Order* (Hurst, 2014), *A Fundamental Fear: Eurocentrism and the Emergence of Islamism* (Zed Books, 2004), and the co-edited volumes *Thinking through Islamophobia: Global Perspectives* (Columbia University Press, 2010), and *A Postcolonial People: South Asians in Britain* (Columbia University Press, 2008). His works have been translated into over half a dozen languages.

SANTIAGO SLABODSKY is the Florence and Robert Kaufman Chair in Jewish Studies at Hofstra University in New York. Slabodsky is co-director of the journal *Decolonial Horizons/Horizontes Decoloniales* at the GEMRIP institute in Latin America and convener of the summer program of Liberation Theologies and Decolonial Thought at the Global Dialogue Center in Spain. In the past he was co-chair of the Liberation Theologies unit at AAR, convener of the PhD program in Religion, Ethics and Society at Claremont School of Theology and associate director of the center for Race, Culture and Social Justice at his current institution. Concurrently to his permanent posts in the US, he has served as visiting professor at institutions in the Netherlands, South Africa, Spain, Costa Rica, Macedonia, and Argentina and has lectured throughout Europe, the Americas, Africa, South East Asia, and the Middle East. His book *Decolonial Judaism: Triumphal Failures of Barbaric Thinking* (2014) received the 2017 Frantz Fanon Outstanding Book Award from the Caribbean Philosophical Association.

INDEX

A
absolute submission, 74n56
abyssal line, 13, 171, 172, 182, 183
abyssal thinking: alternatives to, 15, 172, 180, 181; definition of, 12–13, 17, 18
Adorno, Theodor, 31
Africa: American racial order in, 95; burial rites, 150; decolonial possibilities, 146; European idea of, 161n1; Global North and, 210; Hinduism in, 161n3; languages, 154; "missionary" religions, 161n3; NGOs in, 152–53; possibility of modernity, 78; precolonial, 93–94; Traditional Medicine Day, 156
African Initiated Churches (AICs), 151, 154–55, 158, 163n18
African knowledge: commodification of, 155; about healing, 155, 156, 157–58; modes of production of, 157; suppression of, 154–55
African National Congress (ANC), 158

African religions, 142, 143, 148, 154, 159
Afrikania movement, 159, 163n15
Afrofuturism, 78, 79, 84, 97, 97n5, 98n7
Afropessimism, 93–94, 102n44
Agamben, Giorgio, 108
Agrama, Hussein Ali, 65
Ahmadu, Fuambai, 153
alternative futures, fictional depictions of, 81, 82
altruistic projects, 41, 160
Amir-Moazami, Schirin, 86
Ampofo, Adomako, 151
"analytic bifurcation" of western social thought, 171, 172
Andrić, Ivo, 184, 200n79
Anidjar, Gil, 2, 35, 75n56, 101n34
anticolonial solidarity, 182
anti-Orientalism, 80
antisemitism, 37, 39, 40
Appleby, R. Scott, 26, 179
Arab/Berber-Jews, conflict with Arab/Berber-Muslims, 37–38
Arnfred, Signe, 151

Asad, Talal, 6, 54, 111, 145
asylum seekers, 185
"ATR" (African Traditional Religion), 148

B
Baldwin, James, 204
Balibar, Étienne, 108
Balkanization, 182, 183
Balkans: as boundary space, 18, 182, 183, 185; Byzantium and Ottoman legacies, 200n78; challenge of the abyssal line, 171; critical studies of, 199n75; distinctive status of, 172, 173; ethnic nationalisms in, 177; exclusion from colonial projects, 184; ideal of, 200n79; irrationality of, 199n69; nationalist imaginaries in, 196n44; othering of, 16, 183, 211; as periphery, 190–91, 200n77; refugees in, 171, 172; resistance to the character of, 199n67; studies of, 183–84; wars in, 177, 178, 185; western perception of, 183
Banting, Keith, 174
Barun, Tvrtko: Christian humanism of, 187, 189, 211; in Croatian media, 186; dismissal of religious identitarianism, 188; on experiences of living on the Balkan borders, 189; on identity and culture, 188, 189; interviews, 188; on national attachment, 188; response to the "migrant crisis," 169, 171–72, 184, 187, 189, 191; view of solidarity, 187–88, 189
Bazoum, Mohamed, 102n41
Belgian Muslim community, 50–51
Bernal, Martin, 97n2
Beyer, Gerald, 202n96

Beyer, Peter, 112
Bhabha, Homi, 18
Bible, translations into African languages, 154
Bigo, Didier, 57
Bihać, Bosnia, 186
biopolitics, 51–52
Black Orientalism, 95, 103n47
Black Panther (film): depiction of the future, 78, 79, 81, 96–97; dreams of modernity in, 77; examples of cultural comportments, 80–81; imaginary world of, 78; indeterminate temporality, 79; opening scene of, 95; plot, 95; as postracial fantasy, 95–96; precolonial possibility in, 81; production of, 96; superhero in, 78
Boatcă, Manuela, 32
Bolsonaro, Jair, 26
Bosnia: as bridge between the east and the west, 200n79; refugee crisis, 189; wars in, 178, 179
Bouteldja, Houria, 27
brainwashing, 61–62
Brazil, colonization of, 35
Brenner, Neil, 131
Brown, Wendy, 111
Brubaker, Rogers, 26, 39, 176, 180
Brussels terrorist attack, 50
burial rites, 150
Butler, Anthea, 179

C
Caduff, Carlos, 51
Calhoun, Craig, 176, 191n2
capitalism, 106–7
Cassel, Gustav, 99n16
Casteel, Sarah Phillips, 46n31
Cavanaugh, William, 197n49
Centre for Constructive Theology at the University of KwaZulu-Natal (UKZN), 158

Césaire, Aimé, 40, 88; *Discourse of Colonialism*, 27
Cheyette, Bryan, 41
Chinese Dream, 87, 100n29
Christian European modernity, 3
Christian identity, 197n49
Christianity: colonization and, 161n3; humanism and, 16, 180; as right religion, 29; universalism of, 179, 180; white nationalism and, 179
Christian missionaries: campaigns to eradicate female circumcision, 150–51; Catholic, 144; claim to colonial religion, 146–47; contestation between, 149; legacy of, 148; regulatory strategies, 149; resistances to, 148; strategies vis-à-vis African languages, 154–55; study of, 15; translations of the Bible, 154; types of, 147
churches and religious organizations, 120–21
citizenship, 111, 176
civic nationalism, 171, 176, 177–78, 182, 196n43
Cohn, Normand, 57
Cold War, 27
collective identity formation, 191n2
colonial afterlives, 14, 18
colonialism: alternatives to, 9; anthropology and, 94; vs. coloniality, 5, 161n3; humanitarian trends and, 142; legacy of, 5; modernity and, 5, 78–79, 85, 86; regulatory strategies, 149; religion and, 6; resistance to, 149; violence and, 141, 149, 150
coloniality: "altruistic" dynamics of, 37; vs. colonialism, 5, 161n3; definition of, 5, 19n4, 29, 89; genocidal practices and, 29; global condition of, 209–10; influence of, 29; Jewish persecution and, 37; reproduction of, 32; scholarship on, 7–8, 11; versions of, 39
coloniality of power, 107–8, 121
colonial religion, 142, 146–47, 158–59
colonial/religion nexus, 143
communism, 61, 62, 74n56, 124, 126
conspiracies, 33, 37, 43n8
Contending Modernities (CM) research initiative, 1, 2
cosmological imperialism, 14
cosmology of the mutant strains, 51, 70n6
counterradicalization programs, 87, 101n35
COVID-19 pandemic: neoliberal governance of, 130–31; traditional medicine therapies, 156
critical caretaking, 48n41
Critical Investigations into Humanitarianism in Africa (*CIHA*) blog, 143, 144
Critical Muslim Studies, 80
critical race studies, 45n20
Croatia: border protection, 201n86; migrant crisis, 185–86, 200n85; in Schengen area, 185; wars in, 178, 179

D

Damuah, Osoffo Okomfo, 163n15
da'wa (Islamic proselytization): captivating power of, 63; circulation of, 65, 67; covert, 63, 64; definition of, 60; elusive nature of, 63–67; fetishization of, 68; form of, 65; perceived threat of, 58, 61, 63, 65–66, 68, 69; vs. radical Islam, 60; reification of, 68
decoloniality, 18, 90, 91–92, 144, 155
decolonial religion, 15, 143, 147, 148, 158, 160

decolonial theory, 13, 18, 32
decolonization: vs. decoloniality, 90; project of, 91–92, 158–60
decolonizing religion, 141–42, 160
dehumanization, 8
democratic pluralism, 11
deradicalization policies: aim of, 58, 62, 67, 88; emergence of, 58, 62; as fetish, 53, 57, 58, 67–68; implementation of, 53, 57; mobilization of, 67; of Muslims, 11, 59; ontological dimensions of, 63; as public policy, 53; security and, 57; study of, 8, 9, 16, 49, 52–53, 87; supernatural discourse and, 57–58
Derrida, Jacques, 208
de Witte, Marleen, 159
dictatorial regimes, 38, 47n36
Dillon, Michelle, 194n27
Discourse of Colonialism (Césaire), 27
doctrine of discovery, 6, 146
Doosje, Bertjan, 62
double critique methodology, 14
dualism, 7, 30
Dube, J. L., 158
Du Bois, W. E. B., 182
Dune (film): allure of oriental despotism, 96; celebration of Muslimness, 79; colonial-racial logics of, 96; comparison to epic fantasy, 79; depiction of the future, 79, 81, 96–97; dreams of modernity in, 77; examples of cultural comportments, 80–81; imaginary world of, 78; plot, 79; production of, 96
Dunn, Shannon, 192n8
Durkheim, Émile, 173
Dussel, Enrique, 32
Dutch security agencies, 59–60, 63

E
economism, 212
Eisenstadt, Shmuel N., 82, 83
emergency: agency and, 206–7; Christian humanism and, 211; decision-making during, 206; declaration of state of, 209; fictitious, 213–15; fire as metaphor of, 203–9; global, 207–8, 210; of learning tradition, 215–16; media and, 208; perception of, 205–6; religion and, 214; response to, 208–9, 214; solidarity and, 211
epidemiological imaginary, 51
epistemology of limited knowledge, 125, 126, 129
Escobar, Arturo, 172
ethics of identity, 17, 170, 174, 175, 176, 177, 181
ethics of solidarity, 17, 174, 175, 176, 181
ethnic/civic nationalism binary, 176–78, 179, 195n42
ethnic nationalism, 176, 177
Eurocentrism, critique of, 77
European "new radical right," 192n4
European refugee crisis, 185–86, 187
"European Universalism," 181
Evangelicals, 147
evolutionism, 7, 30

F
Fadil, Nadia, 8–9, 13, 16, 38, 86, 87, 88, 92, 209, 213, 214
Fanon, Frantz, 13, 182
fascism, 118
female circumcision: campaigns against, 151, 152, 153; Christian condemnation of, 150; cultural aspect of, 153; definition of, 164n29; Islamic view of, 151–52; sexuality and, 153; studies of, 151

fetish, concept of, 49, 55, 56, 67, 68, 69, 213
fire, as metaphor of emergency, 203–9
first modernity, 32, 35
First Things, 179
forced inclusion, 31, 41
Foucault, Michel, 28, 51, 66
Francis, Saint, 186
Frettingham, Edmund, 3, 9, 10, 11, 16, 158, 211, 212
From Da'wa to Jihad (report), 60, 63

G
Gaddafi, Muʻammar Muḥammad al-, 38
García Fernández, Javier, 32
Gbodossou, Erick, 157
gender, 34
genealogical approach, 3, 4
genocidal practices: altruism of, 36; coloniality and, 29; historical roots of, 32, 33; liberal values and, 27–28, 29, 30, 31; as norm, 27, 28; right-wing, 39, 40; in second modernity, 36
Gilroy, Paul, 46n31
Glaude, Eddie, Jr., 179
global emergency, 210
Global North: Africa and, 142, 161n1; Muslim diaspora in, 80; as uncontaminated origin, 27, 28, 209–10
Global South: description of, 91; economic development, 99n16; forms of solidarity, 182; othering of, 182; political landscape of, 26
Go, Julian, 171, 181
Göle, Nilüfer, 110
Gopin, Marc, 179
Gorski, Philip, 196n45
governmentality, concept of, 41
Grabar-Kitarović, Kolinda, 201n86

Gramsci, Antonio, 2, 18
Gutkowski, Stacey, 54

H
Habermas, Jürgen, 174
Hafez, Farid, 38
Hauerwas, Stanley, 179
Hayek, Friedrich: critique of Mises, 125, 137n84; on erroneous rationalism, 125; *The Fatal Conceit: The Errors of Socialism*, 122; on "good" and "bad" religions, 127; on institutions, 125; on market, 122–23, 127, 128, 129, 212; on nonfactual beliefs, 126; on political ideologies, 125; postmodernist outlook of, 129; on religion, 121, 122, 124, 125, 129–30; on secularism, 125; on social rules, 123; theory of neoliberalism, 9, 105, 106, 109, 117, 128, 129, 130, 211; on tradition and morality, 122; on true knowledge, 125–26
Heath-Kelly, Charlotte, 57
Hegel, G. W. F., 39
Herbert, Frank, 78, 96
hermeneutics of citizenship, 16
hermeticism, 25
Hindu-Muslim violence, 100n31
Hindutva ideologies, 93, 102n43
Hintsa, king of the Xhosa, 149
history, ancient vs. Aryan model of, 97n2
Hollenweger, Walter, 155
Hollinger, David, 175
Holocaust: coloniality and, 36; European view of, 40; German genocides in Africa vs., 37; interpretations of, 25, 27, 37
Horkheimer, Max, 31
humanism, 180

humanitarianism, 14, 15, 16, 142, 160
human rights, 13
Hurd, Elizabeth Shakman, 73n48
Hussein, Saddam, 38
hybridity, concept of, 18
hysteresis, 54

I
identitarianism, 17, 180
identity: ethics of, 17; solidarity and, 17, 169, 170, 171, 176–80, 190, 192n8
inclusion, 18, 41
India: communal riots in, 100n31; secularism, 10
Indigenous knowledge, 154
Indigenous religions, 142, 147–48
integration, 60–61
"inter-imperiality," 32
Islam, 29, 98n6, 147, 161n3, 213, 214
Islamicate, 79, 83, 92, 95, 96, 98n6
Islamic Relief, 151, 152
Islamofuturism, 80, 84, 97
Islamophobia: 9/11 terrorist attack and, 66; Orientalist trope of, 92; right-wing populism and, 39; roots of, 39; scholarship on, 38; spread of, 40, 87–88
Israel, State of, 37
Israeli-Palestinian conflict, 37

J
Jackson, Sherman, 95, 103n47
Jakelić, Slavica, 4, 7, 14, 15, 16, 17, 18, 210, 211
Jambon, Jan, 50–51
James, Stanlie M., 151
Jesuit Refugee Service, 172, 186
Jewish-Black relations, 46n31
Jews: colonialism and, 44n13, 46n31; constitution of "western frontiers" and, 43n13; ethnic cleansing of, 32; in Muslim-ruled lands, 37; Natives and, 34; non-European, 37; western construction of, 35, 36
jihad, 60
John Paul II, Pope, 187
Johnson, Boris, 130
Joint Learning Initiative on Faith & Local Communities (JLI), 152
Judaism, 29
Judeo-Christian tradition, 44n13, 88–89

K
Kandiyoti, Dalia, 34
Karklin, Rasma, 176
Kazi, Nazia, 38
Keynesianism, 116
Khan, Imran, 102n41
Khosrokhavar, Fahrad, 62, 74n53
Kierkegaard, Søren, 203, 204
Kirby, Jack, 96
knotted intersection of history, 46n31
knowledge, 125–26, 128
Kohn, Hans, 176, 177
Kolb, Anjuli Fatima Raza: *Epidemic Empire*, 51
Krastev, Ivan, 175
Kudzai, Taruona, 158
Kundnani, Arun, 62
Kymlicka, Will, 174

L
Laclau, Ernesto, 170
learning tradition, 215–16
Lee, Stan, 96
Lentin, Alana, 37
Lepore, Jill, 178
liberal democracies, 86, 89–90, 92
liberalism: definition of, 5, 71n23; exclusionary logic of, 89; global dimension of, 88; rational authority of, 118; religion and, 8, 122
liberal-populist marriage, 89

liberal-secular matrix of state power, 86
liberal values, 30
Liberia, 95
Lugones, María, 34
Lupo, Joshua, 142
Lynch, Cecelia, 4, 12, 14, 15, 16, 17, 93, 210
Lyon, David, 110

M
Maasai community in Kenya, 152
MacIntyre, Alasdair, 174, 194n29
Macron, Emmanuel, 196n45
Maelbeek metro station terrorist attack, 50
Maghreb, 37
magic, 57–58, 72–73n36
Mahmood, Saba, 145
Malaysia, freedom of expression laws, 90
Maldonado-Torres, Nelson, 13
Malinowski, Bronislaw, 57–58, 72n36
Mardešić, Željko, 179
market: irrationality of, 127; justification for trusting, 128; neoliberalism and, 212; sacralization of, 121; self-regulated, 212; as system of social coordination, 117, 126
Marshall, Ruth, 55
Martínez, María Elena, 34
Marzouki, Nadia, 180
Masango, Charles, 156
Mavelli, Luca, 3, 9, 10, 11, 16, 54, 158, 211, 212
Mbembe, Achille: notion of *fetish*, 49, 53, 55, 56, 67, 88, 213; *On the Postcolony*, 55; on surplus of meanings, 56
Mbuwayesango, Dora, 154
mechanic solidarity, 173–74, 194n27
Meerloo, Joost, 74n56

Melley, Timothy, 63, 74n56; *The Covert Sphere*, 61
Memmi, Albert, 38
Merkel, Angela, 187
methodological nationalism, 8
Middle East/North Africa (MENA) region, 38
Mignolo, Walter, 32, 173
migration, 175, 185
Míguez, Néstor, 127
Milan, Chiara, 189
Mises, Ludwig von: on churches and religious organizations, 120; on market, 126, 212; modernist outlook of, 129; on neoliberal secularism, 121; promotion of neoliberalism, 9, 105, 106, 117–18, 211; on religion, 109, 119–20, 121, 122, 129; on theocracy, 118–19
modernity: archaeological accounts of, 16; bifurcation of premodernity and, 146; borders of, 85; colonialism and, 5, 16, 78–79, 86; critique of, 95; effects on the political, 85, 86; forms of, 84; identity of, 85; liberal democracies and, 86; material condition and, 99n18; politics of, 100n26; religion and, 108; scholarship on, 2–3, 78, 82–83; standard narratives of, 83; theories of, 77; vs. tradition, 12; west and, 83, 91, 97n2. *See also* multiple modernity theories
Modi, Narendra, 26
Moeti, Matshidiso, 156
Mont Pèlerin Society, 117
Moosa, Ebrahim, 26
Mouffe, Chantal, 170
Mpanzi (NGO), 153
Mudimbe, V. Y., 161n1
multiculturalism, 11–12

multiple modernity theories, 83–84, 91, 98n11
Muslim-African syncretic traditions, 147
Muslim Brotherhood, 64
Muslims: conspiracy theories about, 64; ethnic cleansing of, 32; otherness, 58; political consciousness, 38; rhetoric of coloniality and, 38; study of, 8–9; submissiveness of, 75n56; surveillance of liberal state, 39; western construction of, 35

N
nationalism, ethnic vs. civic, 176–78, 180
nation-state: citizenship as primary identity of, 111; formation of, 54; religion and, 7; secularism and, 105–6, 110, 111; study of, 10, 16
neoliberal capitalism, 9, 16, 106–7, 109, 111
neoliberalism: colonial framework and, 10; definitions of, 107, 115; economic sphere of, 115, 116, 133n15; expansion of, 11, 211–12; founding fathers of, 9; market and, 129; parasitism of, 131; religion and, 105, 106, 130, 213; sources and development of, 116–17; theological anatomy of, 10
neoliberal piety, 107
neoliberal "regime of truth," 130
neoliberal secularism. *See* secularism
Netherlands: deradicalization policies in, 87; Muslim integration problem, 59, 60; Saudi influences in, 62; security services, 59–60
New Christians, 34, 45n25
Ngũgĩ, wa Thiong'o, 149, 154
Niger, political regime, 102n41

nonrational beliefs, 121
non-western societies, industrialization of, 84

O
Occidentalism, 35
Ogega, Kenyan Jackie, 153
Omer, Atalia, 16, 26, 37, 48n41, 142
onto-epistemology, 161–62n5
ontopolitical concern with secular modernity, 52
Orbán, Viktor, 185
organic solidarity, 173
Orientalism, 35, 184

P
Pakistan, political regime, 102n41
pandemic prophecy, 70n6
particularity, vs. universality, 192n6
Parvulescu, Anca, 32
Peck, Jamie, 131
Pentecostal Christians, 147
people with no religion, 30, 31
people without a soul, 34
people with the wrong religion, 29, 31
Perceval, José María, 34
philanthropy, 9
philosemitism, 29, 40
Plenković, Andrej, 200n85
politics of belonging, 18
politics of threatened majorities, 175
populism, 26, 39–40, 89, 170, 179, 180
positionality, 143
post-abyssal thinking, 13, 18
postcolonial humanitarianism, 15, 141, 142–43
postcolonial subject, 56
Powers, Gerard, 179
precolonial imaginary, 2, 92–93
presentism, 94, 102n46
productivity of life, 66

PROMETRA (Promotion of Medicine and Treatment from Africa), 156, 157
property rights, 146
Prudon, Peter, 62
public and private categories, 145
purchasing power parity (PPP), 99n16
purity of blood, 34, 47n31
Pusić, Vesna, 185

Q
Quijano, Aníbal, 19n4, 32, 209

R
race, 6, 28, 52
racism: anti-Muslim, 50; origin of modern, 30, 31, 33, 36, 39; in racialized communities, 32, 35; scholarship on, 26, 32; types of, 29, 35; in the United States, 45n20
radical Islam (Muslim radicalism), 60, 63, 64, 68, 69
radicalization, 51, 62, 74n53
Rawlings, Jerry John, 159
refugees, 185
religion: abyssal lines and, 13; boundaries of, 8, 114; Christianity and, 6, 33; colonialism and, 6, 8, 12; critique of, 145; decolonial analysis of, 6; definitions of, 112, 144–45; deterritorialized forms of, 106; development of, 124; discursive construction of, 65; economic sphere and, 106, 107, 121, 122–23; empire and, 7, 8, 11; as generic category, 10–11; genocidal practices and, 30–31; "good" and "bad," 119–20, 125, 127; humanitarianism and, 142, 160; idea of return to, 4; identitarian vs. belief-centered, 171, 178–81; liberalism and, 118, 122; Marxist view of, 106; modernity and, 106, 108; moral values and, 124–25; nationalism and, 178; neoliberalism and, 107, 108, 115, 125; origins of, 161n4; political sphere and, 4, 6, 114; premodern interpretations of, 145; as private affair, 118, 119, 125; race and, 44n20; "right" and "false," 7, 29; scholarship on, 3–4, 14, 44–45n20, 106–7; scientific conceptions of, 112–13; self-destructive, 124; social and collective role of, 107, 120, 121, 123; state and, 124; survival of, 124; symbols of, 65; theological conceptions of, 112–13; Weberian thesis on, 106. *See also* African religions; Indigenous religions
religious freedom, 65, 73n48, 124
religious groups and organizations, 61, 120
religious nationalism, vs. civil religion, 196n45
Rieger, Joerg, 127
right-wing populisms, 39, 40, 41–42
rite of passage, 150, 151, 152, 153
Robertson, Claire C., 151
Rorty, Richard, 174, 194n31
Rothberg, Michael, 34
Roy, Olivier, 180

S
Sahel kingdom, 147
Said, Edward, 28, 184
Salafis, 147
Santos, Boaventura de Sousa, 12, 17, 18, 171, 181–82
Sayyid, S., 2, 3, 9, 18, 19, 38, 55, 65
Schorsch, Jonathan, 33, 34
science, 114

second modernity, 35, 36
secularism: coloniality of, 107, 109, 116, 131; comparative, 105–6; critique of, 121; definition of, 10, 71n23; diversity in, 113–14; foundations of, 117; models of, 109, 110, 111, 114, 212; national variations in, 10, 111; nation-state and, 105–6, 110; neoliberal rationalities of, 106, 107, 108, 109, 111, 115, 128–29, 131, 212; plural, 109; "political," 128; postmodern neoliberalization of, 122–28; promotion of markets, 115; religious conceptions of, 114, 213; rise of, 145; scholarship on, 3–4, 10, 110; security policies and, 54; structure of suspicion and, 65; studies of, 9, 109; western discourse of, 110
secular modernity, 112
secular sensibilities, 54
security policies, 53–54, 55, 68
self-colonialism, 105, 108, 128, 130, 131, 213
self/other binary, 182
Semites, 89, 101n34
sense of belonging, 190
Sephardic studies, 33
Sheth, Falguni, 52, 66
Shohat, Ella, 28, 34, 35, 36
Shohat, Iraqi, 40–41
Silverblatt, Irene, 34; *Modern Inquisitions*, 33
Slabodsky, Santiago, 4, 5, 7, 8, 9, 11, 12, 16, 86, 87, 88, 89, 92, 143, 209
slavery, 91
Smith, Anthony, 176
social disintegration, 61
socialism, 118
societal differentiation, 113
sociology of absences, 171

solidarity: agency and, 175; belonging and, 190; Catholic teaching about, 202n96; changing notion of, 173; ethics of, 15, 17; ideal of, 174; identity and, 17, 169, 170, 192n8; Jesuit view of, 172; mechanic and organic, 173–74; in pluralistic societies, 174; practices of, 17; problem of achieving, 175; scholarship on, 15, 174; sense of, 194n30, 194n31
sovereign power, 66, 206
Spain: colonial expansion, 6; Inquisition, 39
spirituality, 157
Springs, Jason, 170
Stam, Robert, 28, 35, 36
Stoler, Ann, 34
structure of suspicion, 65
Styers, Randal, 73n36
Sufi brotherhoods, 147
Sung, Jung Mo, 127
supplemental particularity, 194n29

T
Tamir, Yael, 176
taqiyya (the practice of concealing one's faith), 64, 76n68
Taylor, Charles, 145, 146
terra nullius, 146
Thatcher, Margaret, 211
theocracy, 118–19, 120
Theodore, Nik, 131
theological division of the world, 88
Tinsley, Meghan, 171, 182
Todorova, Maria, 183, 184, 196n44, 199n75, 200n79
tradition, 4, 12, 17
Trump, Donald, 130

U
Uganda, colonial legislation of, 90

United States: imperialism of, 101n34; universities, 101n39
Uyghurs, civil rights struggle of, 88

V
Vincent, Andrew, 192n6
virulence of forced exclusion, 160
Volf, Miroslav, 178, 179

W
"War on Terror," 87–88
Weber, Max, 112
West, Cornel, 179
white nationalism, 178, 179
Wittgenstein, Ludwig, 18, 94, 102n42

World Council of Churches (WCC), 155
World Health Organization (WHO), 156
Wynter, Sylvia, 13

X
Xi Jinping, 88, 100n29

Y
Yack, Bernard, 176

Z
Zimmerer, Jürgen, 36–37
Zionism, 37, 38
Zubrzycki, Geneviève, 176

www.ingramcontent.com/pod-product-compliance
Lightning Source LLC
Chambersburg PA
CBHW072359210225
22389CB00007B/719